BIG BLUE MARBLE®
ATLAS

The *Big Blue Marble Atlas* is an unusual atlas of information about and illustrations of the whole Earth — its land, its water, its atmosphere, its neighborhood, and its people. It features maps by Hammond, Inc., and a special section on space, with remarkable new photographs supplied by the National Aeronautical and Space Administration (NASA).

BIG BLUE MARBLE® ATLAS

by Paula S. Brown and Robert L. Garrison

Illustrated by John Trotta

A Rutledge Book

IDEALS PUBLISHING CORP.

Milwaukee, Wisconsin

Prepared and produced by Rutledge Books, Inc.
25 West 43rd Street, New York, New York 10036

Published and distributed by Ideals Publishing Corp.
Post Office Box 1101, Milwaukee, Wisconsin 53201

First Edition 1980

Printed in the United States of America

Library of Congress Cataloging in Publication Data

Brown, Paula S.
Big blue marble atlas.
SUMMARY: An atlas of the whole earth, its land, water, atmosphere, and people. Includes information about outer space.
1. Atlases. [1. Atlases] I. Garrison, Robert L. II. Trotta, John. III. Title.
G1021.B77 1980 912 80-675234
ISBN 0-89542-924-1

Cover Design: David Grupper

"Big Blue Marble" is the first worldwide television series for young people. At present it is broadcast weekly in 200 cities in the United States and in 65 other countries. The programs are produced and provided to U.S. stations without charge by International Telephone and Telegraph Corporation (ITT) to encourage international understanding among all people, especially the coming generations.

To complement that series, which has received honors such as the Peabody Award, several Emmys, and other prizes and commendations, this information atlas has been prepared. It shows how peoples of the world are affected by geography. In addition, a section is included on how and where the planet Earth fits into its universe. There is also a practical *Big Blue Marble* Book of Lists, as well as maps of all countries with supporting illustrations and pictures. *Big Blue Marble Atlas* is an ideal reference book for everyone interested in the living world.

To Berry Brown and to Lauri, Greg, and Kathy Garrison, along with all the other members of the generation who will soon be responsible for the care and keeping of our beautiful Big Blue Marble.

Acknowledgments

Appreciation is extended to the following organizations for their information and the opportunity to share it:

The Blue Marble Company, ITT, New York
City of New York Public Libraries, New York
Field Enterprises Educational Corp., Chicago
The Geographer, U.S. Department of State, Washington, D. C.
Hammond, Inc., Maplewood, New Jersey
Map Library of the United Nations, New York
National Aeronautics and Space Administration, Washington, D. C.
Statistical Office of the United Nations, New York
U.S. Board on Geographic Names, Washington, D. C.
U.S. Committee for UNICEF, New York
World Bank, Washington, D. C.
World Book — Childcraft International, Inc., Chicago

Thanks also to the following persons for their interest and cooperation in this project:

Nathaniel O. Abelson, map librarian of the United Nations
Dr. Henry Brown, Ph.D., University of Michigan
Sally Garrison Conrad, B.A., M.A., Michigan State University; Ed. D. (cand.), Wayne State University
Clare Lynch O'Brien, consultant to "Big Blue Marble"

Special thanks to Allan Mogel, art director; Deborah Weiss and Jay Hyams, editors; Cynthia Parzych; Sharyn S. Perlman; and Randi Goldstein.

Population figures used in this atlas are the latest figures obtainable. There are notable variations in the methods of keeping track of the numbers of people within a political area. Nevertheless, the census figures and estimates used are to the most practical degree of accuracy and according to the most reliable sources.

With the encouragement of the United Nations and its members, efforts are being made to standardize the names of cities, countries, and geographic areas of the world, usually in the language of the country or countries in which they exist. For example, in Italy the city that was once known as Turin is now preferred as Torino; the city that was once Leghorn is now preferred as Livorno. Such changes are being made today in keeping with a practical rate of acceptance and assimilation.

The U.S. Board on Geographic Names in Washington, D. C., publishes current listings of accepted and anticipated name changes.

In this atlas, major amendments to maps contained herein are noted in the margins on the pages on which the primary presentation of the city, country, or geographic area is offered.

Also note that the short forms of the names of many countries are given for ease of referral. For example, East and West Germany and North and South Korea are acceptable for informal usage.

Contents

The Key to Reading this Atlas

The *Big Blue Marble®* *Atlas* contains maps called general reference maps. They represent the lay of the land and the political boundaries of countries and states.

The lay of the land is the physical or natural features of the land; it is the geography of the land.

Following is the key to elevation of the land, from the highest to the lowest, from the highlands to the lowlands, from the mountains to sea level.

Mountains
Highlands
Lowlands
Sea level

Political boundaries, states, nations, or countries are the people-made borders of the land.

- International boundary
- Boundary between states or between groups of countries
- Capital of a country
- Capital of a state
- Major city

This scale is important in order for you to have an accurate idea of the size (area) of a continent, a country, or a state. Pay attention to it!

THE WORLD
Scale at Equator
0 1000 2000 3000 MI.
0 1000 2000 3000 KM.

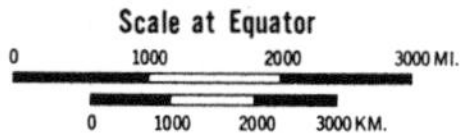

To see the actual relationship of a country, group of countries, a state, or group of states to other countries, states, or the entire continent, look at the continental maps in the beginning of each map section.

Whether it's an individual country or a group of countries (the same is for states), some maps in this book have been enlarged to show details. For example, although the map of India and the map of Iran each fill most of a page, the countries are *not* the same size. That's the reason for the scale, which appears in every map. It will help you determine the comparative size of each country. All the better to be explored by you!

So don't forget to check the scale and check it twice, because distance is noted in both kilometers and miles.

FOREWORD:

It's a Small World!

Ring-a-Ling
Good morning!
It's time to get up!
Wake up! It's 6:45.

The first mechanical clocks were made in Italy in 1335. Remember, though, that before there were clocks, there were roosters to wake you up. Wake up!

But it's still dark out.
Then turn on the light!

It has been only about a hundred years since the invention of electric lights. Thomas A. Edison of the United States got the bright idea around 1879. The metal tungsten is the light bulb's filament — that part of the light bulb that glows. Tungsten ores mainly come from countries like Canada, China, and Russia.

It's time to get ready for school!
Eat a balanced breakfast:
Orange juice
Cereal with bananas on top
Cocoa

In the United States, orange juice is made from oranges grown in Florida and California. Around 1000 BC the Chinese were the first to cultivate sweet oranges and other citrus fruit. The first packages of breakfast cereal hit the table in 1880 in Michigan. Since then they have become popular, and most grains for cereals in this country (corn, wheat, oats) come from America's Great Plains.

The bananas you eat come from Central and South America; they are grown in countries like Honduras and Ecuador. Cacao beans from Ghana, Brazil, Colombia, Mexico, and Ecuador are the source for your cocoa.

Go wash your face!

Did you forget to use soap? The first soaps were made from tallow and wood ashes more than 3,000 years ago. It wasn't until the late 1700s that soap, as we know it today, was developed in France. In fact, the first bar of soap wasn't

made in the United States until 1830. Coconut oil is an important ingredient of soap. It comes from places like India, Indonesia, Malaysia, Papua New Guinea, the Philippines, and Sri Lanka.

Brush your teeth!

And keep them sparkling! The first false teeth were made by the Etruscans in 700 BC. But the best teeth are your own — so be sure to brush them *regularly!*

It's cold outside.
Better dress warmly!

Be careful — don't button up your cotton flannel shirt incorrectly. Ever since about 2500 BC in the Indus Valley of Pakistan, cotton has been a major fiber in textiles (clothing). Today cotton also grows in the American cotton belt: Alabama, Arkansas, Georgia, Louisiana, Mississippi, and Texas. It grows in California and Oklahoma, too. Buttons have been closing clothing for nearly 5,000 years.

Put on your blue jeans.

Indigo, a natural dye, has been popular for over 4,000 years. Today it is made synthetically and is the "blue" in blue jeans. Blue jean (or denim) was originally used for work clothes because it was a heavy-duty material. Wearing blue jeans while doing homework might not be the same as working in the fields or in a factory. . . but whoever said homework was easy?

Remember your wool sweater!

Wool is the first woven fiber known to have been used by human beings. Wool comes from sheep. Great flocks of sheep are raised in Argentina, Australia, New Zealand, Texas, and Wyoming.

Hey! You can't go too far barefooted!
Put on your shoes!

Shoes were first worn in Egypt in 1500 BC. If your shoes are leather, chances are the leather came from Argentina.

You are running a little late so ride your bike today!

The wheel, a real great invention, may have been used as early as 3500 BC in Mesopotamia or what is now a part of the Middle East. In 1690 the first bicycle with two wheels was built in France. It didn't have rubber tires, even though in the 1200s a soft natural rubber had been developed by the Maya and the Aztec Indians of the Americas. Today, natural rubber comes from trees that grow in India, Indonesia, Malaysia, Sri Lanka, and Thailand. Rubber for the tires of your bicycle wheels is probably synthetic (man-made).

Whew! Made it on time to school!
There is an assembly first hour. Go to the gymnasium quietly and sit on the bleachers.

The first gymnasiums were in Greece. Their name comes from the Greek word meaning "to exercise." They were outdoor arenas for men only! Today they're inside — for girls as well as boys! Gymnasiums have come a long way!

MATH CLASS

0 1 2 3 4 5 6 7 8 9 are Arabic numerals that originated in India 2,500 years ago. People have been calculating since the beginning of civilization. The abacus was first used in ancient China and Greece. If you forget your calculator, you can do your addition the long way. Although it may be slow, the answer will be the same.

GEOGRAPHY CLASS

It's a pop quiz.
Get out paper and pencil.

Paper comes from trees from places like

Canada and Scandinavia. The first paper was used in Egypt, around 3000 BC. But then it was made from papyrus reeds instead of trees. Pencils were invented in Switzerland in 1565.

Answer the following questions:

What is the difference between a *continent* and an *island*?

Size! about two million square miles.

Australia is the smallest continent: 7,686,848 square kilometers (2,967,909 square miles).

Greenland is the largest island: 2,175,600 square kilometers (840,000 square miles).

Both are land surrounded by water.

What is the difference between an *ocean* and a *sea*?

Both oceans and seas are large bodies of salt water. Seas can sometimes be oceans. Do you know when a sea is not an ocean? When it is partially surrounded by land. The South China Sea, the world's largest, 3,380,000 square kilometers (1,300,000 square miles), is but a drop in the bucket of the world's largest ocean, the Pacific, 166,884,000 square kilometers (64,186,000 square miles).

Ninety-eight percent of Earth's water is in the oceans and seas. The remaining 2 percent is in the lakes, rivers, glaciers, ground water, and water vapor in the air.

It's lunch time!
Peanut butter and grape jelly.
A glass of milk.
And an apple!

In the United States peanuts come from Alabama, Georgia, Texas, and Virginia. Grape jelly comes from grapes grown mostly in California, New York, Washington, and Ontario, Canada.

Milk comes from cows raised in the dairy regions of many states, such as Iowa, Michigan, Minnesota, New York, Ohio, Pennsylvania, and Wisconsin. Did you know that using a drinking glass was a luxury less than 200 years ago? The apple you eat can come from Washington, New York, or Michigan.

ART CLASS
Assignment: Decorate the bulletin boards. The theme is: Small World! The materials: newsprint, construction paper, chalk, and paint.

The bulletin board is made of cork — the bark of certain trees that grow mainly in Portugal. Newsprint and construction paper are made from wood pulp of Canadian trees. The chalk could very well be from Arkansas' great Chalk Bluff. Paint? People have been using it for years. Close to 20,000 years ago paint was first used by Stone Age artists in the Lascaux and Altamira caves in France and Spain.

GYM CLASS
Today you're going outside to play soccer.
One swift kick and... Oops! Your seam in your shorts has split.
The teacher has a safety pin.
Get back in there and score some points!

Use your head — not your hands! Soccer is one of the most popular sports in the world. It is believed that a game very similar to modern soccer was first played in China over 2,000 years ago, about 400 BC. In 1848 the first rules of the game were decided upon in Cambridge, England.

To fix your split seam use safety pins. They have been around since the Bronze Age (2000 BC, almost 4,000 years ago), when they were first used in the eastern Mediterranean region.

Tie game! You played well! You'll win the next time.

ENGLISH CLASS
Assignment: Write an essay answering the question, "If you could visit any place in the world, where would you go? Why?"

The only book you can use is an atlas. The essay is due at the end of the hour.

Get busy! No talking please!

According to Greek mythology Atlas was a Titan — a real giant of a fellow. As punishment for being on the losing side of a battle, he had to carry the weight of the world on his shoulders.

Today, Atlas continues to carry the world because an *atlas* is a book or collection of maps. A *map* is a graphic representation of either part of or all of the Earth.

"What do you want me to do? Draw you a map?" Maybe this was first said in Mesopotamia more than 5,000 years ago. The first map, carved on a clay tablet, was found in the Middle East. It dates back to 3800 BC.

In AD 150, Claudius Ptolemy, a Greek scholar living in Alexandria, Egypt, published 26 regional maps of Europe, Africa, and Asia. This was the first major collection of maps ever.

The name atlas was not given to a book of maps until the 1500s. The map maker, Gerhardus Mercator, was the first to use the name officially.

This *atlas* is a book of maps that represents the Big Blue Marble — our planet, Earth.

INTRODUCTION:

The Magical Spherical Miracle

Without water, life on Earth would not be possible. There would be no plants, no animals, no birds, no fish, and no people. In our solar system, the planet Earth, often referred to as a "Big Blue Marble," is covered with water — 70 percent of its surface, in fact. Its color, when viewed from space, is a beautiful watery blue. The Earth is the only planet that we know so far to have all this liquid water. Earth's oceans of water mean there is much life here.

How did the planet Earth luck out? No one knows for sure, but maybe the right "timing" had something to do with it!

THE RIGHT TIME

Roughly 4,600,000,000 (4.6 billion) years ago, it seems that conditions were right for life to

eventually begin. A whirling mass of gas and dust was pulled together by gravitational attraction. This started the process of *condensation*: the gas and dust materials were squeezed together into a much smaller space. As this happened, the center of our planet was formed. It became very hot at the same time. The Earth's center, or inner core, is made up of white-hot (5,000°C/9,000°F) liquid iron-nickel metal. Over this very hot core a layer of molten rock (silicate), often called the Earth's mantle, formed. Its temperature is about 870°C/1,600°F. On top of the mantle is the Earth's crust.

THE RIGHT PLACE

Earth, the third planet in our solar system, is 148,000,000 kilometers or 93 million miles from the Sun. Earth's place in space is just right for most of its water to be in a liquid state. Unlike Venus, the second planet, 107,200,000 kilometers (67 million miles) from the Sun, Earth's not too hot. The small amount of water on Venus is in the form of vapor. And it's not too cold, like Mars, the fourth planet, 227,200,000 kilometers (142 million miles) from the Sun. The small amount of water on Mars is in the form of ice.

THE RIGHT SIZE AND WEIGHT

The Earth is 12,656 kilometers or 7,910 miles in diameter and weighs 5,900,000,000,000,000,000 or 5.9 quintillion tonnes (6.6 sextillion tons)! It is this combination that produces the gravitational attraction necessary to hold on to an atmosphere like ours.

The Atmosphere

The atmosphere, the original security blanket, surrounds Earth. It is the very air we, and all living things, breathe. Without the right combination of elements — 78 percent nitrogen, 21 percent oxygen, 1 percent other gases and water vapor — life would not be possible. Venus, for example, has no life, because approximately 98 percent of its atmosphere is carbon dioxide. There is only a trace of oxygen and water vapor. Our own moon has no atmosphere. No one lives there but the "man in the moon," who is really just a crater formation that looks like a man's face when viewed from Earth.

Speaking of the moon's craters, they are constantly being formed by meteors that bombard the moon's surface. The Earth's atmosphere protects us from the same never-ending meteor shower. It is estimated that nearly 200 million meteors hit the Earth's atmosphere every day! Most of them, however, burn up before they reach the Earth's surface.

The Lithosphere

The lithosphere is the Earth's crust, its rock bottom. From the highest continental point in the world, Mount Everest, to the lowest oceanic point in the world, the Marianna Trench, the lithosphere is like a fantastic trophy that sits on top of the Earth's mantle, the molten layer of rock under the Earth's crust. The thickness of this crust varies. Under the continents it is about 32 kilometers (20 miles) thick and under the ocean floor it is about 8 kilometers (5 miles) thick. Crust is crust whether above or below water. It is no small surprise then that there are underwater valleys, canyons, and mountain ranges. In fact, the greatest mountain range in the world is under water! Extending from the Gulf of Aden (Saudi Arabia) all the way to the Gulf of California (Mexico) and measuring 30,720 kilometers (19,200 miles) in length, it is called the Indian-East Pacific Ocean Cordillera.

Did you know that at one time the six giant landmasses upon which the seven continents of the world are located did *not* exist? Scientists believe that nature may have taken around 200 million years to create them. The story is as follows: Once there was a lone landmass named Pangaea adrift in the only ocean in the world, named Panthalassa. Eventually, Pangaea split in two, forming Gondwanaland and Laurasia. Gondwanaland drifted slowly to the south, splitting into what are today Africa, the Indian subcontinent, Australia, Antarctica, and South America. Laurasia drifted to the north and split into what are today the

landmasses of Eurasia (the world's largest) and North America.

So you see, continents, and landmasses in general, change with time. They have never been permanent in shape or place. They are not glued, nailed, taped, or stapled down. For the last 4.6 billion years, and even this very minute, the continents have been drifting. It is real *slow motion* though! Continents move from 1.3 centimeters to 10 centimeters (½ inch to 4 inches) a year.

What makes the Earth's surface (crust, lithosphere) move? The Earth's crust is made up of about twenty massive formations called plates. These plates carry continents and ocean floors with them as they "float" on the *asthenosphere,* or mantle, the soft molten rock beneath the crustal plates. The plates do not begin and end where continents and oceans meet. One way to tell where the edges are is to check for some outstanding crustal formations like mountains, ocean ridges, ocean-floor trenches, or volcanoes, above or below water.

When one plate slips and slides past another plate, an edge can be pushed up to form a mountain, or pushed down to form a deep trench. If two plates pull apart an ocean floor can be created.

When these plates shake, rattle, or roll, we have what is called an *earthquake!* An earthquake can last for seconds or minutes. It is usually caused by the slow motion squeezing and stretching of rocks at the plate's edges. Finally, when the rocks can't take the pressure, they rupture. These ruptures are called *faults.*

Three, two, one, zero . . . Blast off! Hot gases and rock fragments burst into the air from a volcano! This explosion results from the slow motion of melted rocklike material coming from deep within the Earth. It makes its way to an opening in the crust and then . . . off it goes into the wild blue yonder!

The Earth quakes over a million times in a year. More than three-quarters of these quakes take place in an area called the Ring of Fire, which is the Pacific Ocean plate. In many places its edges are trimmed with volcanic mountains and volcanic islands, not all of which are active. The Ring of Fire includes the Aleutian Islands in the Bering Strait near Alaska, the Pacific Coastal Ranges along the extreme western border of the North American continent, the Andes Mountains on the South American western coast all the way across the South Pacific to the volcanic islands of New Zealand, Papua New Guinea, Indonesia, the Philippines, and Japan.

The effect of earthquakes and volcanoes on the Earth's changing face can be dramatic. Islands may come and islands may go, with the eruption of an ocean volcano.

Other, less dramatic but effective processes also change the Earth's surface, including landslides, rockslides, mud slides, and snowslides, also known as avalanches.

Water

Whether in the form of rain, snow, or ice, a river, lake, or ocean, water has greatly affected the

Earth's surface. Never underestimate its power. With a depth of 1.6 kilometers (1 mile) and a length of 347 kilometers (217 miles), the Grand Canyon ("Gorgeous Gorge") is the world's largest canyon. It was and is being carved out of rock by the Colorado River.

The glaciers (ice lakes) of the last ice age in North America created the Great Plains, the Great Lakes, and other geographic formations as they started to retreat some 20,000 years ago. This great glacial period ended about 12,000 years ago.

Look What the Wind Blew in . . .

Sand dunes . . . and if the wind is strong enough, sand and loose top soil can eventually cover a forest.

Wind and water can change the shape of mountains. For example, the Appalachians is the oldest range on the North American continent. The Appalachians have been around more than 255 million years with winds and waters constantly eroding their surface. That's one good reason why they are round and smooth and not too high. The Rocky Mountains are much younger — 65 million years young! They are jagged, rough, and high. Maybe 160 million years from now, with the wind and water weathering process, they'll look like the Appalachians. Do you ever wonder what the Appalachians will look like then?

The Biosphere

The biosphere, including the atmosphere and the lithosphere, is where life is found! The first biosphere on the planet Earth was the *hydrosphere*. The hydrosphere consists of the water areas of the Earth, and they make up 70 percent of its surface. Without liquid water there would be no life. Life on Earth had its beginnings in the sea nearly 600 million years ago.

From Algae to Algae

The first forms of life on Earth appeared in the sea. They were tiny, microscopic one-celled algae and bacteria. And just think, these first living things, algae, could be an essential source of food in the future if today's world population explosion continues. Our planet's land may not be able to grow enough food to feed everybody!

Be careful! There are sharks in those waters! During the Earth's next 375 million years, evolution

continued at a snail's pace, but fortunately it never clammed up. There were all kinds of shellfish like snails and clams. The first plants to appear on land were ferns. And then some fish decided they could live on dry land as well as in the water — and they became amphibians. *Life had made a landing!* (Were they trying to get away from the sharks?)

It was after this initial landing that life on Earth blossomed. There were evergreen trees and there were dinosaur-size dinosaurs who ruled the Earth. It was during this period, 120 to 160 million years ago, that some members of the reptile family took to the air and became birds. And in the last 65 million years great varieties of plants, animals, fish, and birds continued to develop. Our first relatives appeared 2.5 million years ago. They survived by picking wild berries and fruits and by hunting animals for food and clothing.

About 10,000 years ago the life-style changed. In areas where there was a good drinking-water supply, enough rainfall, and favorable weather, people learned to plant and harvest wild grains and to cultivate fruit trees and vegetables. Once they grew their own food, they no longer needed to travel far and wide to feed themselves. Eventually they grew more than they could eat, so there was a surplus, or lots of extra food. This meant that not everyone needed to be a farmer and some could do other things, like making tools, baskets, and clothes. Others could open shops. This is how life as we know it started! Then small villages became *towns*, and towns became *cities*. A city, as you know, is a community where *many* people live and work. Eventually some cities became "civilizations" where new customs, ideas, and ways of living resulted.

THE RIGHT CONDITIONS

All the earliest known civilizations had the following in common:

- They were located in the Eastern Hemisphere, which is often called the "Old World." (A **hemisphere** means half of a sphere. An example of a sphere is the Earth.)
- They all were located along a river, or rivers.
- The climate was subtropical, just right for farming.

Modern societies have long histories. From the oldest to the youngest, the four "cradles of civilization" were the following:

- The oldest (3500 BC) was in the Tigris-Euphrates River valley, also known as the Fertile Crescent. It was located where Israel, Lebanon, Syria, Iraq, and Iran are today.
- In nearby Egypt 500 years later (3000 BC) the Nile River valley was a major center of civilization.
- It took another 500 years (2500 BC) until the Indus River valley (Pakistan) became a central location of civilization.
- The youngest ancient civilization appeared in the Hwango Ho (Yellow River) and Yangtze River valleys in what is now China, in 1500 BC.

The Western Hemisphere (often referred to as the "New World") has been new for a long, long time! You see, people first appeared in Africa, then they migrated to Europe and Asia. By the time they crossed the Bering Strait that linked Asia (at Siberia) to the Americas (at Alaska) lots of time (thousands of years) had passed.

The first civilizations known in the Americas are a little more than 2,000 years old (young compared with the Tigris-Euphrates valley, which is almost 5,500 years old!). Interestingly enough, these ancient American Indians, the Mayan Indians of Central America and the Incas of South America, like their earlier Eastern Hemisphere counterparts, also started out as farmers and craftspeople.

This "Magical Spherical Miracle," the planet Earth, is home sweet home for all the living things we know. Life is constant growth. Life has been constantly changing since it first appeared in the form of tiny one-celled plants and animals over 600 million years ago. It is slowly changing even today. However, not all of the Earth's "natural" changes are for the good.

Earthquakes and volcanoes can destroy cities. Wind and water weathering can turn fertile land into barren land.

People have been on Earth for a comparatively short period of time (2.5 million years out of 4.6 billion years). Yet people have done a lot to change the Earth. Earthquakes and volcanoes cannot be stopped, that's for sure, but there are ways to improve the Earth's environment. *Reservoirs* have been built to collect water to be used for irrigation. With this water, unproductive desert land can become rich cropland. Dams on rivers provide *water power,* which means electricity, which means energy. And we all know how important that is!

However, not all people-made changes have been for the good, either. In the past, it seems that people didn't give much thought to the Earth's future and always did what was easiest and fastest. Vast forests have been cleared. What does that mean? Besides there being no trees, birds and animals that live in the forest have no homes. What happens to them? Where do they go?

Water has been used as a dumping ground for waste materials from homes and industry. As a result many streams, rivers, and lakes are polluted. What does that mean besides not being able to drink the water or go swimming? Plants and fish live in water. What happens to them? Where do they go?

Nature gave us fog. We added pollution and smoke to it and we got smog. What needs air? All living things: plants, animals, birds, fish, and you. What will happen if the air becomes unbreathable? Where do we go?

Life on Earth is up to all of us. Civilization must practice conservation for the preservation of this Magical Spherical Miracle — in order to keep it in "living color" for future generations.

Hemispheres, or the Sphere's Other Half

The Earth is a sphere. If it were possible to split it in half crosswise in an east-west direction at the equator, the top half would be the Northern Hemisphere, the bottom half would be the Southern Hemisphere.

Or, if it were possible to split it lengthwise in a north-south direction from the Atlantic Ocean to the Pacific Ocean, the left side would be the Western Hemisphere (the Americas) and the right side would be the Eastern Hemisphere (Europe, Asia, Africa, and Australia). And that's the way it is!

AS THE EARTH TURNS

The Earth spins like a top on its tilted axis. It takes 24 hours (one whole day) to make one complete turn!

The sun's rays will always give you the time of day! Look on the brighter side. It's daytime. Look on the darker side. It's nighttime.

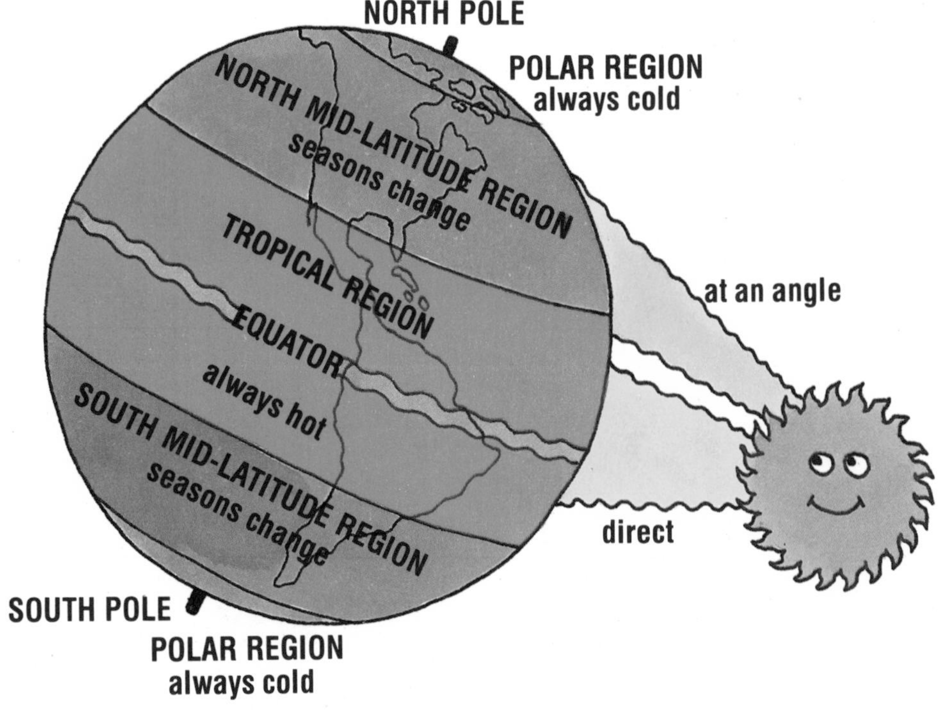

The world has 24 time zones that correspond to the Earth's 24-hour complete spin!

Greenwich, England, was chosen to be the location of what is called the *prime meridian,* or 0° longitude. Meridians, or lines of *longitude,* are imaginary lines running north-south from the Earth's North and South poles. They measure distances east and west of Greenwich. At Greenwich, when the sun is directly overhead, it is 12 noon Greenwich mean time (GMT). Don't forget the Earth is spinning in a west to east direction, so it is later in the day the farther east you go!

In fact, traveling east, by the time you get all the way (halfway, actually) to the mid-Pacific Ocean from Greenwich you'll run into another "very real imaginary" line, the *international dateline,* zigzagging the length of the Pacific Ocean from the North to the South Pole. The dateline separates calendar days. Say it is 3 PM Sunday. You are in the mid-Pacific and you travel west across the dateline, it would now be 3 PM Monday — the next day! Are you hungry? According to the calendar you should be. Not only did you miss Sunday dinner, but also Monday breakfast and lunch.

Time marches on! Days turn into weeks, into months, into years!

While the Earth rotates on its tilted axis each day (and night), it also travels around the sun. It takes 365¼ days (one year) for the Earth to make one complete trip around the sun.

Spring . . . summer . . . fall . . . winter. Seasons depend on the Earth's latitude and its "leaning" toward and away from the sun. This tilting causes the seasons to change by affecting the range of the sun's rays four times a year in both the Northern and Southern hemispheres.

Lines of *latitude,* or parallels, are imaginary lines running in an east-west direction around the Earth. They measure distances north and south of the equator. Latitude, like longitude, is measured in degrees (°). The equator is 0° latitude.

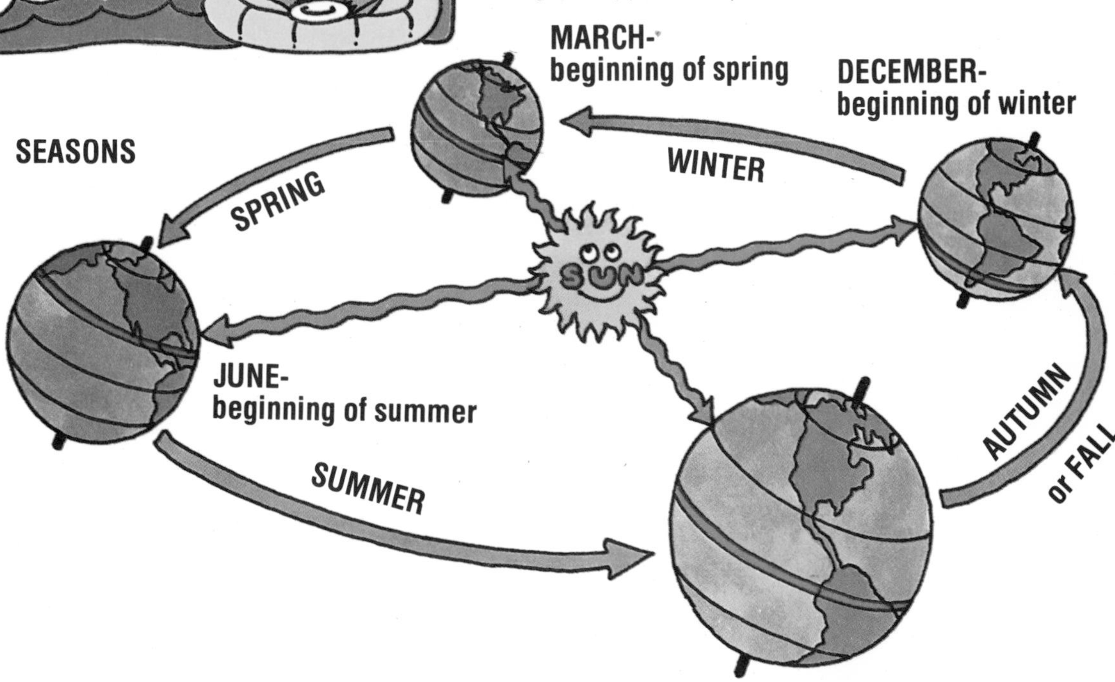

The More, the Warmer!

In the Northern Hemisphere, the first day of summer is in June. The Earth is at full tilt, leaning its northernmost part toward the sun. It is no wonder then that the first day of summer is the longest day, or the shortest night, of the year (which means there are more hours of daylight). The more sunlight, the warmer the weather. What is happening on this same day in June in the Southern Hemisphere? The southern part of the Earth is leaning *away* from the sun. The days are short and the weather is cold. This is the first day of winter in the Southern Hemisphere—the shortest day, or the longest night, of the year (which means there are more hours of darkness).

Remember the north mid-latitude region in the Northern Hemisphere and the south mid-latitude region in the Southern Hemisphere are alike in that they both have four seasons. But they are different, too. When it is summer in the Northern Hemisphere, it is winter in the Southern Hemisphere. The four seasons are always opposite throughout the entire year!

Some regions never change or change only very slightly.

When it's hot, it's hot at the equator, which is the Earth's middle and extends north to the north tropic line (Tropic of Cancer) and south to the south tropic line (Tropic of Capricorn). The sunlight is direct, the hours of daylight long. These tropic regions are hot all year around.

When it's cold, it's cold, like at the North Pole (Arctic) and at the South Pole (Antarctic). At the extreme ends of the Earth, the sunlight is indirect and the hours of daylight are short. These polar regions are cold all year around.

WHERE IN THE WORLD IS...?

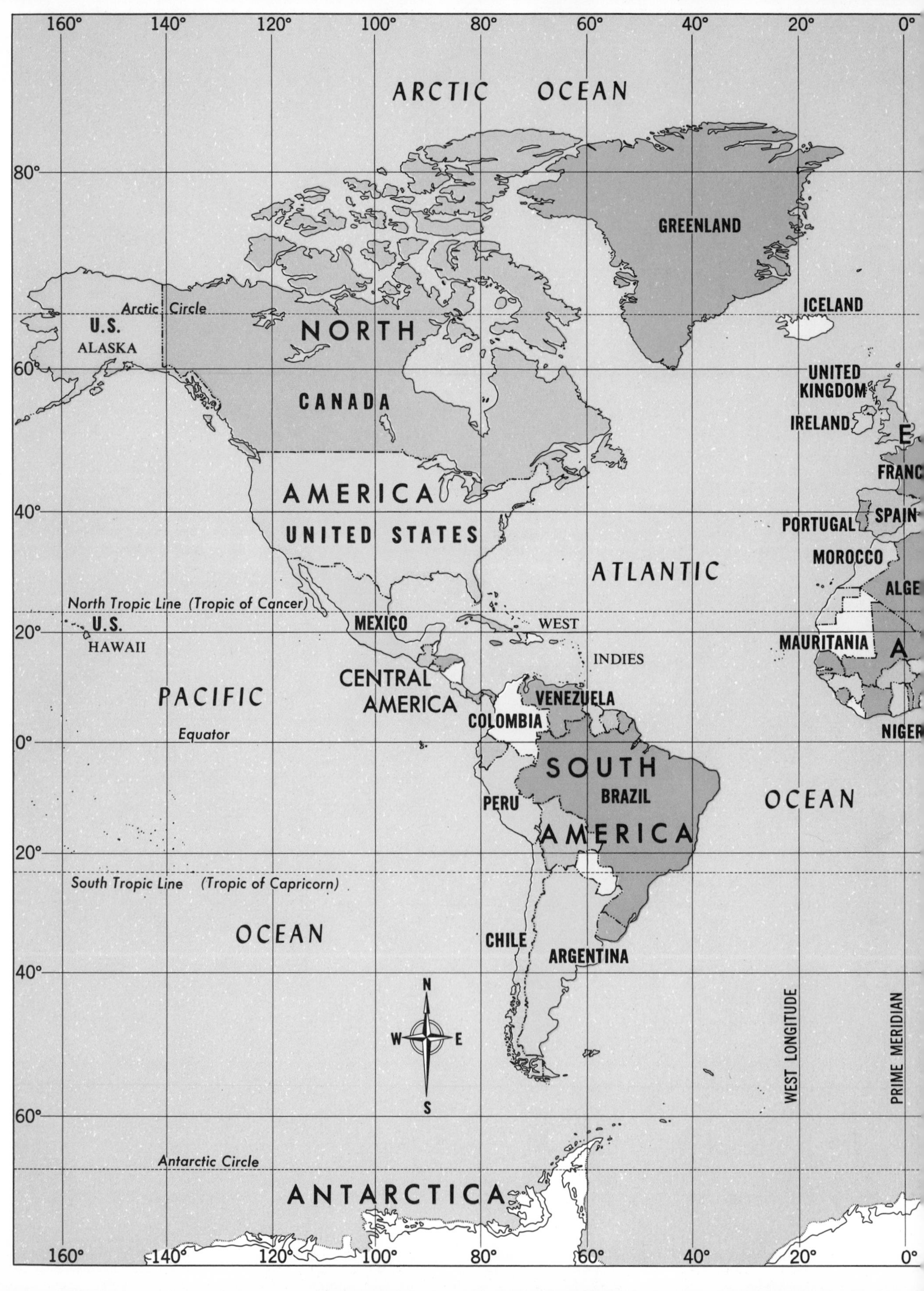

160°
140°
120°
100°
80°
60°
40°
20°
0°
ARCTIC OCEAN
80°
GREENLAND
ICELAND
Arctic Circle
U.S.
ALASKA
NORTH
60°
UNITED KINGDOM
CANADA
IRELAND
E
FRANC
AMERICA
40°
UNITED STATES
PORTUGAL
SPAIN
MOROCCO
ATLANTIC
ALGE
North Tropic Line (Tropic of Cancer)
U.S.
HAWAII
MEXICO
WEST
INDIES
20°
MAURITANIA
A
CENTRAL AMERICA
PACIFIC
VENEZUELA
COLOMBIA
Equator
NIGER
0°
SOUTH
BRAZIL
PERU
OCEAN
AMERICA
20°
South Tropic Line (Tropic of Capricorn)
OCEAN
CHILE
ARGENTINA
40°
N
W
E
S
WEST LONGITUDE
PRIME MERIDIAN
60°
Antarctic Circle
ANTARCTICA
160°
140°
120°
100°
80°
60°
40°
20°
0°

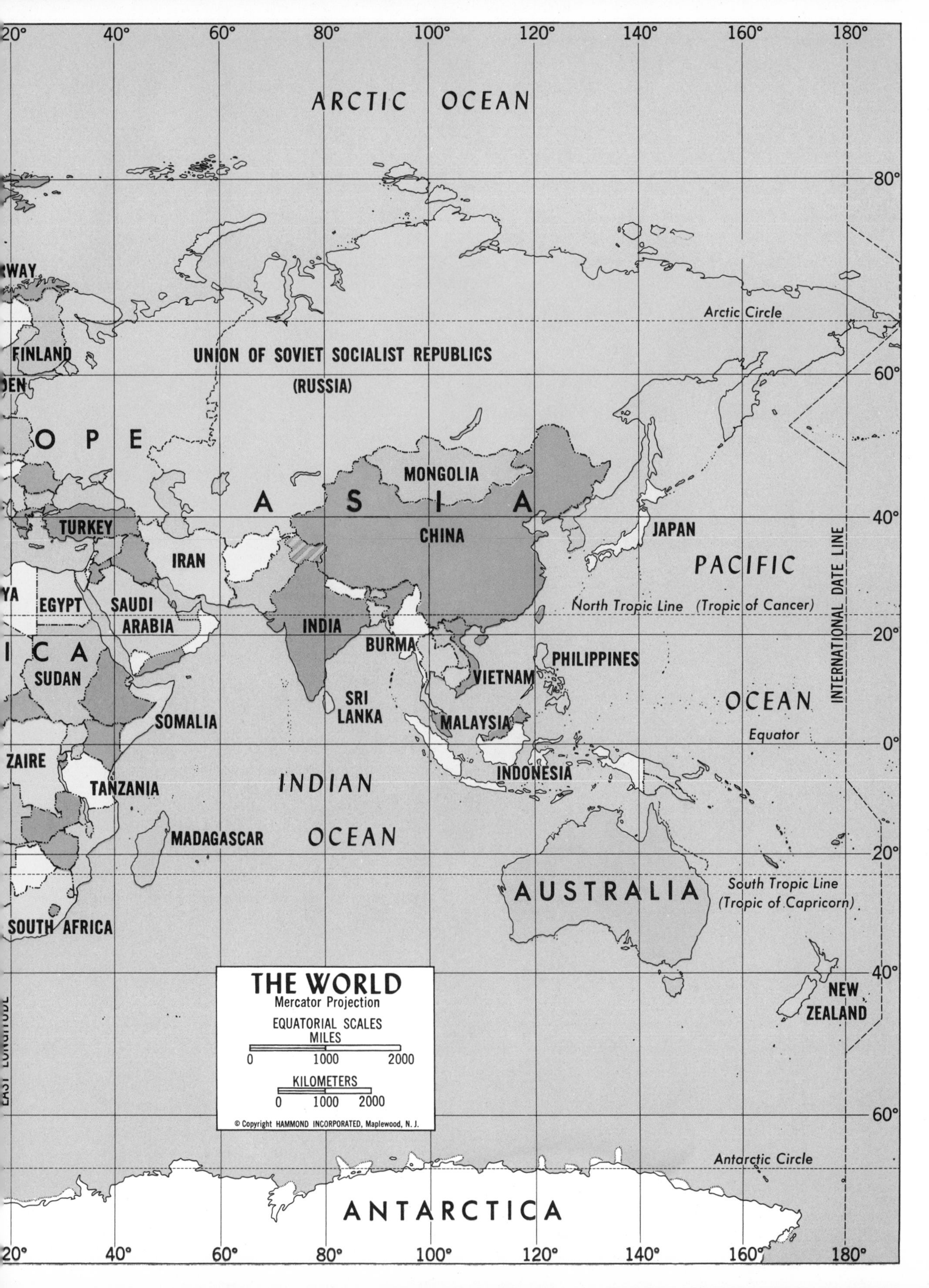

ARCTIC OCEAN
UNION OF SOVIET SOCIALIST REPUBLICS
(RUSSIA)
FINLAND
MONGOLIA
A S I A
TURKEY
CHINA
IRAN
JAPAN
PACIFIC
EGYPT
SAUDI ARABIA
INDIA
North Tropic Line (Tropic of Cancer)
BURMA
PHILIPPINES
SUDAN
VIETNAM
SRI LANKA
OCEAN
SOMALIA
MALAYSIA
Equator
ZAIRE
INDONESIA
TANZANIA
INDIAN
OCEAN
MADAGASCAR
AUSTRALIA
South Tropic Line
(Tropic of Capricorn)
SOUTH AFRICA
NEW ZEALAND
Arctic Circle
Antarctic Circle
ANTARCTICA
INTERNATIONAL DATE LINE
THE WORLD
Mercator Projection
EQUATORIAL SCALES
MILES
0 1000 2000
KILOMETERS
0 1000 2000
© Copyright HAMMOND INCORPORATED, Maplewood, N. J.

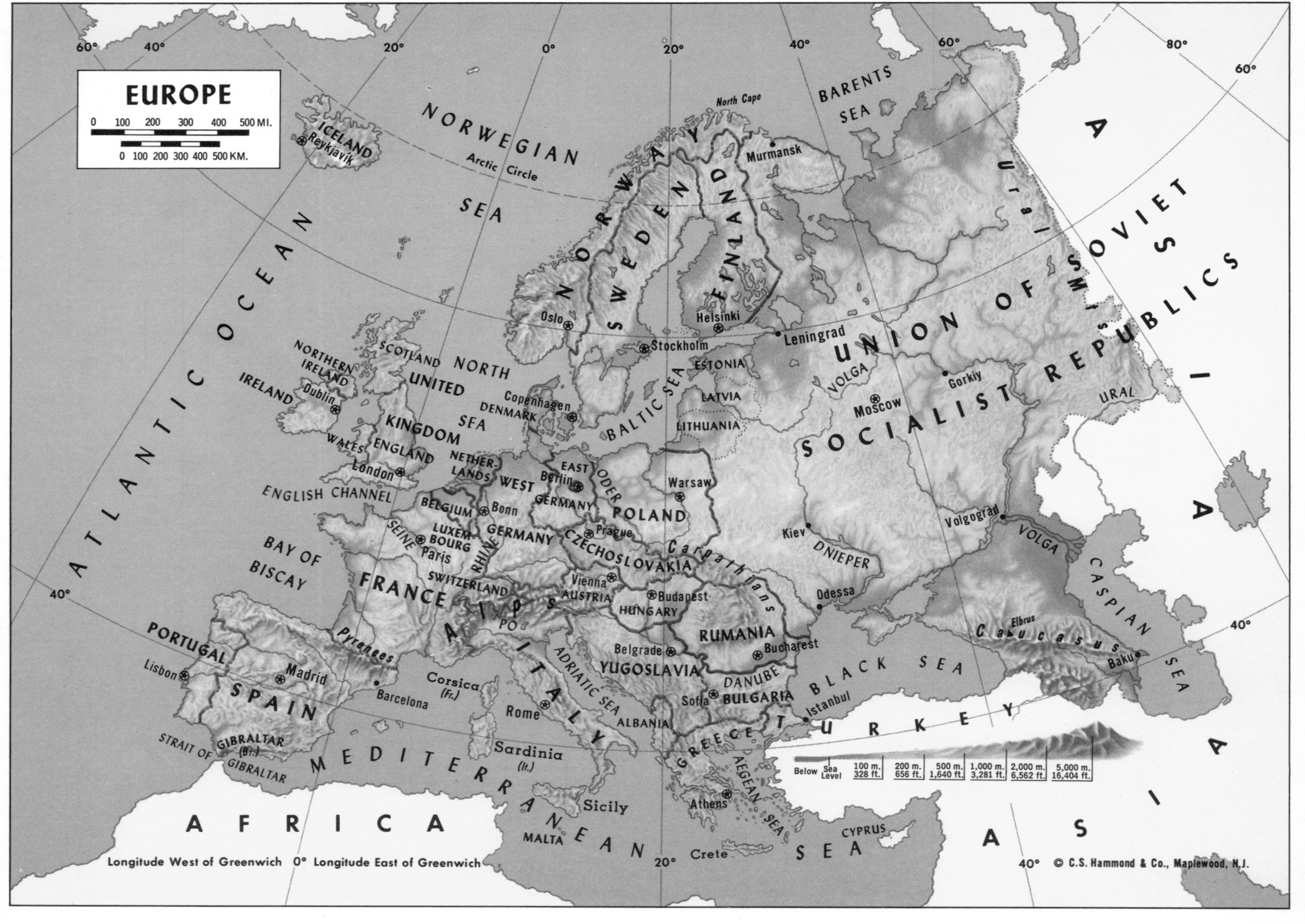
EUROPE
0 100 200 300 400 500 MI.
0 100 200 300 400 500 KM.
NORWEGIAN SEA
Arctic Circle
ATLANTIC OCEAN
ICELAND
Reykjavik
North Cape
BARENTS SEA
Murmansk
NORWAY
SWEDEN
FINLAND
Oslo
Stockholm
Helsinki
Leningrad
UNION OF SOVIET SOCIALIST REPUBLICS
Urals
URAL
VOLGA
Gorkiy
Moscow
ESTONIA
LATVIA
LITHUANIA
BALTIC SEA
NORTHERN IRELAND
IRELAND
Dublin
SCOTLAND
UNITED KINGDOM
WALES
ENGLAND
London
NORTH SEA
Copenhagen
DENMARK
NETHERLANDS
EAST GERMANY
Berlin
WEST GERMANY
Bonn
ODER
POLAND
Warsaw
ENGLISH CHANNEL
BELGIUM
LUXEMBOURG
SEINE
Paris
RHINE
Prague
CZECHOSLOVAKIA
Carpathians
Kiev
DNIEPER
Volgograd
CASPIAN SEA
BAY OF BISCAY
FRANCE
SWITZERLAND
Vienna
AUSTRIA
Alps
Budapest
HUNGARY
Odessa
PO
RUMANIA
Bucharest
Elbrus
Caucasus
Baku
PORTUGAL
Lisbon
Pyrenees
Madrid
SPAIN
Barcelona
Corsica (Fr.)
ITALY
Rome
ADRIATIC SEA
Belgrade
YUGOSLAVIA
DANUBE
Sofia
BULGARIA
ALBANIA
BLACK SEA
Istanbul
TURKEY
GREECE
Athens
AEGEAN SEA
STRAIT OF GIBRALTAR
GIBRALTAR (Br.)
Sardinia (It.)
Sicily
MALTA
MEDITERRANEAN SEA
Crete
CYPRUS
AFRICA
ASIA
Below Sea Level
100 m. 328 ft.
200 m. 656 ft.
500 m. 1,640 ft.
1,000 m. 3,281 ft.
2,000 m. 6,562 ft.
5,000 m. 16,404 ft.
Longitude West of Greenwich 0° Longitude East of Greenwich
© C.S. Hammond & Co., Maplewood, N.J.

EUROPE

Europe is the second smallest continent in the world. About the same size in area as the United States, it is made up of 34 different countries. Suppose that you lived in Austria and wanted to go skiiing in neighboring Switzerland. Besides skis and poles, you had better remember to pack your passport, foreign language dictionary, and, of course, warm clothes.

The continent of Europe shares the Eurasian landmass, the world's largest, with the continent of Asia. Their common border is made up of the Ural and Caucasus mountains and the largest lake in the entire world, the Caspian Sea. The Romans named it *Mare Caspium.* Although the water tastes

salty, it's not as salty as the ocean. Therefore, both freshwater and saltwater fish are found here. Despite its name, the Caspian Sea is landlocked, and that makes it a *lake!*

Geographically Speaking

There are four major land regions in Europe:

- The Northwest Mountains include the mountains of Ireland, Great Britain, northwest France, Norway, Sweden, northern Finland, and the northwest corner of European Russia.
- The Great European Plain stretches from the Soviet Union to France and includes southeastern England. How, you might ask, can a plain cross the water? Once upon a time, early in the formation of the Earth, England was attached to the main continental body.
- The Central Uplands are centrally located. They're found in Czechoslovakia, Germany, France, Spain, and Portugal.
- The Alpine Mountain System, which you'll find in the south, includes Switzerland, France, Italy, and Austria. But it also includes the Sierra Nevada elevations in Spain; the Pyrenees on the French-Spanish border; the Apennines in Italy; the Dinaric Alps of Yugoslavia and Greece; the Balkans of Bulgaria; and the Carpathians of central Czechoslovakia, southern Poland, western Russia, and Rumania. These mountains are among the youngest on Earth — a mere 65 million years old.

Maptalk

A **peninsula** is a portion of land that is almost completely surrounded by water. In Europe, there are five:

- Scandinavian Peninsula: Norway and Sweden
- Jutland Peninsula: Denmark
- Iberian Peninsula: Portugal and Spain
- Apennine Peninsula: Italy
- Balkan Peninsula: Yugoslavia, Albania, Bulgaria, and Greece.

Did you know that some geographers consider the European continent itself to be a peninsula of the Eurasian landmass?

Spanish National Tourist Office

No Kidding!

The oldest center of advanced civilization in Europe was in Greece around 500 BC. Geography played a key role. The Greek peninsula and islands became ideal rest areas for their seafaring neighbors. It was through this contact with foreign, more advanced cultures like Phoenicia and Egypt that knowledge spread.

In fact, at this very moment you are experiencing a result of this contact. The Greeks borrowed the Phoenicians' written alphabet. They made some changes. The most outstanding change was reversing the direction of writing. Words had been written from right to left, but they changed the direction from left to right. You are reading from left to right right now. Right?

Stonehenge: Sandstone pillars completed about 2150 BC stand on England's Salisbury Plain.

British Tourist Authority

How did Greek civilization influence al Europe? Remember there were no newspap TV to spread ideas. But there were Romans, a they were militarily powerful. They conquered Greece, took over its land, and adopted its civilization, making their own contributions along the way. As the Romans continued their conquests, they passed on their knowledge throughout Europe.

Did you know that many European countries can trace back their national boundaries 2000 years to the ancient Roman Empire?

How's the Weather?

Much of Europe enjoys mild weather, mostly due to the Gulf Stream. As the Gulf Stream flows, it transports warm water from the Gulf of Mexico to Europe's western coast. As there are no sizable mountains on Europe's western shores to act as a windbreaker, winds blowing in from the Atlantic Ocean across the continent are warmed by these waters. Putting it mildly, where else but in Europe would you expect to find a Mediterranean climate —hot, dry summers and mild, rainy winters? The warm waters of the Mediterranean Sea make the weather quite nice for Spain, France, Yugoslavia, Greece, and Italy.

Is That a Fact?

	Europe
Area:	10,523,000 sq. km. (4,063,000 sq. mi.)
Total population:	676,000,000
Children aged 0–14:	195,235,000
High spot:	Mount Elbrus, USSR 5,633 m. (18,481 ft.)
Low spot:	Caspian Sea, USSR 28 m. (92 ft.) below sea level
Smallest country:	Vatican City 0.44 sq. km. (0.17 sq. mi.)
Largest country:	USSR (Europe) 4,975,000 sq. km. (1,920,750 sq. mi.)
City with most people:	Moscow, USSR
Northernmost town:	Vest Spitsbergen, Norway

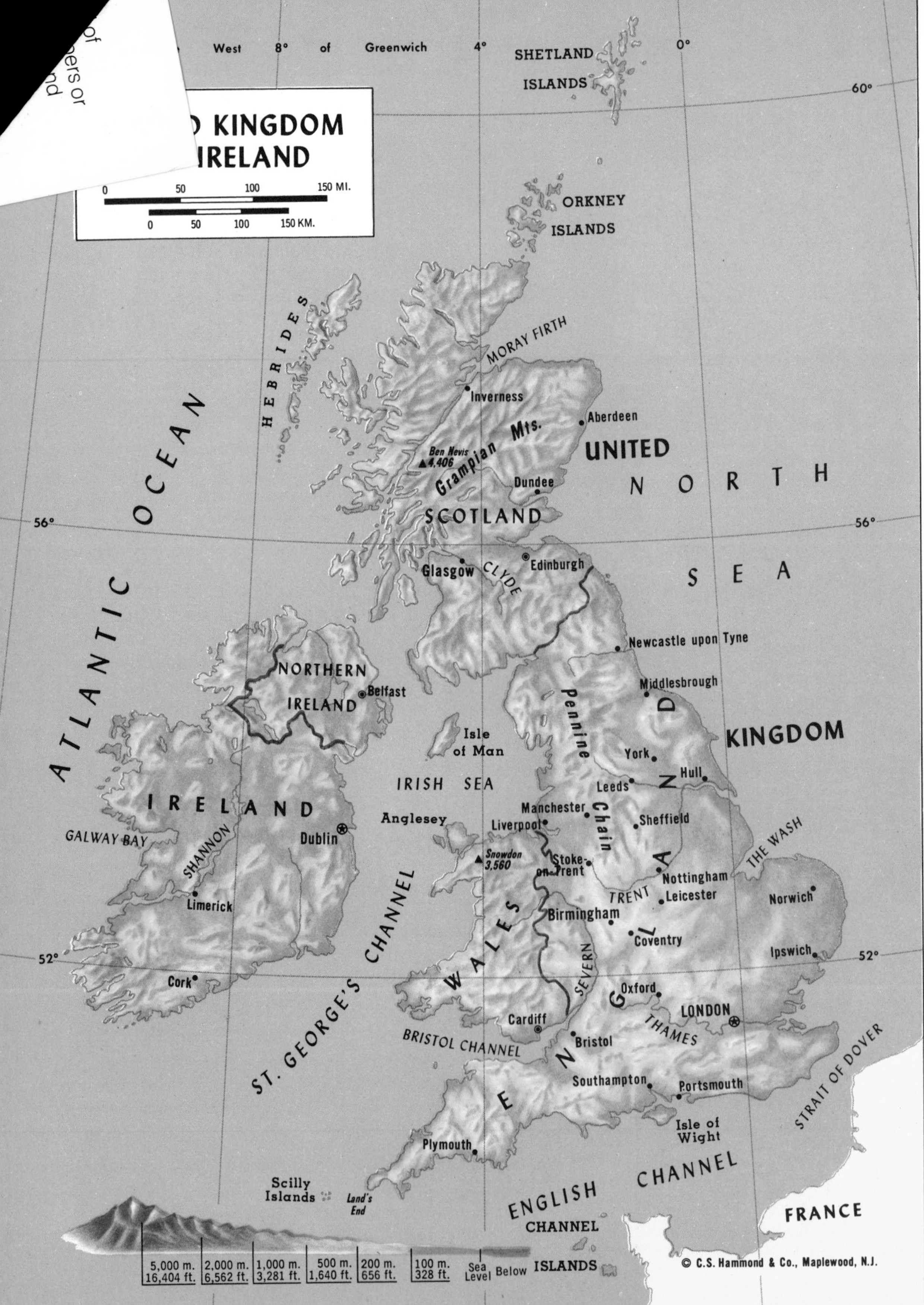

D KINGDOM
IRELAND
0
50
100
150 MI.
0
50
100
150 KM.
West
8°
of
Greenwich
4°
0°
60°
56°
52°
SHETLAND
ISLANDS
ORKNEY
ISLANDS
HEBRIDES
MORAY FIRTH
Inverness
Aberdeen
Grampian Mts.
Ben Nevis
4,406
UNITED
NORTH
SEA
KINGDOM
Dundee
SCOTLAND
Edinburgh
Glasgow
CLYDE
ATLANTIC
OCEAN
Newcastle upon Tyne
Middlesbrough
NORTHERN
IRELAND
Belfast
Isle
of Man
Pennine
Chain
York
Hull
Leeds
IRISH SEA
IRELAND
Manchester
Anglesey
Liverpool
Sheffield
GALWAY BAY
SHANNON
Dublin
Snowdon
3,560
Stoke-
on-Trent
THE WASH
Nottingham
Limerick
TRENT
Leicester
Norwich
Birmingham
Coventry
WALES
ST. GEORGE'S CHANNEL
Ipswich
SEVERN
Cork
Oxford
LONDON
Cardiff
THAMES
Bristol
BRISTOL CHANNEL
ENGLAND
Southampton
Portsmouth
STRAIT OF DOVER
Isle of
Wight
Plymouth
ENGLISH CHANNEL
Scilly
Islands
Land's
End
FRANCE
CHANNEL
ISLANDS
5,000 m.
16,404 ft.
2,000 m.
6,562 ft.
1,000 m.
3,281 ft.
500 m.
1,640 ft.
200 m.
656 ft.
100 m.
328 ft.
Sea
Level
Below
© C.S. Hammond & Co., Maplewood, N.J.

United Kingdom and Ireland

Geographically Speaking

The British Isles are made up of more than 5,000 islands. The two main islands are Great Britain and Ireland. There are three countries on the island of Great Britain, which is the seventh largest island in the world: England, Scotland, and Wales. There are two countries on the island of Ireland: Ireland and Northern Ireland.

What is the United Kingdom, or as it is more accurately called, the United Kingdom of Great Britain and Northern Ireland? The countries in the United Kingdom are England, Scotland, Wales, and Northern Ireland. What about Ireland? It is an independent country. But when you say British Isles, Ireland is included!

It's only 61 meters to 91 meters (200 feet to 300 feet) deep. It's one of the world's most important waterways and is 563 kilometers (350 miles) long. Many attempt to swim across it, even though it's 34 kilometers to 160 kilometers (21 miles to 100 miles) wide. It's the English Channel. Why is it so shallow? Geologists believe that this is where England and France were once connected.

Naturally

The great white cliffs of Dover in England are made of chalk! They were formed by deposits of millions of lime-shelled protozoa (single-cell animals). This happened over 225 million years ago.

Even though Wales produces one-quarter of Great Britain's steel, its coal and iron-ore deposits are running low. Coal and iron ore are nonrenewable resources, and that means when the deposits are used up, they're not replaceable.

Instead of bringing coal to Newcastle, England, take it to Ireland; the bins are empty. But the Irish are not bogged down; they are rich in peat, which they use for heat.

The Wales slate quarry is not wiped clean! It is one of the world's largest quarries and is still producing slate.

A Natural W.O.W. (Wonder of the World)

Have you ever walked across a creek or a river on a natural bridge of stepping stones? Off the coast of Northern Ireland there is a giant one made of 40,000 stepping stones. These stepping stones are actually six-sided columns that are 6 meters (20 feet) high. They were formed by volcanic lava that was cooled by the sea. This bridge is called Giants Causeway, *naturally.*

It's a small world and the Industrial Revolution certainly helped to make it that way. The roar of power-driven machinery which marked the beginning of the Industrial Revolution in England in the 1700s was heard around the world.

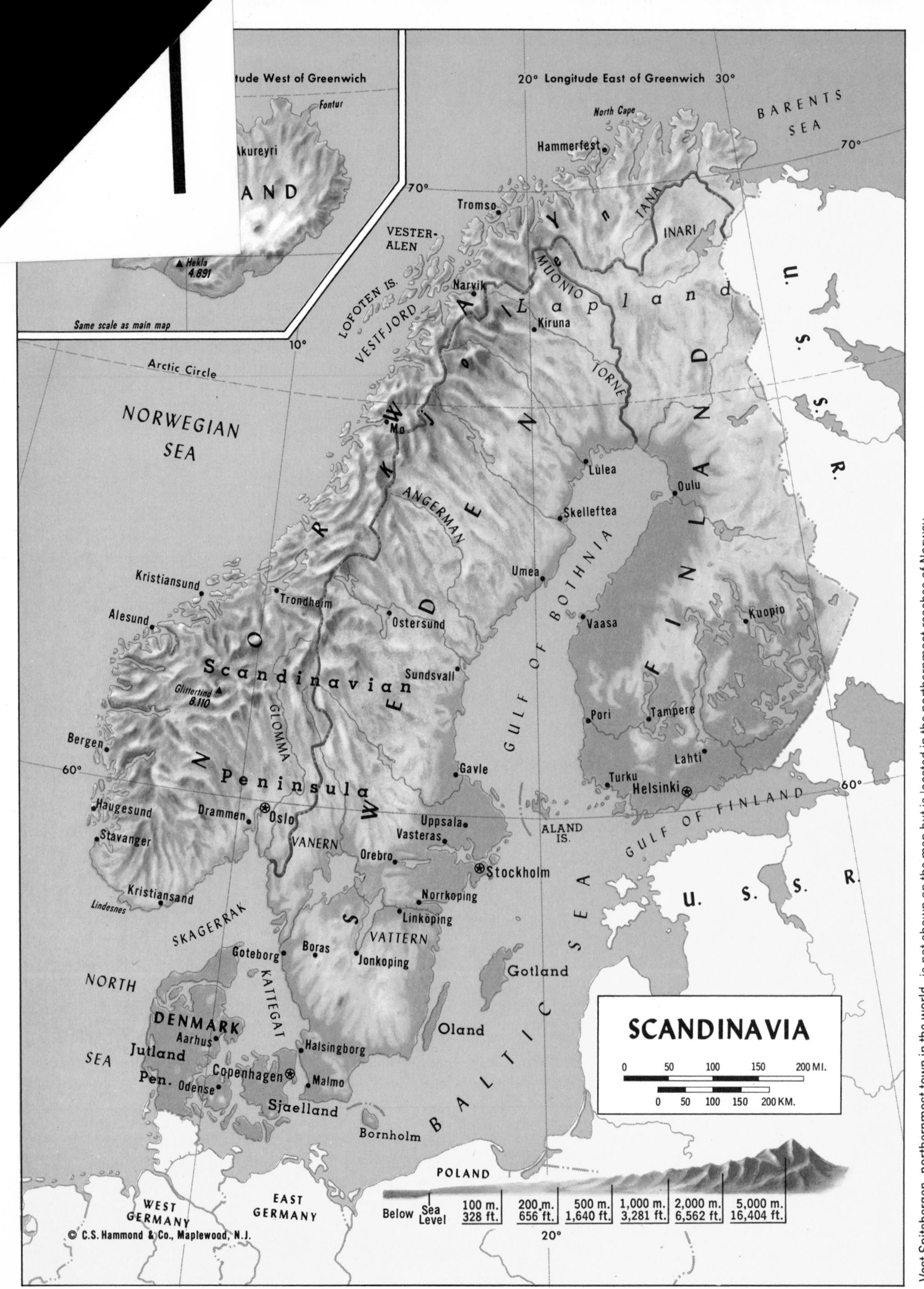

Vest Spitsbergen, northernmost town in the world, is not shown on the map but is located in the northernmost reaches of Norway.

Scandinavia

"Big Blue Marble" Photograph

Geographically Speaking

Arctic Circle, icebergs, and reindeer. Cross-country skiing is not just a sport here, it is a way of life. The average temperature along the western coast of Norway is 7°C (45°F) in *January*. Not what you would expect? The fact is, the climate is rather mild, especially along the low-lying coastal areas. The Gulf Stream is the reason.

The "Land of the Midnight Sun" is in the northernmost parts of Iceland, Norway, Sweden, and Finland. During approximately two and one-half months in the summer, the Sun doesn't "set." There are 24 hours of daylight because of the Earth's tilt on its axis and its position relative to the Sun. What happens in the winter? Although the name doesn't change to the Land of the Noonday Moon, there can be as few as six hours of daylight.

Lapland, above the Arctic Circle, is land that belongs to Norway, Sweden, Finland, and the Soviet Union, but this land is inhabited by the Lapps — 34,000 Asiatic nomadic people. They have lived there for thousands of years, much like their ancestors did, tending herds of reindeer, the very key to their survival.

Maptalk

A **geyser** is a spring that shoots hot water and/or steam into the air. The word "geyser" comes from the famous Icelandic hot spring called *Geysir,* which sends water 59 meters (195 feet) into the air. Iceland has more hot springs and sulfur-steam areas than any other country in the world. Iceland also has about 200 volcanoes and as much glacier-covered land as all of Europe. No wonder Iceland is often referred to as the "Land of Frost and Fire."

Finland has 60,000 lakes!

Fiord, or fjord, is the Norwegian word for a deep bay or water inlet situated between steep rocky walls of land. Millions of years ago glaciers shaped fiords and rivers deepened them. The Sogne Fiord in Norway is 160 kilometers (100 miles) long; the walls are 1,500 meters (5,000 feet) high.

Norway is really up there when it comes to mountains, plains, and towns!

Glittertinden is northern Europe's tallest mountain: 2,470 m. (8,104 feet).
Hardanger Plateau is Europe's largest highland plain: 11,700 sq. km. (4,500 sq. mi.).
Vest Spitsbergen is the northernmost town in Europe and the world.

Naturally

"Timber," or its equivalent in Norwegian, Swedish, and Finnish, can usually be heard in the vast forest regions of this neck of the woods. These three countries are leaders in paper and wood-pulp manufacturing. Finland is the world's top producer of plywood.

Because the Scandinavian peninsula and islands are surrounded by water, these countries have *naturally* "gone fishing."

Sweden has some of the world's largest iron-ore deposits.

No Kidding!

In Iceland, many people have the same name. So, for easy identification, names *and* occupations are listed in the telephone book: "Hello, is this my friend Jon the fisherman?"

The Vikings were mighty seafarers and explorers from Norway, Sweden, and Denmark. The most famous, Leif Ericson, came to North America in about AD 1000.

BELGIUM, NETHERLANDS
and LUXEMBOURG
0 20 40 60 MI.
0 20 40 60 KM.
NORTH SEA
WEST FRISIAN ISLANDS
Waddenzee
Leeuwarden
Groningen
Friesland
IJsselmeer
Vechte
Holland
Haarlem
AMSTERDAM
Hilversum
Apeldoorn
IJssel
Enschede
NETHERLANDS
The Hague
Leiden
Utrecht
Arnhem
Rotterdam
Lek
Goeree
Nijmegen
Schouwen
Dordrecht
Waal
Rhine
Maas
Walcheren
Breda
Tilburg
Flushing
Eindhoven
WEST
Ostend
Bruges
Antwerp
Albert Canal
Flanders
Ghent
Mechelen
Genk
Scheldt
Lys
Courtrai
Aalst
Louvain
BRUSSELS
Maastricht
GERMANY
BELGIUM
Tournai
Liège
Seraing
Namur
Mons
Charleroi
Meuse
Botrange
2,277
Sambre
Ardennes
Bastogne
LUXEMBOURG
FRANCE
Mosel
Semois
Luxembourg
Esch-sur-Alzette
Below Sea Level
100 m. 328 ft.
200 m. 656 ft.
500 m. 1,640 ft.
1,000 m. 3,281 ft.
2,000 m. 6,562 ft.
5,000 m. 16,404 ft.
4°
6°
52°
50°
6° Longitude East of Greenwich

Belgium, Netherlands, and Luxembourg

Geographically Speaking

The countries of Belgium, the Netherlands (often called Holland), and Luxembourg are equal in size to two and one-half states of Maryland and one state of Rhode Island.

Maptalk

A **canal** is a narrow man-made waterway used for transportation and/or irrigation.

The "Canal Connection." The Netherlands has a network of rivers and canals measuring 6,400 kilometers (4,000 miles). That's a lot when you consider the Netherlands' greatest distance in a north-south direction is just 315 kilometers (196 miles). East to west it is just 269 kilometers (167 miles).

A **polder** is the Dutch name for land at or below sea level that has been reclaimed from the sea.

What does "below sea level" make you think of? Underwater, right? Well, much of the Netherlands, often called the Lowlands, *is* below sea level, a pretty unique situation. Here's why. From out of the sea comes the land. Two-fifths of the Netherlands was once covered by the sea. Windmills provided the power to run the pumps that drained the sea-water off the land. Dikes and other barriers were built to hold back the sea, revealing rich farmland, *naturally*.

As a matter of fact, the Zuider Zee, formerly the Netherlands' largest bay, is now part of its richest farmland.

Prince Alexander polder is the lowest point in the Netherlands, 6.7 meters (22 feet) below sea level.

The "Lowlands" do have their high points, though. In Belgium it is Botrange Mountain at 694 meters (2,277 feet). In the Netherlands it is Vaalser Berg at 322 meters (1,057 feet). In Luxembourg it is Buurgplaatz at 559 meters (1,835 feet).

Naturally

Belgium, with its coal, and Luxembourg, with its iron ore, got together to make steel; then the Netherlands joined them, bringing its farm products to the union. The economic alliance of Benelux in 1958 was the result.

No Kidding!

The expression, "To meet your Waterloo," means to meet your defeat or, more simply, to lose. Waterloo is the name of a town located in central Belgium. The French Emperor Napoleon, who was busy conquering Europe, was the first person ever to meet his Waterloo at Waterloo in 1815.

"Who is that clomping around in the kitchen?" It can't be a Dutch person wearing *klompen,* the wooden shoes worn to work in the fields. Before someone wearing klompen comes inside, he or she takes them off first.

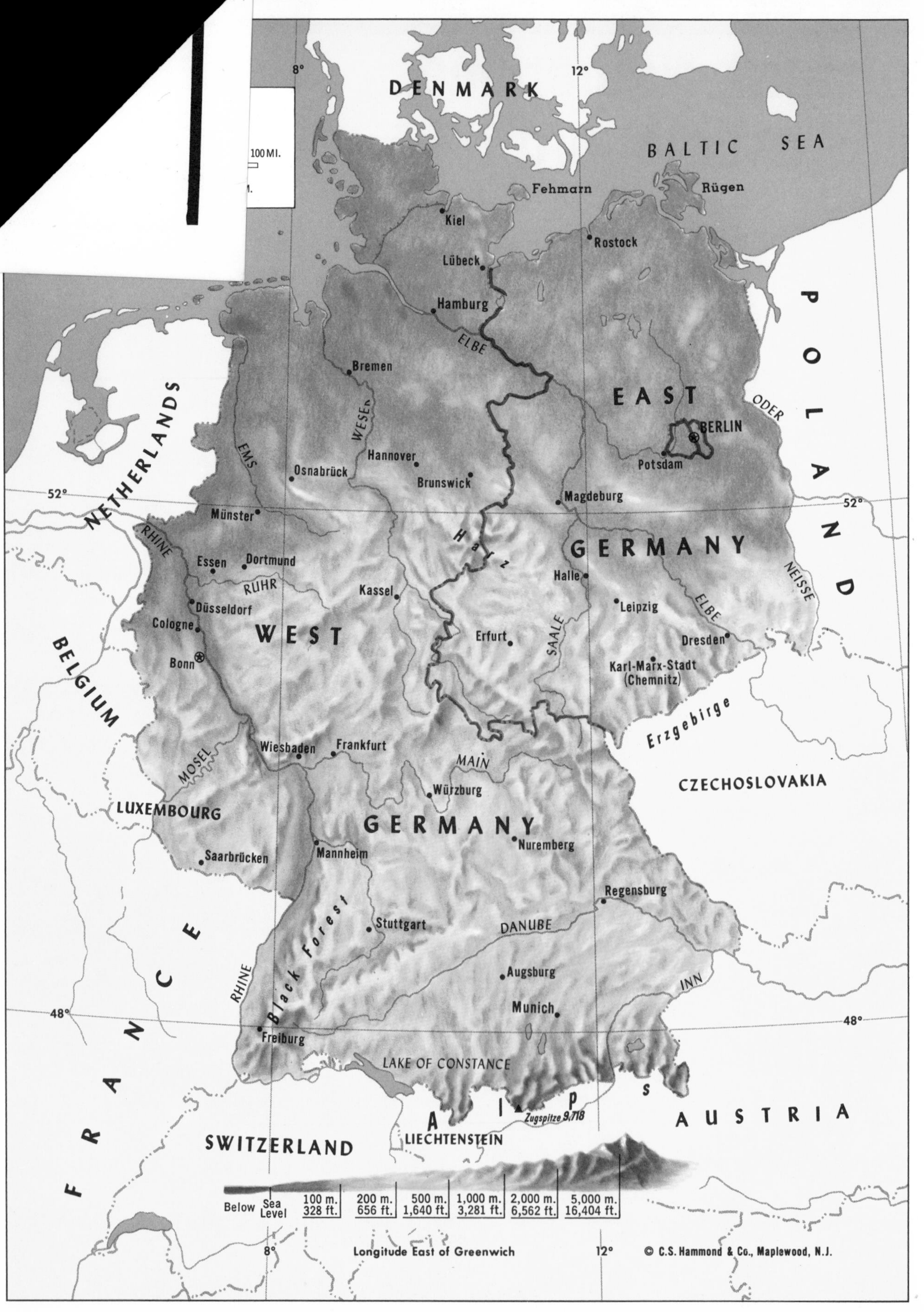

DENMARK
BALTIC SEA
Fehmarn
Rügen
Kiel
Rostock
Lübeck
Hamburg
ELBE
Bremen
WESER
EAST
ODER
BERLIN
Potsdam
POLAND
NETHERLANDS
EMS
Hannover
Osnabrück
Brunswick
Magdeburg
52°
Münster
RHINE
Harz
GERMANY
Essen
Dortmund
RUHR
Kassel
Halle
NEISSE
Leipzig
ELBE
Düsseldorf
Cologne
WEST
Erfurt
SAALE
Dresden
BELGIUM
Bonn
Karl-Marx-Stadt
(Chemnitz)
Erzgebirge
Wiesbaden
Frankfurt
MOSEL
MAIN
CZECHOSLOVAKIA
Würzburg
LUXEMBOURG
GERMANY
Nuremberg
Saarbrücken
Mannheim
Regensburg
Stuttgart
DANUBE
Black Forest
FRANCE
RHINE
Augsburg
INN
48°
Munich
Freiburg
LAKE OF CONSTANCE
Alps
Zugspitze 9,718
AUSTRIA
SWITZERLAND
LIECHTENSTEIN
8°
12°
100 MI.
Below Sea Level
100 m. 328 ft.
200 m. 656 ft.
500 m. 1,640 ft.
1,000 m. 3,281 ft.
2,000 m. 6,562 ft.
5,000 m. 16,404 ft.
Longitude East of Greenwich
© C.S. Hammond & Co., Maplewood, N.J.

Germany

Geographically Speaking

From its western boundaries to its eastern boundaries, the great German Plain "drain" involves some of Europe's most famous rivers: the Rhine, the Ems, the Weser, the Elbe, and the Oder. All these rivers flow from the south to the north, draining into the North Sea (northwest) and the Baltic Sea (northeast).

The north German Plain lies low, less than 91 meters (300 feet) above sea level, and it is as flat as every other plain. In between the great wide river valleys with their fertile soil is other land that is covered with gravel and sand. The Germans call this the *heathlands*. The heathlands were formed way before any of us was born — 10,000 years ago — when the glaciers of the last ice age pulled back, leaving gravel and sand in their tracks.

In the Central Highland plateaus, Germany's rivers have been cutting away at the rock and soil for thousands of years. The steep narrow valleys of gorges that were formed are gorgeous. The Rhine River valley is just one of these scenic gorges. Its medieval castles peeking out through the trees make this a sight to be seen.

You may have heard of the delicious Black Forest cake, but the *real* Black Forest is the home of fairy tales and elves. It is a mountainous region with peaks that reach an average height of 760 meters to 910 meters (2,500 feet to 3,000 feet). The ragged slopes are covered thickly with lush dark fir and spruce trees.

Germany has its Alps, German style. They are called the Bavarian Alps. These snow-capped mountains rise 1,800 meters (6,000 feet), making them Germany's highest peaks!

Sure-footed sheep graze in the south German hills. There's such good grazing land in Germany that beef, dairy cattle, and hogs get their fill.

In western Germany, where the Moselle and Rhine rivers twist and wind around, grows Germany's famous fruit of the vine — grapes, used to make wine.

The Ruhr River region is one of the busiest industrial areas in the world and it comes by its features *naturally*. The Ruhr is an easy source of transportation and water power, and there are large deposits of coal nearby.

No Kidding!

No artificial ingredients, no artificial preservatives added! This label could have been applied over 100 years ago when the Germans, in an attempt to prevent cabbage from spoiling, added some vinegar. They were successful! The cabbage didn't spoil, although it tasted a little sour. Sauerkraut became world famous!

German Information Center

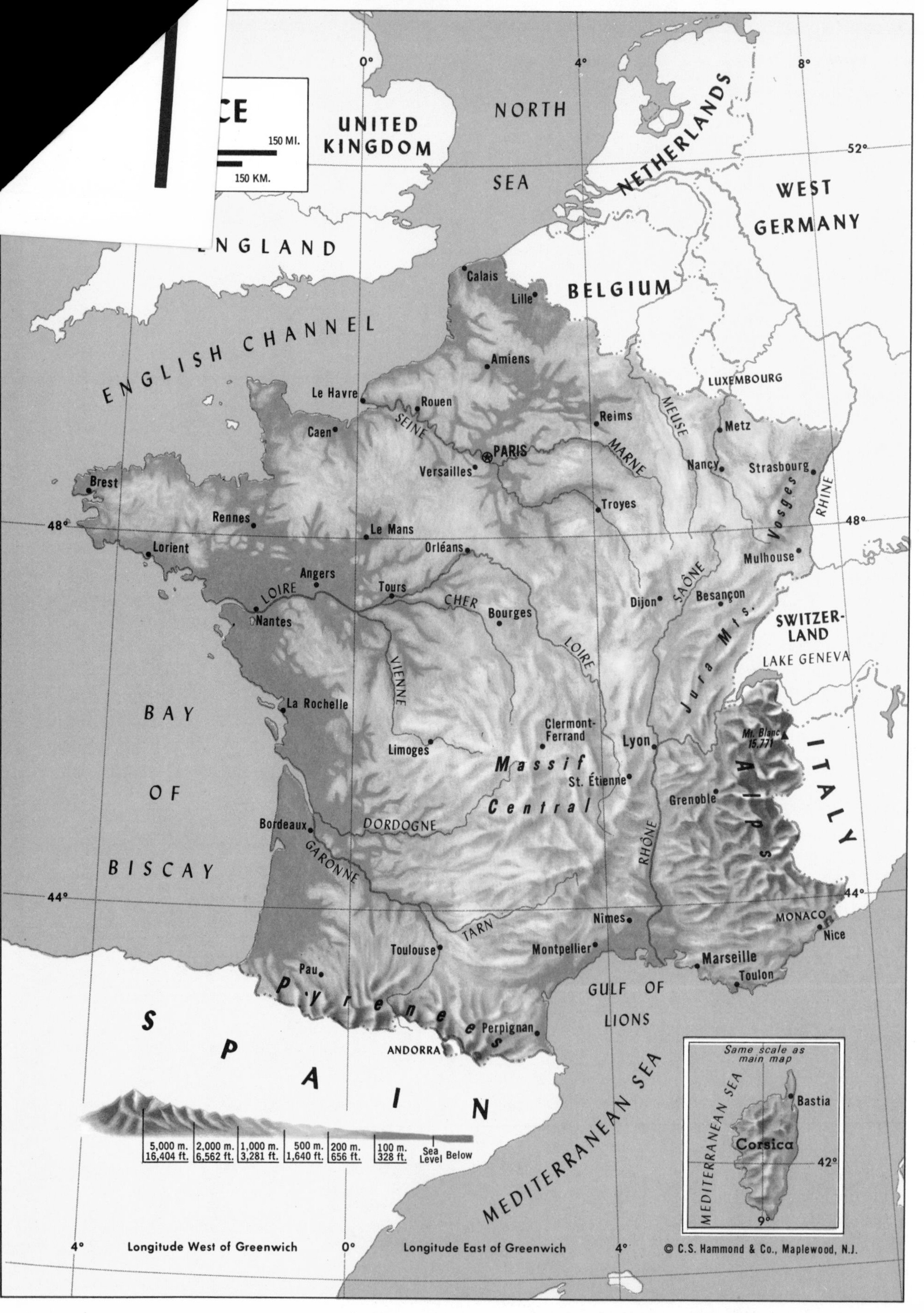

CE
150 MI.
150 KM.
UNITED KINGDOM
NORTH SEA
NETHERLANDS
WEST GERMANY
ENGLAND
BELGIUM
LUXEMBOURG
ENGLISH CHANNEL
Calais
Lille
Amiens
Le Havre
Rouen
Caen
SEINE
Reims
MEUSE
MARNE
Metz
PARIS
Versailles
Nancy
Strasbourg
Vosges
RHINE
Brest
Rennes
Troyes
Le Mans
Lorient
Orléans
Mulhouse
Angers
Tours
LOIRE
CHER
Bourges
Dijon
SAÔNE
Besançon
Nantes
Jura Mts.
SWITZER-LAND
LAKE GENEVA
VIENNE
LOIRE
BAY OF BISCAY
La Rochelle
Clermont-Ferrand
Lyon
Mt. Blanc 15,771
Limoges
Massif Central
St. Étienne
Grenoble
Alps
ITALY
Bordeaux
DORDOGNE
RHÔNE
GARONNE
MONACO
Nice
Nîmes
TARN
Toulouse
Montpellier
Marseille
Toulon
Pau
Pyrenees
GULF OF LIONS
Perpignan
ANDORRA
SPAIN
MEDITERRANEAN SEA
Same scale as main map
MEDITERRANEAN SEA
Bastia
Corsica
5,000 m. 16,404 ft.
2,000 m. 6,562 ft.
1,000 m. 3,281 ft.
500 m. 1,640 ft.
200 m. 656 ft.
100 m. 328 ft.
Sea Level
Below
4°
0°
4°
8°
9°
42°
44°
48°
52°
Longitude West of Greenwich
Longitude East of Greenwich
© C.S. Hammond & Co., Maplewood, N.J.

France

Geographically Speaking

All along France's west-coast lowlands that border on the Bay of Biscay is great grape-growing country. The climate is fine for the vines that produce the grapes that make some of France's world-famous grape "juice"—wine!

The rivers Garonne and Dordogne water Bordeaux's great vineyards. Bordeaux is natural gas and oil country, too.

France's northwestern corner (with the cities of Brest, Lorient, and Rennes) has many of the world's oldest mountain formations. The Brittany-Normandy hills are no longer the great big mountains they probably once were. Today they are low, rounded, rolling hills.

The central northern plain has flat to rolling terrain. In the center of the plain is the Paris basin, which is drained by the river Seine and other major rivers. Ninety percent of France has fertile soil and much of it is found here, where sugar beets and wheat are grown and cattle and sheep graze.

The city of Lille, near Belgium, has *more than a little bit* of coal.

Northeastern France is plateau country, and in the Vosges Mountains there is iron ore. France is a world-leading producer. *Coal plus iron equals steel.*

France's eastern border with Germany is the Rhine River, the main inland waterway of Europe. Besides being a busy, bustling avenue for boats, the Rhine River is bordered on both sides by truck routes and railroad lines and its slopes are covered with trees and more grapevines.

The massive central highland plateau called Massif Central is both large and centrally located. Here, the Loire River, the longest river totally contained in France, originates. It flows north and west 1,050 kilometers (650 miles) to the coast and empties into the Bay of Biscay.

The Jura Mountains and the French Alps, part of the European Alpine Mountain System, border on Italy and Switzerland.

Many of France's fruits and vegetables are grown in its sunny Mediterranean lowlands and the Rhône-Saône River valleys. Here they are shielded by the Alps from the cold north wind called the *Mistral*. Every once in a while the Mistral "jumps" the Alps and blows into the valleys and damages the crops.

A Man-made W.O.W.

The Eiffel Tower is considered one of the modern wonders of the world. When it was built in 1889, this tower was the highest structure in the world, 300 meters (984 feet) from its base to its top.

"Big Blue Marble" Photograph

SPAIN AND PORTUGAL
0 50 100 150 MI.
0 50 100 150 KM.
Below Sea Level
100 m. 328 ft.
200 m. 656 ft.
500 m. 1,640 ft.
1,000 m. 3,281 ft.
2,000 m. 6,562 ft.
5,000 m. 16,404 ft.
Longitude West of Greenwich
Longitude East of Greenwich
BAY OF BISCAY
FRANCE
Pyrenees
ANDORRA
Cantabrian Mts.
Iberian Peninsula
SPAIN
PORTUGAL
ATLANTIC OCEAN
MEDITERRANEAN SEA
ALGERIA
MOROCCO
El Ferrol
La Coruña
Cape Finisterre
Oviedo
Gijón
Santander
San Sebastián
Bilbao
Vitoria
Pamplona
León
Burgos
EBRO
MIÑO
Vigo
Orense
Braga
Oporto
DOURO
Valladolid
Saragossa
Lérida
Sabadell
Barcelona
Salamanca
Coimbra
Sa. da Estrêla
MADRID
Toledo
TAGUS
Castellón de la Plana
GULF OF VALENCIA
Valencia
JÚCAR
Lisbon
Setúbal
Évora
GUADIANA
Badajoz
Albacete
Sierra Morena
Alicante
Córdoba
GUADALQUIVIR
Murcia
Cartagena
Jaén
Huelva
Seville
Granada
Mulhacén 11,411
Sa. Nevada
Almería
Faro
Cape St. Vincent
GULF OF CÁDIZ
Jerez de la Frontera
Cádiz
Málaga
GIBRALTAR (Br.)
STRAIT OF GIBRALTAR
Ceuta (Sp.)
Alborán (Sp.)
Minorca
Majorca
Palma
Ibiza
BALEARIC ISLANDS (Spain)
8°
4°
0°
40°
36°

Spain and Portugal

Spanish National Tourist Office

Geographically Speaking

Portugal and Spain make up the Iberian Peninsula of Europe. It is surrounded on three sides by water: the Bay of Biscay to the northwest, the Atlantic Ocean to the west, and the Mediterranean Sea to the south and east.

Portugal is the "west coast" of Europe. It is easy to understand why Portugal, with the white-wavy, wild blue yonder of the Atlantic at its back door, was a front-runner, or "front-explorer," during the 1400s' Age of Exploration, when Europe began to search for new lands and trade routes.

In the Douro River valley and Tagus River valley vineyards are where the great grapes of Portugal grow, making Portugal a world-leading wine producer.

The Guadalquivir River basin is also rich and fertile farmland, thanks to irrigation, without which the land would be hot and dry. Together, these two river basins, along with the Mediterranean coastal plains, bring cereals, olives, oranges, and lemons from Spain.

Will the real plain in Spain please stand up? The plain in Spain is mainly on the high and dry plateau that is called a *meseta.* The plains are broken up by hills and low mountains with forests scattered about. The soil is poor for farming, but the goats and sheep don't care because it's great for grazing.

The Tagus River rises in the meseta and takes its course due west as it flows through Spain and Portugal for 1,007 kilometers (626 miles) to the Atlantic Ocean.

The Balearic Islands — Majorca, Minorca, and Ibiza — belong to Spain, and their names give you an idea about their sizes. Majorca is the major, the biggest island of the three; then comes Minorca, which is a minor compared to Majorca; and the smallest is itsy-bitsy Ibiza.

The Sierra Nevada and the Pyrenees are part of the great Alpine Mountain System.

The mercury may rise, the mercury may fall. It is at nature's beck and call. Nature may supply the weather, but Spain supplies much of the world's mercury. Put that in your thermometer or barometer and measure it!

Maptalk

A **strait** is a narrow body of water connecting two larger bodies of water.

At the southern end of Spain there is Gibraltar, with an area of 6 square kilometers (2.3 square miles). The Strait of Gibraltar connects the Atlantic Ocean and the Mediterranean Sea.

¡Olé! Bullfighting is a popular sport in Spain, and most towns have rings (bullfighting arenas). To be a matador, you have to want to challenge the bulls. If you win, you are a national hero. If you lose, it could be quite painful.

Portugal packs sardines like sardines! It is a leading exporter of sardines.

A Natural W.O.W.

As far back as 20,000 years ago, prehistoric man was making an attempt to record history. In caves like the ones at Altamira, Spain, and Lascaux, France, wonderfully detailed drawings have been found. From these walls we learn of our ancestors' lives as hunters and about the deer, bison, and boar they hunted. And maybe the handprints found all over these caves are the first human signatures.

Turin is now Torino. Leghorn is now Livorno.

Italy

Geographically Speaking

It looks like Italy is giving Sicily a kick, with the tip of its boot, that is! Maybe that is why Sicily's active volcano, Mount Etna, is known to blow its stack so often.

Italy is located on the Apennine Peninsula and the Apennine Mountains run the length of Italy's tall boot. In the northern regions, these rugged mountains are covered with beautiful forests. In the central area, the mountains are high and fantastic for grazing. In the south, the mountains are dry. They are known to have earthquakes that cause a lot of landslides. Italy is surrounded on three sides by seas, *naturally*. From west to east, Italy provides a shore for the Ligurian Sea, the Tyrrhenian Sea, the Mediterranean Sea, the Ionian Sea, and the Adriatic Sea.

Italy means "land of grazing" and it has more than its fair share of sheep, cattle, and goats grazing there.

Italy's got the Alps, too. In the north, the Italian Alps' steep slopes are great pasturelands for sure-footed sheep and goats. Its tumbling waterfalls provide energy for the Po River valley located below. In the summer, the melting of snow from the mountains provides an important water supply for farming areas.

The Po River valley is Italy's richest natural resource. This fertile farmland is the best-managed and one of the most highly productive regions in all of Europe. Corn, rice, sugar beets, and wheat grow along the Po.

In the Po, they don't miss a chance! Did you know that even though grapes don't grow on trees, in Italy grapevines are strung between the trees! That's using space wisely and practically.

Ninety percent of the island of Sardinia is covered by mountains. It's great for grazing sheep and growing wheat.

Naturally

Carrara marble for building buildings and sculpting sculpture comes from Italy's Carrara quarry.

Is there any reason why olives are sometimes served when people are drinking wine? Probably not. However, in Italy, as in other Mediterranean countries, olive trees and grapevines grow side by side.

Did you hear about the day Mount Vesuvius blew its top back in AD 79? The city of Pompeii, Italy, was covered with lava that flowed from this volcano more than 1,900 years ago. Although destructive, this lava acted as a preservative. Today, the buildings look the same as they did the day Mount Vesuvius erupted.

No Kidding!

Guess what fish is found in the waters around Sardinia? It isn't tuna, but it *is* sardines.

Italy's got the littlest: Vatican City is the smallest independent state in the world — 44 hectares (109 acres).

Italy's got the biggest: Sicily is the largest island in the Mediterranean Sea — 25,708 square kilometers (9,926 square miles).

Any way you twirl it — on a fork, on a fork with a spoon, or even on a chopstick! Chopstick? That's right! Spaghetti originally comes from China. In his travels to the Far East in the late 12th century, Marco Polo first tasted these noodles and then brought back to Italy recipes telling how to make them.

SWITZERLAND
and LIECHTENSTEIN
0 10 20 30 40 MI.
0 10 20 30 40 KM.
WEST GERMANY
FRANCE
AUSTRIA
LIECHTENSTEIN
SWITZERLAND
ITALY
JURA
Lake of Constance
Schaffhausen
Thur
Winterthur
St. Gallen
Rhine
Basel
Baden
Wettingen
Limmat
Zürich
Uster
Lake of Zürich
Delémont
Birs
Olten
Aarau
Reuss
Doubs
Aare
Grenchen
Solothurn
Langenthal
Zug
Biel
La Chaux-de-Fonds
Vaduz
Burgdorf
Lucerne
Schwyz
Neuchâtel
Lake of Neuchâtel
Bern
Köniz
Lake of Lucerne
Altdorf
Glarus Alps
Chur
Davos Platz
Fribourg
Thun
Yverdon
Saane
Bernese Oberland
Rhaetian Alps
Inn
Lausanne
Vevey
Montreux
Lake Geneva
Lepontine Alps
St. Moritz
Sierre
Sion
Rhône
Geneva
Bellinzona
Locarno
Martigny
Pennine Alps
Zermatt
Lake Maggiore
Lugano
L. of Lugano
Lake Como
Matterhorn 14,780
Dufourspitze 15,203
Great St. Bernard Pass
Below Sea Level
100 m. 328 ft.
200 m. 656 ft.
500 m. 1,640 ft.
1,000 m. 3,281 ft.
2,000 m. 6,562 ft.
5,000 m. 16,404 ft.
6°
7°
8°
9°
10°
47°
46°
Longitude East of Greenwich

Switzerland and Liechtenstein

Geographically Speaking

Alps by any other name are one and the same as the Swiss Alps!

- Bernese Oberland
- Pennine Alps
- Glarus Alps
- Lepontine Alps
- Rhaetian Alps

The Swiss Alps in the southern part of Switzerland are in the heart of the Alpine Mountain System. There are more mountains in the north. They are part of the Jura range.

The snow-capped, glacier-covered Swiss Alps are the source of the great European river connection. The following rivers run their course north, south, east, and west, finally emptying into seas, *naturally!*

The Rhine River flows north to the North Sea.
The Rhône River flows south and west to the Mediterranean Sea.
The Inn River flows inland east to the Danube River and the Danube River flows east to the Black Sea.
The Ticino River flows south to the Po River and the Po River flows east to the Adriatic Sea.

Switzerland is loaded with glacier lakes. Lake Geneva in the southwest and the Lake of Constance in the northeast were formed by glaciers thousands of years ago.

Naturally

Approximately 60 percent of Switzerland is mountainous. This makes it a real powerhouse. Just think of those glacier-fed rivers running rapidly down the mountainsides. *Hydroelectricity* is the power of water.

Where do the cows whose milk makes the world-famous Swiss cheese graze? In between the northern (Jura) mountains and the southern (Alps) mountains there is a high plateau where people live and work and where grasslands for grazing grow.

No Kidding!

It's nice to be able to borrow a cup of sugar from a neighbor. Liechtenstein (lying between Switzerland and Austria) has more than a neighbor in neighboring Switzerland. Liechtenstein uses Swiss money and stamps. Switzerland represents Liechtenstein in foreign-trade and other business matters.

"Big Blue Marble" Photograph

AUSTRIA, CZECHOSLOVAKIA AND HUNGARY
0 25 50 75 100 MI.
0 25 50 75 100 KM.
5,000 m. 16,404 ft.
2,000 m. 6,562 ft.
1,000 m. 3,281 ft.
500 m. 1,640 ft.
200 656
EAST GERMANY
WEST GERMANY
POLAN
CZECHOSLOVAKIA
CZECH SOCIALIST REPUBLIC
SLOVAK SOCIALIST REPUBLIC
AUSTRIA
HUNGARY
YUGOSLAVIA
RUMANIA
ITALY
SWITZER-LAND
LIECHTENSTEIN
U.S.S.R.
Erzgebirge
Sudeten Mts.
Bohemian Forest
Beskids
Carpathians
Alps
Gerlachovka 8,707
Grossglockner 12,461
PRAGUE
VIENNA
BUDAPEST
Bratislava
Usti nad Labem
Liberec
Hradec Kralove
Plzen
Ceske Budejovice
Olomouc
Ostrava
Brno
Kosice
Miskolc
Debrecen
Linz
Salzburg
Innsbruck
Wiener-Neustadt
Leoben
Graz
Klagenfurt
Gyor
Szombathely
Kecskemet
Bekescsaba
Szeged
Pecs
LAKE OF CONSTANCE
LAKE BALATON
DANUBE
VLTAVA
MORAVA
HRON
INN
DRAU
DRAVA
TISZA
12°
16°
20°
48°
Longitude East of Greenwich
© C.S. Hammond & Co., Maplewood, N.J.

Austria, Czechoslovakia, and Hungary

Geographically Speaking

Czechoslovakia's western and northern borders are mountainous, *naturally!*

The western region of Czechoslovakia is called Bohemia. In the Bohemian mountain range are the Ore Mountains. You couldn't ask for more. Not only is there plenty of coal for energy and industry, there is also uranium ore galore — the largest and richest deposit of this nuclear fuel in Europe.

The Bohemian forest has lots of timber.

The Vltava and Elbe rivers, which form the Bohemian basin, are good for farming: potatoes, rye, sugar beets, and wheat; and good for living: Prague,the capital and largest city,is locatedhere.

From the Morava River where the southern Bohemian highland meets the Moravian highlands, the mountains are lower in altitude as the Morava flows north toward Poland. Near Ostrava, in what are called the Moravian lowlands, lies Czechoslovakia's industrial ace in the hole, coal.

They're surrounded! Czechoslovakia and its neighbors to the south — Austria and Hungary — are *landlocked,* meaning they are surrounded entirely by land.

But they will never give up! They don't have to because of the Danube River, Europe's great west-east connection. The beautiful blue Danube flows through all three countries, linking them with all points east, and with Asia, where the Danube empties into the Black Sea.

Alps are alps are alps. There are three separate ranges that make up the Austrian Alps' part of the European Alpine Mountain System. The Northern Limestone Alps are high plateaus and rugged peaks made of limestone. Next to them there is a series of valleys. Then, the Central Alps rise high into the sky. Big granite mountains with glaciers on top, they precede another series of valleys. Finally, the Southern Limestone Alps, which are limestone, form the other side, the third range. Kind of like a granite Alp sandwich between two pieces of limestone.

"Big Blue Marble" Photograph

Seventy-five percent of Austria's total area is mountainous. Like Switzerland, Austria produces a lot of important hydroelectric power.

Austria has some of the largest deposits of magnesite, a resource used in making heat-resistant bricks and plaster. Get out your pencil and take notes! Austria also has some of the largest deposits of graphite, the form of lead used in pencils for writing.

Hungary's western hilly region is a continuation of the Austrian Alps.

Lake Balaton in Hungary is the largest lake in Central Europe. It covers 596 square kilometers (230 square miles).

The Danube and Tisza river basins are separated by sandy dunes that are roughly 120 meters (400 feet) high.

Hungary is a champion and deserves a medal when it comes to the lightweight metal, aluminum. Hungary has some of the world's largest deposits of bauxite, which can be made into aluminum.

A Natural W.O.W.

Czechoslovakia and Hungary have got what it takes in the Aggtelek caverns. There are stalactites and stalagmites and a 450-meter (1,500-feet) underground lake.

THE BALKANS

0 50 100 150 200 MI.

0 50 100 150 200 KM.

Below Sea Level | 100 m. 328 ft. | 200 m. 656 ft. | 500 m. 1,640 ft. | 1,000 m. 3,281 ft. | 2,000 m. 6,562 ft. | 5,000 m. 16,404 ft.

20° Longitude East of Greenwich

Rumania is sometimes Romania. The latter spelling is preferred by the country, according to the United Nations. Salonika (Greece) is now Thessaloniki. Candia (Crete) is now Iraklion.

The Balkans

Geographically Speaking

Rumania is not part of the Balkan Peninsula. However, because of its close historic and political associations with Bulgaria, Yugoslavia, Albania, and Greece, it is often considered to be part of it.

The Danube River is an important commercial link between Europe and Asia. It is Europe's second-longest river, flowing west to east to the Black Sea. For 2,858 kilometers (1,776 miles), it goes through seven countries, three of which are in the Balkans. They are: Yugoslavia, Bulgaria, and Rumania.

Water, water, everywhere! There isn't any part of Greece that is farther than 137 kilometers (85 miles) from water. In fact, one-fifth of Greece is made up of islands.

The Dinaric Alps of Greece and Yugoslavia, the Balkan Mountains of Bulgaria, and the Carpathians of Rumania are part of the Alpine Mountain System.

Naturally

Yugoslavia is a leading producer of bauxite in Europe.

Rumania has the second-largest oil and natural gas resources in Europe. The USSR is first.

Urban outdoor murals may have their origins in Rumania. In medieval times, Rumanians painted beautiful paintings on the outside of church walls to inspire, to remind, and to teach people as they passed by.

The Olympic games are a 2,500-year-old tradition. The first Olympics on record took place in Olympia, Greece, in 776 BC.

In ancient times, plays were performed in huge, open-air amphitheaters. The largest one seated 17,000 people. Would you say today's drive-ins are twentieth-century amphitheaters? The Greek dramatic forms of comedy and tragedy are the basis for many of today's plays and movies.

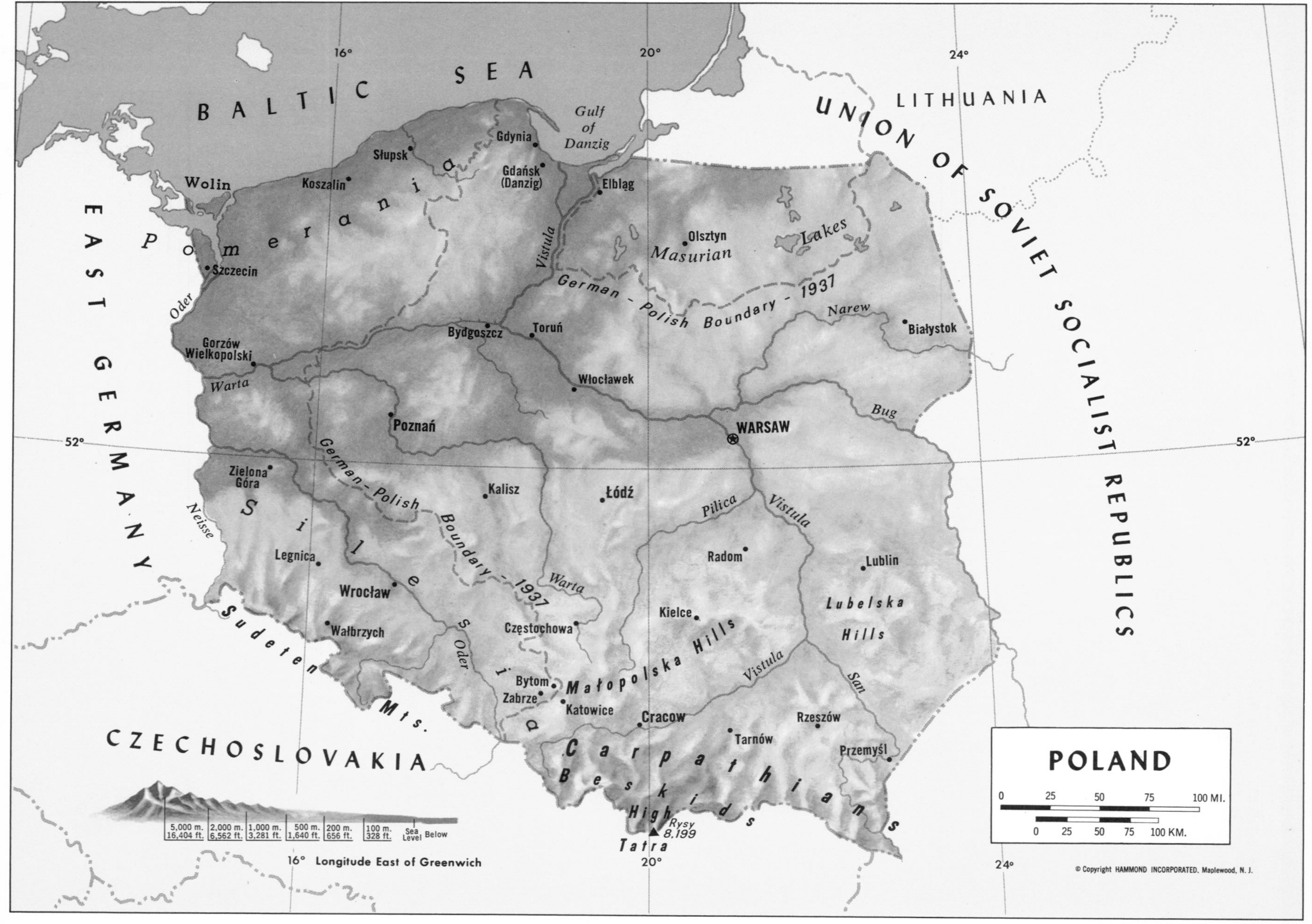
POLAND
0 25 50 75 100 MI.
0 25 50 75 100 KM.
BALTIC SEA
Gulf of Danzig
LITHUANIA
UNION OF SOVIET SOCIALIST REPUBLICS
EAST GERMANY
CZECHOSLOVAKIA
Pomerania
Silesia
Masurian Lakes
German - Polish Boundary - 1937
Lubelska Hills
Małopolska Hills
Sudeten Mts.
Carpathians
Beskids
High Tatra
Rysy 8,199
WARSAW
Wolin
Szczecin
Koszalin
Słupsk
Gdynia
Gdańsk (Danzig)
Elbląg
Olsztyn
Białystok
Bydgoszcz
Toruń
Gorzów Wielkopolski
Włocławek
Poznań
Zielona Góra
Kalisz
Łódź
Legnica
Wrocław
Wałbrzych
Częstochowa
Radom
Kielce
Lublin
Bytom
Zabrze
Katowice
Cracow
Tarnów
Rzeszów
Przemyśl
Oder
Warta
Neisse
Vistula
Narew
Bug
Pilica
San
16°
20°
24°
52°
5,000 m. 16,404 ft.
2,000 m. 6,562 ft.
1,000 m. 3,281 ft.
500 m. 1,640 ft.
200 m. 656 ft.
100 m. 328 ft.
Sea Level
Below
16° Longitude East of Greenwich
© Copyright HAMMOND INCORPORATED, Maplewood, N. J.

Poland

Geographically Speaking

The coastal lowlands of Poland lie along the Baltic Sea. The northern half of Poland, called the Baltic Lakes region, is a vacation land during all seasons. Get out your fishing gear, there are thousands of lakes here.

Poland's name comes from the Slavic word *polane,* which means plain or field. So it shouldn't be a surprise that Poland has a plain that is centrally located. The Central Plains stretch across the entire country!

Plains are just about the same everywhere. They are level expanses of land, good for grazing, good for farming, and good for living! Poland's major cities of Poznań and Warsaw are located on the Central Plains.

Vistula here, Vistula there, everywhere Vistula! The Vistula River's source is in the Carpathians in the south of Poland. It flows east, meets the San River, and changes its course by flowing north. It then meets the Pilica River, continues flowing north, then west, then northeast, and finally empties into the Gulf of Danzig in the Baltic Sea, *naturally!* The Vistula is 1,086 kilometers (675 miles) long.

The Sudeten Mountains and the Carpathians are both part of the Alpine Mountain System that forms a natural border between Poland and its neighbor, Czechoslovakia.

Naturally

Poland's plains produce many of the principal crops, but when it comes to potatoes and rye, Poland ranks among the top world producers.

Poland has more than potatoes in its fields. In the upland region covered with hills, low mountains, and plateaus, near the city of Katowice, coal is king industrially. It is the largest coalfield in the world. But "king coal" is not alone; there are also copper, lead, and zinc.

Mime: *the universal language* "Big Blue Marble" Photograph

"Big Blue Marble" Photograph

UNION OF SOVIET SOCIALIST REPUBLICS

0 200 400 600 800 1000 MI.

0 200 400 600 800 1000 KM.

Below Sea Level	100 m. 328 ft.	200 m. 656 ft.	500 m. 1,640 ft.	1,000 m. 3,281 ft.	2,000 m. 6,562 ft.	5,000 m. 16,404 ft.

Longitude East of Greenwich

C. S. Hammond & Co., Maplewood, N. J.

New Siberian Islands are now Novosibirskiye Ostrava.

Union of Soviet Socialist Republics (Russia)

Geographically Speaking

A country in two continents at one time? The Union of Soviet Socialist Republics (USSR), the largest country in the world with 22 million square kilometers (8.7 million square miles), occupies area in two continents: Europe and Asia. Don't forget, both the continents of Europe and Asia share the largest landmass in the world named Eurasia. Europe is in the west and Asia is in the east.

Russia's Ural Mountains, the Caspian Sea (the world's largest saltwater lake), and the Caucasus Mountains form the "natural" boundary between the continents of Europe and Asia and between European Russia and Asian Russia, often called Siberia.

The Ural Mountains are old, low, rounded mountains. Their average height is 610 meters (2,000 feet). However, several mountains peak at 1,500 meters (5,000 feet).

The Karagiye Depression, located just east of the Caspian Sea, is really low as far as Russia's altitude goes! It is the lowest point in the USSR: 132 meters (433 feet) below sea level.

"Big Blue Marble" Photograph

Between the Caspian and the Aral seas in Soviet Central Asia, there is a checkerboard of desert lands: the Kara Kum and the Kyzyl Kum, Black Sands and Red Sands, respectively.

Siberia stretches from the Ural Mountains east to the Pacific Ocean. It is only the northeastern part that is the freezing Siberia we think of. The temperature can drop to minus 51° C (minus 159° F).

Maptalk

A **plateau** is a highland plain or elevated area of generally level land, sometimes containing deep canyons.

Central Siberia is plateau country. It lies between the Yenisey River on the west and the Lena River on the east. In the southeastern edge of the plateau is Lake Baykal. This lake is the deepest freshwater lake in the world — 1,741 meters (5,712 feet) deep.

In the south-central plateau area near the city of Krasnoyarsk is the largest hydroelectric power station in the world. The Yenisey River is the water supplier.

The western Siberian Plain stretches from the Yenisey River in the east to the Ural Mountains in the west. The western Siberian Plain is no ordinary plain. Its level terrain is the largest expanse of flat land in the world — 2.6 million square kilometers (1 million square miles)!

Mountains and plateaus make up the Eastern Siberian Highlands. The mountains rise as high as 3,000 meters (10,000 feet). There is a series of mountain ranges along the east coast of the USSR that continue onto the Kamchatka Peninsula and into the Sea of Okhotsk, forming the Kuril Islands, *naturally.*

The Kamchatka Peninsula is alive and flowing! There are 25 active volcanoes here. Snow-topped Mount Klyuchevskaya is the highest at 4,750 meters (15,584 feet).

Permafrost is permanently frozen soil.
Tundra is cold, barren (treeless) land.
Taiga is subarctic (below the Arctic Circle) evergreen forest land.
Steppes are mid-latitude grasslands, prairies, or plains.

Much of the northern USSR lies within the Arctic Circle. The Ob, Yenisey, and Lena rivers empty into the Kara Sea and the Laptev Sea, both of which are part of the Arctic Ocean and remain frozen much of the year. This is Russia's frozen *tundra,* where the soil is *permafrost,* permanently frozen. Nothing can grow here except moss and lichen, a simple fungus and alga that grow together as a single plant.

Below the Arctic Circle is the USSR's evergreen-covered *taiga.* Forests cover one-third of the USSR from the Urals to the Pacific Ocean. *Lumber, timber, paper!* Russia leads the world in production of these goods because of its tremendous forests of evergreen trees.

Russia has a *black belt!* Oops, be careful, watch your step. Russia's *steppes* in the extreme southwest, from the Ukraine to southwest Siberia, are top-quality farmland (dark, rich, fertile soil) and pastureland. With more farmland than any other country in the world, the USSR is a leading producer of barley, rye, potatoes, flax, sugar beets, and wheat — those are the facts!

No Kidding!

There is a difference of a mile! Mount Elbrus, located in the Caucasus Mountains on the European side of Russia, is 5,633 meters (18,481 feet) high. It is also the highest point on the European continent.

However, the highest point in the USSR happens to be Communist Peak, which peaks at 7,495 meters (24,590 feet). It is located on Russia's southern Asian border in the Pamir Mountains near China, Pakistan, India, and Afghanistan!

Russia's Volga River is Europe's longest. It is 3,690 kilometers (2,293 miles) long. Russia's longest river, however, is the Lena River in Central Siberia, the Asian portion of the USSR. It is 4,270 kilometers (2,653 miles) long. Russia has a tremendous river connection that is helped along by canals. It's the Volga-Don-Dneiper waterway. Russia's super-river highway.

Seventy-five percent of Russia's total population lives in the steppe region of European Russia. Taking care of everyone, seventy-five percent of Russia's doctors are women.

How's the Weather?

Would you believe the winters are long and cold and the summers are short and warm? You should believe it, it's true, except in the Black Sea region. This region is an exception to the general Russian weather rule. Near the Black Sea there is a real Mediterranean climate. After all, it is not too far from the Mediterranean — just through the Dardanelles at the southwest end of the Black Sea. There are warm summers here and mild rainy winters! It's Russia's vacationland!

Naturally

This giant-size country has giant-size amounts of minerals! It leads the world in the production of manganese, which is found in Georgia and the Ukraine. Manganese is used to make steel!

The Ural Mountains and Kazakhstan are chock full of minerals, making Russia among the world's top-ten producers of nickel, lead, zinc, tin, and the precious metal, gold.

When it comes to the fossil fuels of coal, oil, and natural gas, Russia is hard to surpass. Russia's largest coal mines are in the Donets River basin in the Ukraine and in the Karaganda and Kuznetsk basins in Siberia. Most of Russia's oil and natural gas comes from the Volga-Ural oil fields.

Russia, not to be outdone, has lots of asbestos, sulfur, petroleum, mercury, iron ore, chromium, copper, silver, and platinum, as well.

"Big Blue Marble" Photograph

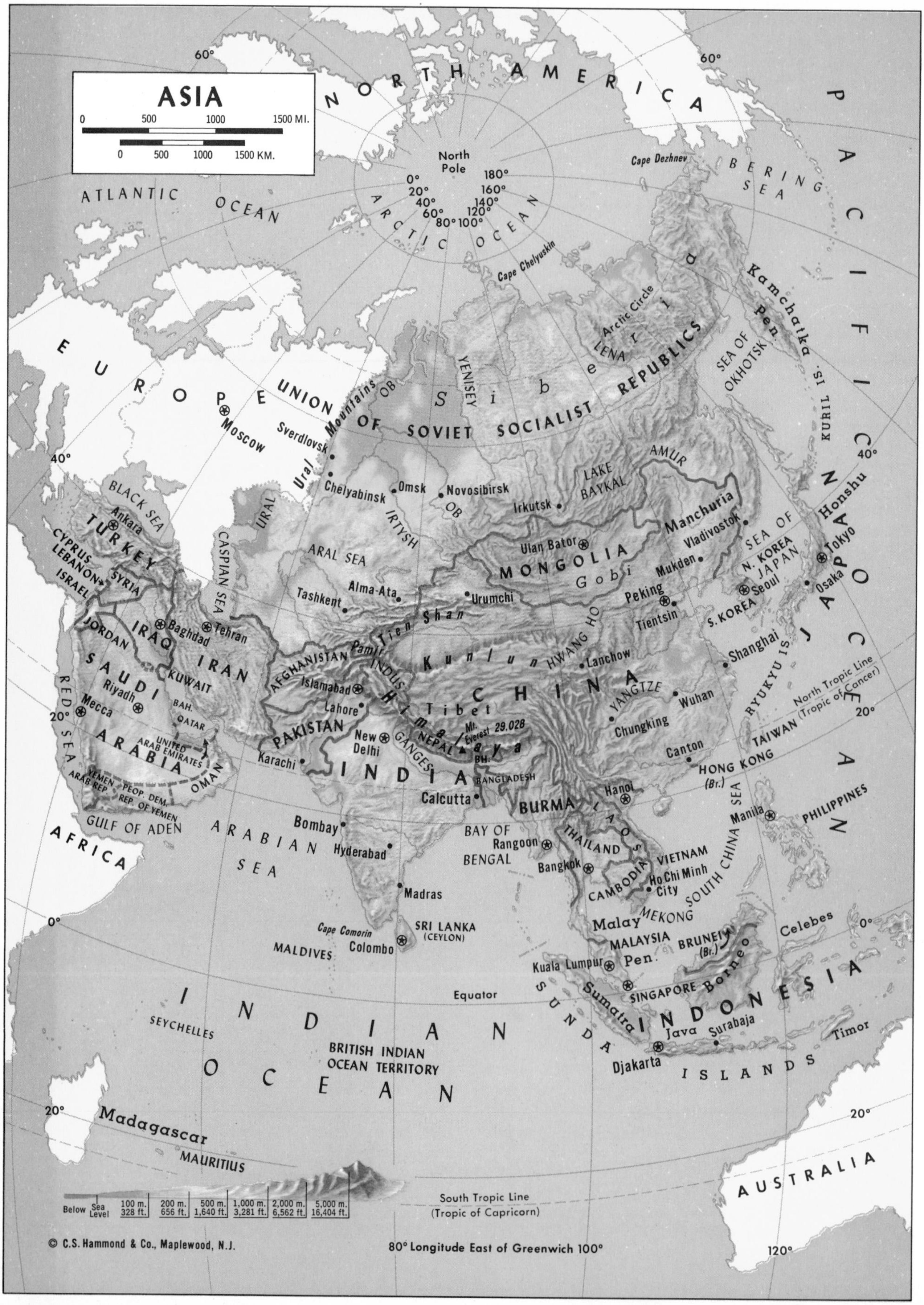

ASIA

0 500 1000 1500 MI.

0 500 1000 1500 KM.

NORTH AMERICA
PACIFIC OCEAN
ATLANTIC OCEAN
ARCTIC OCEAN
North Pole
0° 20° 40° 60° 80° 100° 120° 140° 160° 180°
Cape Dezhnev
BERING SEA
Cape Chelyuskin
Kamchatka Pen.
Arctic Circle
LENA
Siberia
SEA OF OKHOTSK
KURIL IS.
EUROPE
Moscow
UNION OF SOVIET SOCIALIST REPUBLICS
OB
YENISEY
Ural Mountains
Sverdlovsk
Chelyabinsk
Omsk
Novosibirsk
IRTYSH
URAL
LAKE BAYKAL
Irkutsk
AMUR
Manchuria
Vladivostok
SEA OF JAPAN
Honshu
Tokyo
Osaka
JAPAN
N. KOREA
S. KOREA
Seoul
Mukden
Peking
Tientsin
BLACK SEA
Ankara
TURKEY
CYPRUS
LEBANON
SYRIA
ISRAEL
CASPIAN SEA
ARAL SEA
Tashkent
Alma-Ata
Urumchi
Ulan Bator
MONGOLIA
Gobi
Tien Shan
Pamir
HWANG HO
Lanchow
Kunlun
JORDAN
IRAQ
Baghdad
Tehran
IRAN
AFGHANISTAN
KUWAIT
SAUDI ARABIA
Riyadh
Mecca
BAH.
QATAR
UNITED ARAB EMIRATES
OMAN
YEMEN ARAB REP.
PEOP. DEM. REP. OF YEMEN
RED SEA
GULF OF ADEN
AFRICA
Islamabad
INDUS
Lahore
PAKISTAN
Karachi
Tibet
Himalaya
Mt. Everest 29,028
NEPAL
BH.
New Delhi
GANGES
INDIA
BANGLADESH
Calcutta
CHINA
YANGTZE
Wuhan
Chungking
Shanghai
RYUKYU IS.
North Tropic Line (Tropic of Cancer)
TAIWAN
Canton
HONG KONG (Br.)
BURMA
Hanoi
LAOS
THAILAND
Rangoon
Bangkok
VIETNAM
CAMBODIA
Ho Chi Minh City
MEKONG
SOUTH CHINA SEA
PHILIPPINES
Manila
Bombay
Hyderabad
Madras
ARABIAN SEA
BAY OF BENGAL
Cape Comorin
SRI LANKA (CEYLON)
Colombo
MALDIVES
Malay Pen.
MALAYSIA
Kuala Lumpur
SINGAPORE
BRUNEI (Br.)
Borneo
Celebes
Sumatra
INDONESIA
Java
Surabaja
Djakarta
Timor
SUNDA ISLANDS
Equator
INDIAN OCEAN
SEYCHELLES
BRITISH INDIAN OCEAN TERRITORY
Madagascar
MAURITIUS
AUSTRALIA
60° 40° 20° 0° 20° 120°

Below Sea Level	100 m. 328 ft.	200 m. 656 ft.	500 m. 1,640 ft.	1,000 m. 3,281 ft.	2,000 m. 6,562 ft.	5,000 m. 16,404 ft.

South Tropic Line (Tropic of Capricorn)

80° Longitude East of Greenwich 100°

Mecca (Saudi Arabia) is the religious capital of Islam. Djakarta (Java) is now Jakarta.

ASIA

The continent of Asia is the largest in the world. It occupies the eastern portion of the great Eurasian landmass. All of North and South America and most of Australia combined would just about equal the size of Asia!

More people—over half the world's population—live in Asia than any other continent.

Civilization began in Asia more than 5,000 years ago. The first systems of law began then, too.

The zero, sometimes called a goose egg when it appears on the top of a test paper, is part of the Hindu-Arabic numbering system and also one of the greatest ideas ever. Before the zero, there was no easy way to determine the value of a number. The zero became a placeholder, giving a number value by its position. It makes the difference between four (4 ones) and forty (4 tens, no ones) easy to understand. The zero made possible the development of higher mathematics.

Asia is the birthplace of the world's great religions: Buddhism, Christianity, Confucianism, Hinduism, Islam, Judaism, Shintoism, and Taoism.

It Started Here! Asia is the home of three of the "four cradles of civilization." The earliest civilization known on Earth began about 3500 BC in the Tigris-Euphrates River valley, called the Fertile Crescent (Jordan, Israel, Lebanon, Syria, and Iraq). A thousand years later, around 2500 BC, the Indus River valley (Pakistan) became a flourishing civilization. Then, in 1500 BC, the Hwang Ho (Yellow River) and Yangtze River valleys bustled. Each of these civilizations grew, developed, and spread to influence other areas.

How's the Weather?

Asia has all kinds of weather from the Arctic cold to the tropical hot, but "Look what the wind blew in!" The "wind" is the *monsoon.* A monsoon is a wind for all seasons. It blows regularly in definite seasons. In the winter, monsoon winds out of the north bring cold, dry air. In the summer, it is just the opposite; winds out of the south bring hot, humid, and often rainy weather.

Maptalk

A **peak** is the top of a mountain. A **mountain** is high, elevated land that rises steeply above its surroundings. Mountains that are connected to each other form a mountain chain or mountain range.

Naturally

The source of many great Asian rivers is in and around the mountains of Tibet. The Mekong River flows all the way to Southeast Asia and empties into the South China Sea; the Hwang Ho, also known as the Yellow River, flows to the Yellow Sea; and the Yangtze River runs to the East China Sea, all quite *naturally.*

In South Asia the rivers' source is in the mountainous north. Pakistan's Indus River and the Brahmaputra and Ganges rivers of India and Bangladesh all flow south to the Arabian Sea.

In Southwest Asia there's the Tigris-Euphrates River valley. Both rivers begin separately in Turkey. They meet in Iraq and join forces, following the same course to the Persian Gulf.

Much of Asia is deserted . . . when it comes to deserts, that is. The Rub' al Khali desert covers most of the Saudi Arabian Peninsula. There's also the Taklamakan desert in western China, and the Gobi desert, second largest in the world, in Mongolia and China.

It is a three-meal, double-feature movie flight to go from eastern Siberia all the way west to Turkey's Aegean shore, a distance of about 9,600 kilometers (6,000 miles).

2

Geographically Speaking

Asia has more mountains than any other continent in the world. In fact, sometimes Asia is called the "roof of the world," because here the USSR, China (Tibet), Afghanistan, Pakistan, and India meet. All of Asia's great mountain ranges are tied together at the Pamir Knot. Those mountain ranges are the Tien Shan, the Altay Mountains, and the Kunlun in China and Mongolia; the Himalayas in India, Nepal, and Bhutan; the Hindu Kush in Afghanistan (which becomes the Plateau of Iran) and the Pontic and Taurus mountains that all surround the Plateau of Anatolia in Turkey; and the Karakoram in Pakistan.

River valleys and river deltas are the "room and board" for millions of Asians. People live in and around rivers because of fertile farmland and plenty of water for irrigation and transportation.

The plains in Asia are mainly in northern India and eastern China.

Asia is a six-peninsula continent:

- Saudi Arabian Peninsula
- Indian Peninsula
- Indochinese Peninsula
- Malayan Peninsula
- Korean Peninsula
- Kamchatka Peninsula

Is That a Fact?

	Asia
Area:	43,976,000 sq. km. (16,979,000 sq. mi.)
Total population:	2,535,333,000
Children aged 0–14:	760,484,000
High spot:	Mount Everest, Nepal 8,848 m. (29,028 ft.), the highest in the world
Low spot:	Dead Sea, Israel-Jordan 396 m. (1,299 ft.) below sea level, the lowest in the world
City with most people:	Shanghai, China, the most populated city in the world
Largest country:	USSR (Asia) 17,427,000 sq. km. (6,728,750 sq. mi.)
Smallest country:	Macao 16 sq. km. (6.2 sq. mi.)
Longest river:	Yangtze, the fourth longest in the world
World's highest "land" mountain range:	Himalayan-Karakoram 7,620 m. (28,000 ft.) average

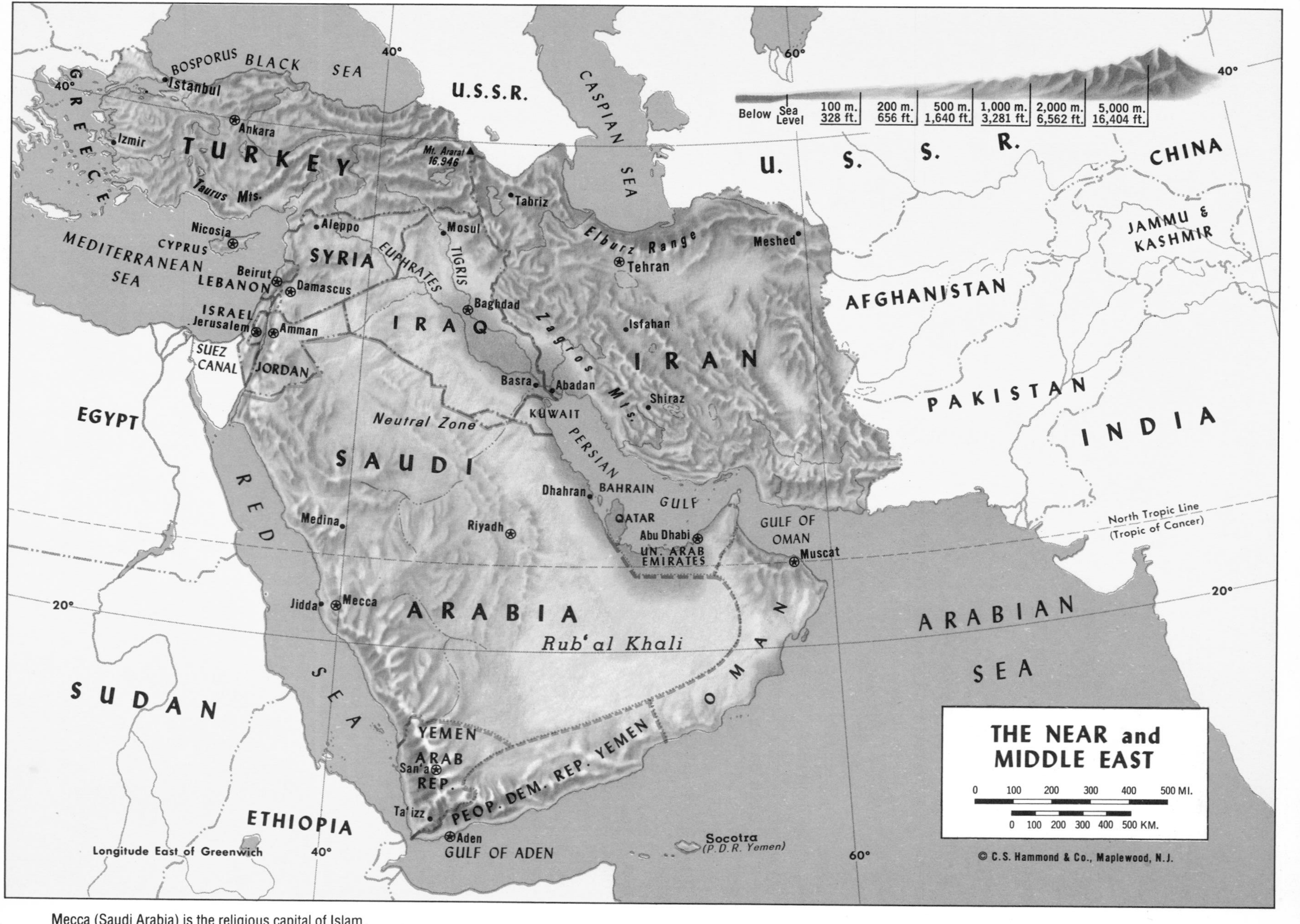

Mecca (Saudi Arabia) is the religious capital of Islam.

The Near and Middle East

Geographically Speaking

Turkey is the keeper of the key for the entranceway to the Mediterranean from the Black Sea. Often called the Straits, this passage, or narrow natural channel, is made up of the Bosporus, the Sea of Marmara, and the Dardanelles.

The Turkish mountains called the Eastern Taurus are the source of the Tigris and Euphrates rivers. These two rivers meet in Iraq and form the moon-shaped Fertile Crescent, the site of Earth's oldest known civilization. Damascus and Aleppo, two ancient cities, are located here. They date back 4,000 years. Talk about old! There is a stone tower at Jericho that dates back 10,000 years.

The Saudi Arabian Peninsula is the world's largest peninsula. On it is the Rub' al Khali, a Texas-size desert, that happens to be about the same size as that American state.

The land of the Jordan River valley in Jordan and Israel is good for farming. Of course, there's not a lot of land here, and it is awfully hot.

To the south is the Dead Sea, the lowest spot on Earth—396 meters (1,299 feet) below sea level. Its concentration of salt is nine times greater than that of an ocean. It is the only place in the world where a nonswimmer can float and read a newspaper at the same time . . . without drowning himself or the paper.

Today, the Dead Sea is used as a source of water for irrigation. To make it worth its salt, the Dead Sea's salt water is undergoing a process called *desalinization.* This means the salt is being taken out of the salt water. Once the salt is out, the water can be used to help turn desert sand into green fertile land.

Bedouins (nomads) tend their flocks of sheep and goats in much the same way as their ancestors did thousands of years ago. They lead their herds from watering hole to watering hole across the great desert expanses.

No Kidding!

Did you know that every 21 minutes an oil tanker passes through the Strait of Hormuz, which links the Gulf of Oman and the Persian Gulf? These shipments represent 60 percent of the world's oil trade.

Naturally

This region is mostly hot and dry desert, without many areas of fertile soil. But where there is sand, there might happen to be *oil.* Kuwait, Qatar, Saudi Arabia, Iran, and Iraq have much of the world's supply.

How about a date? Iraq is one of the world's largest producers of dates. They do grow on trees — date palm trees, that is.

If you don't like to drink it you can read it! It's Turkish coffee! It is said that your fortune can be found by reading the coffee grounds!

From this warm-weather region come materials that everyone can cotton to when the weather starts becoming quite cool. Camels give us camel hair; goats give us mohair; sheep provide wool; and don't forget there's a lot of wonderful cotton!

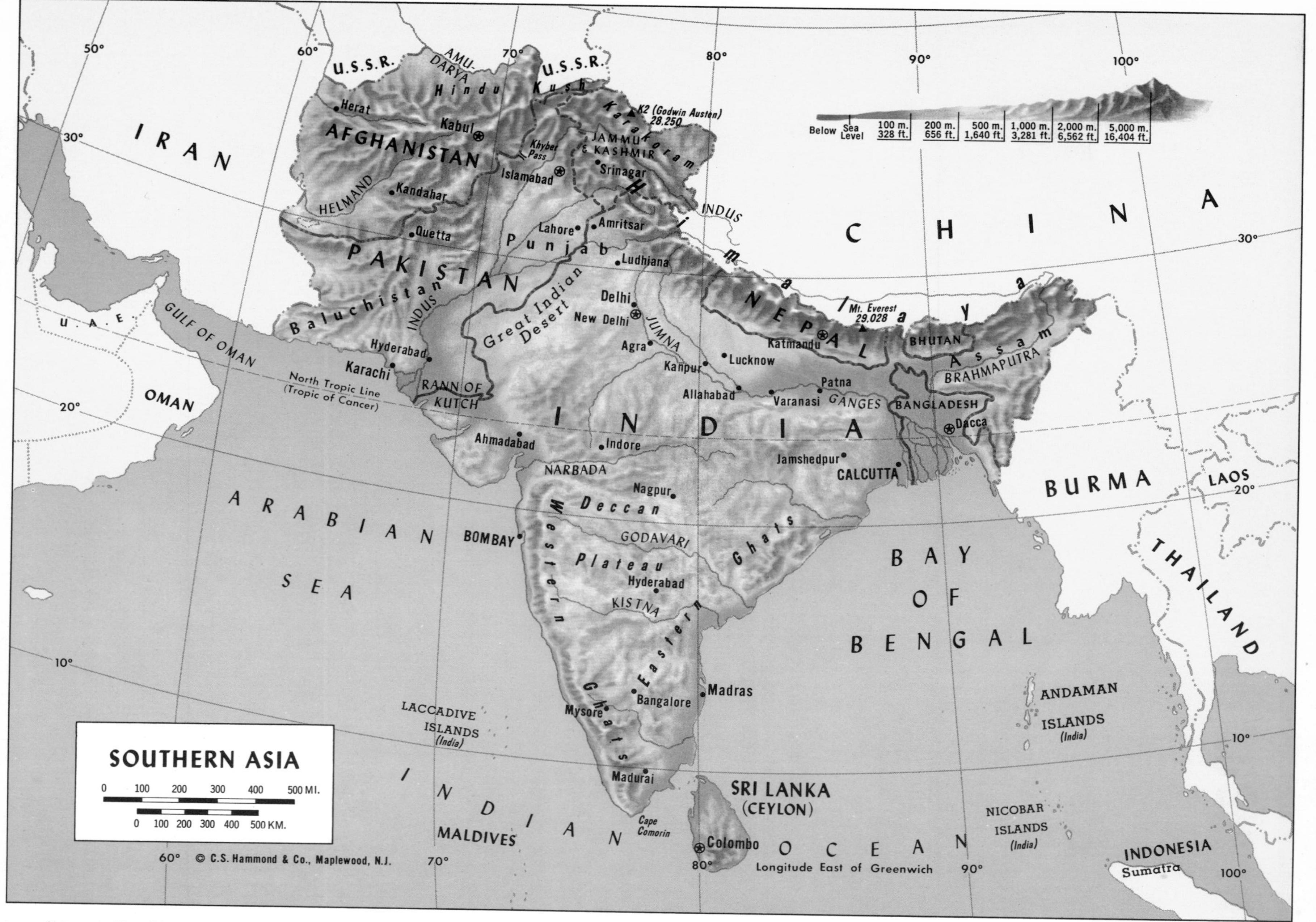

Katmandu (Nepal) is now Kathmadu.

Southern Asia

Geographically Speaking

Want to know about the Indian subcontinent? First, a *subcontinent* is a large land area, but it is smaller than the "recognized" continents and more or less self-contained. The Indian subcontinent stretches to the Himalayas and is made up of the Indian Peninsula and Pakistan!

The Karakoram mountain range of Afghanistan, the Hindu Kush range of Pakistan, and the Himalaya mountains of India are tied into the Pamir Knot. They, along with all the other Asian mountain ranges, meet there.

Ever hear of a "collision" taking thousands of years to happen? According to the continent-formation theory, what is known today as India "bumped" into the landmass known as Eurasia millions of years ago. The result of this incredibly long "smash up" was the Himalayan mountain range, the highest in the world. It stretches across northern India, Nepal, and Bhutan.

Much of the Indian Peninsula is plateau. The Deccan Plateau covers the southern portion of the peninsula and ends where the northern plains begin.

Maptalk

Alluvial land is rich soil that has been deposited by the running water of a river as it empties into a larger body of water. A **delta** is alluvial land in the shape of a triangle or a fan that is found at the mouth of a river.

Great rivers! Great deltas! To the west, there is the Indus River delta and to the east, two rivers: the Ganges and the Brahmaputra. Where these rivers meet is one huge delta that is shared by two countries, India and Bangladesh. They also share its great fertile land.

The Khyber Pass, in the Hindu Kush, is only 53 kilometers (33 miles) long and is probably the most famous pass in the world. For centuries caravans of camels and donkeys have been passing through on this famed trade route to the Orient in search of gems, spices, and silks. Little has changed today, except that caravans of trucks and cars have joined the camels and donkeys.

However, an alternate route is along the Karakoram highway. It passes from Pakistan to China and is 800 kilometers (500 miles) long. It winds its way *over* the mountains rather than passing through them.

A Natural W.O.W.

Mount Everest, in the Himalayan-Karakoram range, is the highest spot on Earth — 8,848 meters (29,028 feet), almost 6 miles high!

Naturally

India leads the world in the production of sugar cane, pepper, tea, and peanuts, too!

Bangladesh leads the world in growing jute, which is used to make rope.

Christopher Columbus was looking for a sea route to trade for spices like cinnamon and curry, not to mention fabulous gems like aquamarine, tourmaline, moonstones, and zircon from Sri Lanka; sapphires and topaz from Afghanistan; lapis lazuli, amethysts, and emeralds from India; and diamonds and rubies from all three.

Do you think that maybe there are used-elephant and used-buffalo lots in Nepal? These animals are the primary means of transportation here.

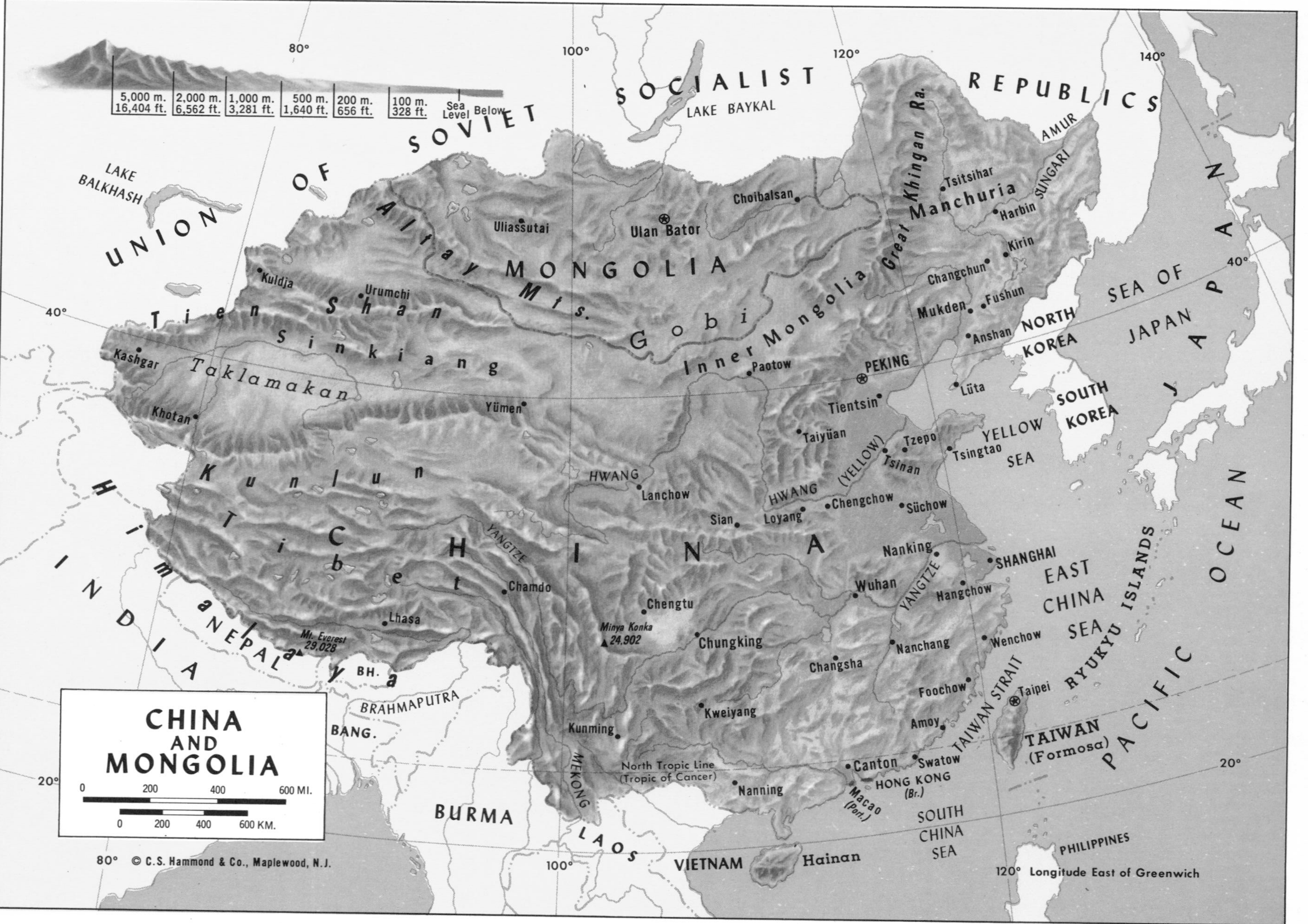

All names of cities and places are being revised to the new Pinyin system of transliteration. For example, Peking, the capital, is now Beijing.

China and Mongolia

Geographically Speaking

The Altay mountains in the north; the Tien Shan mountains in the west; the Kunlun mountains in the south—all do their best to keep China isolated from her neighbors, *naturally.* In fact, nearly two-thirds of China is mountainous.

These great mountain ranges are not deserted when it comes to deserts! They surround the Taklamakan desert in western China. The Taklamakan extends east to the Gobi desert and the desert plateau of Mongolia.

Manchuria was the winning candidate for the plain named the Manchurian Plain in northeastern China.

Farther south but still in northern China is the large, wide, flat North China Plain in the Hwang Ho (Yellow River) valley.

How did the Hwang Ho get its name? West of the North China Plain is an area called the Loess Highlands. Loess is pronounced "less" and consists of land made up of silt and sand. The Hwang Ho actually gets its start in the Loess Highlands, where it cuts deep gorges and picks up yellow-colored loess. It is this loess that makes the Hwang Ho yellow.

The Yangtze Plain lies alongside the Yangtze River valley in southern China. The river's water helps to cover fields, and that is perfect for growing rice. These water-covered fields are called *rice paddies.*

China has been a major agricultural country for over 4,000 years. Besides farming in the Hwang Ho and Yangtze river deltas, terrace farming is used so crops can be cultivated on the rich land on the slopes of hills and mountains. The island of Taiwan, whose very name means "terraced bay," farms in much the same way.

Naturally

China leads the world in the production of rice and tobacco; it's second in corn and cotton; third in tea and wheat!

In southern China the main grain eaten is rice, but in northern China it's wheat that people eat!

China can steal the show as far as minerals go! There's coal and iron ore, and that is best when it comes to making steel.

In China the lights are on. It is a world-ranking producer of tungsten, used in light bulbs.

"Follow the lime brick road" could have been the directions for the horsemen's roadway known today as the Great Wall of China. The top of the wall (the roadway) is 5 meters (15 feet) wide, and it stands 8 meters (25 feet) tall. In 221 BC the Chinese decided to build the wall to protect themselves against roving bands of northern nomads. More than 1,400 years and 2,410 kilometers (1,500 miles) later, the wall was completed. The year was 1644.

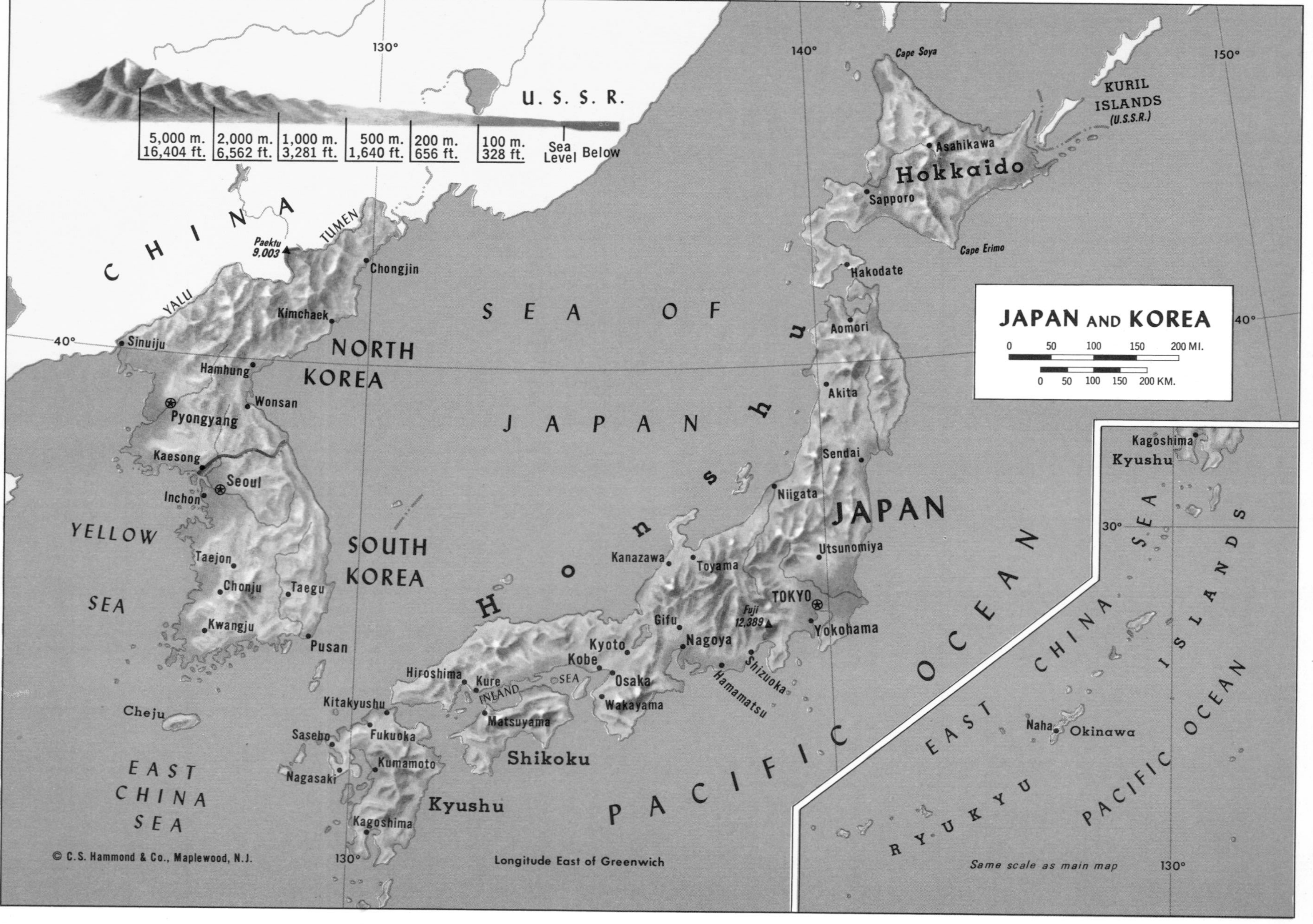
JAPAN AND KOREA
0 50 100 150 200 MI.
0 50 100 150 200 KM.
5,000 m. 16,404 ft.
2,000 m. 6,562 ft.
1,000 m. 3,281 ft.
500 m. 1,640 ft.
200 m. 656 ft.
100 m. 328 ft.
Sea Level
Below
U. S. S. R.
CHINA
KURIL ISLANDS (U.S.S.R.)
Cape Soya
Asahikawa
Hokkaido
Sapporo
Cape Erimo
Hakodate
Aomori
Akita
Sendai
Niigata
JAPAN
Utsunomiya
TOKYO
Yokohama
Fuji 12,389
Shizuoka
Hamamatsu
Toyama
Kanazawa
Gifu
Nagoya
Kyoto
Kobe
Osaka
Wakayama
Honshu
SEA OF JAPAN
INLAND SEA
Hiroshima
Kure
Matsuyama
Shikoku
Kitakyushu
Fukuoka
Sasebo
Nagasaki
Kumamoto
Kagoshima
Kyushu
PACIFIC OCEAN
EAST CHINA SEA
YELLOW SEA
Cheju
NORTH KOREA
SOUTH KOREA
Paektu 9,003
TUMEN
YALU
Chongjin
Kimchaek
Sinuiju
Hamhung
Wonsan
Pyongyang
Kaesong
Seoul
Inchon
Taejon
Chonju
Taegu
Kwangju
Pusan
Naha
Okinawa
RYUKYU ISLANDS
Same scale as main map
130°
140°
150°
40°
30°
Longitude East of Greenwich
© C.S. Hammond & Co., Maplewood, N.J.

Japan
Korea–North and South

Geographically Speaking

The countries commonly called North Korea and South Korea are on the Korean Peninsula, which is located off the southwestern Chinese coast. The peninsula is 1,078 kilometers (670 miles) long and 515 kilometers (320 miles) wide at its widest point.

There are approximately 3,000 islands that belong to Korea, the largest being the island of Cheju.

The Northern Mountains are in northern North Korea. The highest mountain in all of Korea is on the northern border between North Korea and China. Its name is Paektu San. It stands 2,744 meters (9,003 feet) tall, and that's not all! From the Paektu San the Yalu River flows to the Yellow Sea; on the other side of the mountain the Tumen River flows to the Sea of Japan. These two rivers divide the lands of China and North Korea, *naturally!*

The west coast of the peninsula from northern North Korea to southern South Korea can boast about its land. It is a plain divided now and again by rolling hills. It's good for farming; it's good for industry; it's good for living!

The east coast from northern North Korea to southern South Korea is much the same as the west coast. It, too, is a fertile plain!

Mountains of mountains. Japan is 85 percent mountains and hills — but all islands. Its main islands number four, which are surrounded by thousands more. These islands are located in the uppermost part of a great mountain chain that arises from the north Pacific Ocean's floor!

Honshu, Japan's largest island, has Alps — Japanese style — called the Honshu Alps. To the east of these mountains is a chain of volcanoes that cuts across the center of the island.

There are more than 200 volcanoes in Japan. Shikoku is the only major island that doesn't have any volcanoes. The other three — Honshu, Hokkaido, and Kyushu — do. The most famous volcano is Mount Fuji, or Fujiama. It hasn't erupted in almost 300 years.

The Japanese don't complain because they have the Kanto Plain — good for farming and good for living. Tokyo, Japan's largest city, is located here.

The coastline of Japan is the same length as the east coast of the United States. The winters are cold in Hokkaido, just like in Maine, and warm in Kyushu, much like in Florida. That makes sense! Or does it? Japan lies farther north latitudinally than the United States, so it should be much colder. Thanks to the Japan current, which flows northward toward this country from the warm South Seas, southern Japan is nice and warm. The Oyashio current cools the already cold weather in northern Japan.

Naturally

What eats mulberry tree leaves and spins a cocoon of silk thread? In Japan, silkworms do. Their cocoons are taken to factories where the silk threads are undone and then spun onto spools. From there they are woven into fabric called silk. That's quite a *natural* trick.

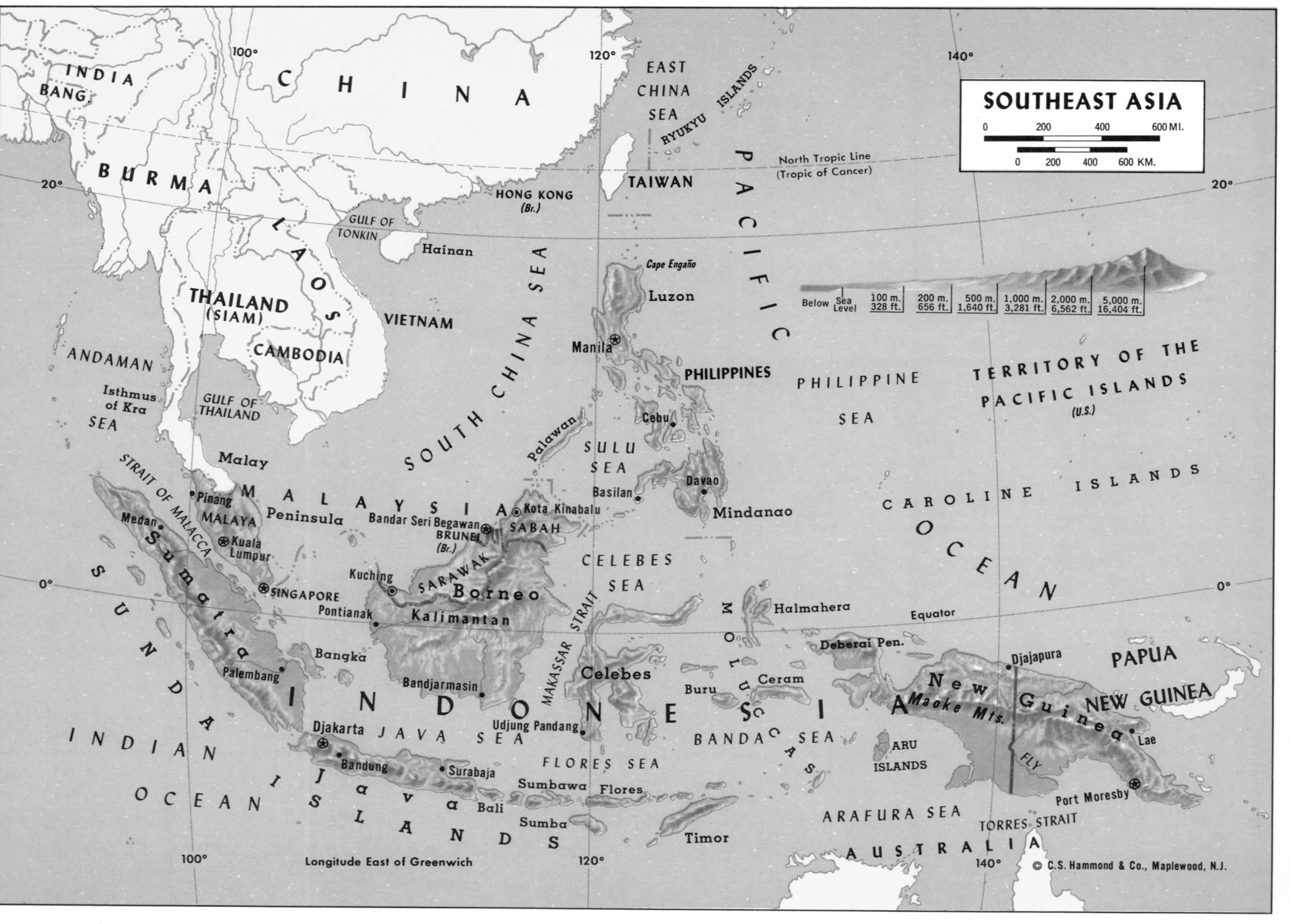

Djakarta (Java) is now Jakarta. Chiengmai (Thailand) is now Chaing Mai. Cambodia is also Kampuchea. Legaspi (Luzon) is now Legazpi.

Indonesia, Papua New Guinea, and Philippines

Geographically Speaking

Indonesia is the largest country in Southeast Asia. It consists of 13,667 separate islands. The Philippines has half as many—only 7,100! A thousand islands in Indonesia and 730 in the Philippines have people living on them. The rest are uninhabited and have no names.

Indonesia is located on the equator. It extends over one-eighth the distance of the Earth's circumference!

The islands of Indonesia, New Guinea, and the Philippines dot the Indian Ocean, South China Sea, and Pacific Ocean. They make up the East Indian archipelago, which lies between Southeast Asia and Australia.

Maptalk

An **archipelago** is a group of islands that are close together. Or, another way of putting it, it's an area of water, a sea or an ocean, that is dotted with islands.

The East Indian archipelago was formed by great underwater volcanic mountain chains. Many of these volcanoes are active, making fire and smoke a common sight. Volcanic ash, when it is spewed out over the land, becomes nature's very own rich fertilizer.

In this enriched soil cassava (a starch), coffee, sweet potatoes, and rice grow.

A **volcano** is a cone-shaped mountain with an opening at the top that reaches all the way down into the Earth's crust. When it is active, or erupting, steam and lava, which is hot molten rock, bubble and shoot out of the opening.

In 1883 the volcano Krakatoa blew its stack. It erupted from a sea bed between Sumatra and Java, causing tidal waves so violent that all of Southeast Asia was affected. Clouds of volcanic ash from its eruption circled the whole world!

Naturally

In Indonesia the world's largest flower grows. It is a water lily named rafflesia. The blossom can be as large as 1.8 meters (6 feet) across.

Abacá, a fiber that makes Manila hemp, is used in making a kind of rope that comes from the Philippines.

Pepper, nutmeg, cinnamon, and cloves are some of the spices of life grown in the Moluccas—the original Spice Islands.

Wild, wild animals live here. Crocodiles 5 meters (18 feet) long; giant pythons 9 meters (30 feet) long; lizards; rhinoceroses; orangutans; parrots; and cockatoos are just a few different inhabitants of this part of the world.

INDOCHINESE AND MALAYAN PENINSULAS

0 100 200 300 MI.
0 100 200 300 KM.

CHINA
INDIA
BANGLADESH
BURMA
THAILAND (SIAM)
Indochina
CAMBODIA
VIETNAM
MALAYA
MALAYSIA
INDONESIA
SINGAPORE
Hkakabo Razi 19,296
100°
110°
20°
10°
5,000 m. 16,404 ft.
2,000 m. 6,562 ft.
1,000 m. 3,281 ft.
500 m. 1,640 ft.
200 m. 656 ft.
100 m. 328 ft.
Sea Level
Below
North Tropic Line (Tropic of Cancer)
Myitkyina
IRRAWADDY
Shwebo
Mandalay
Shan Plateau
MEKONG
Lao Cai
RED
Hanoi
Hoa Binh
Haiphong
GULF OF TONKIN
Nam Dinh
Hainan
Sittwe
Magwe
Luang Prabang
Vinh
SALWEEN
Pye
Chiengmai
Lampang
Vientiane
BAY OF BENGAL
Henzada
Bassein
Rangoon
Tak
Khon Kaen
Savannakhet
Hue
Da Nang
Moulmein
Cape Negrais
GULF OF MARTABAN
Nakhon Ratchasima
Pakse
Surin
Ayutthaya
Qui Nhon
Tavoy
Bangkok
Battambang
TONLE SAP
ANDAMAN SEA
Mergui
MERGUI ARCHIPELAGO
Kompong Chhnang
Da Lat
Phan Rang
Phnom Penh
Bien Hoa
Ho Chi Minh City
GULF OF THAILAND (SIAM)
Isthmus of Kra
Long Xuyen
Pte. de Ca Mau
Nakhon Si Thammarat
Malay Peninsula
SOUTH CHINA SEA
Songkhla
Kota Baharu
Pinang (Georgetown)
Ipoh
STRAIT OF MALACCA
Kuala Lumpur
Melaka
Longitude East of Greenwich

Pye (Burma) is now Prome. Cambodia is now Kampuchea.

Indochinese and Malayan Peninsulas

"Big Blue Marble" Photograph

Geographically Speaking

At first glance it seems that the Malayan Peninsula is the Indochinese Peninsula's peninsula. On second glance two distinct peninsulas become apparent. From north to south, Burma, Thailand, and Malaya are on the Malayan Peninsula; from west to east, Cambodia, Laos, and Vietnam are on the Indochinese Peninsula.

It's rice and rivers all the way! See the rice paddies along the Mekong River? This roving river not only forms the western border of landlocked Laos, separating it from Thailand, *naturally,* but it is also Laos' main highway. The Mekong flows through Cambodia and Vietnam, and 4,184 kilometers (2,600 miles) along, it empties into the South China Sea.

Vietnam is a double-delta country. In the northern part is the Red River delta; in the southern part is the Mekong River delta.

It flows in both directions, but not at the same time! In Cambodia the Tonle Sap River gets its water from the Great Tonle Sap Lake. This river flows southeast to Cambodia's capital, Phnom Penh, where the Tonle Sap runs into the Mekong River. In the dry season there is hardly a splash. In the rainy season it's a different story. When the rains come to the Mekong River's source, the snow melts and the level of the river rises. Are you ready for one of nature's surprises? During the rainy season, at Phnom Penh when these rivers meet again, the Mekong River is much higher and this makes the Tonle Sap flow northwest, back to the lake from which it came. So the river flows in two opposite directions, depending on the time of year.

Rivers, rivers, everywhere. The rivers in the north are the Mekong and the Salween; the Chao Phraya River flows down through the center of Thailand. Do you know what that means? Houses are boats, cars are boats, markets are boats. Much of Thailand is afloat!

The river Salween is the natural border between Thailand and Burma. The Irrawaddy River flows to the capital of Burma—Rangoon—and forms a fertile fan-shaped delta there.

Malaya's independent Singapore is the gateway to the Far East! It's located at the tip of the country and peninsula of the same name. Singapore is one of the world's busiest seaports. Every year 40,000 ships come and go.

Naturally

Elephants are living fork-lift trucks! In Burma and Thailand, world-leading sources for teakwood, elephants transport teakwood logs. They lift the teak tree trunks with their own trunks, place them on their tusks, and lumber over to the teak "depository."

In Burma's jewel box is the world's best jade, along with sapphires, rubies, and lapis lazuli.

In Thailand, ancient Siam, thousands of different kinds of birds are faithfully watched by Siamese cats.

Tin cans, tin foil. When it comes to tin, Malaysia and Thailand certainly win!

Rubber bands, rubber boots, rubber hoses! Much of the world's rubber grows abundantly in Malaysia.

"Excuse me, you have a banana in your ear." "I'm sorry, I can't hear you. I have a banana in my ear." This can be repeated 18 times over in Thailand, because here they grow 18 different varieties of bananas. It's bananas!

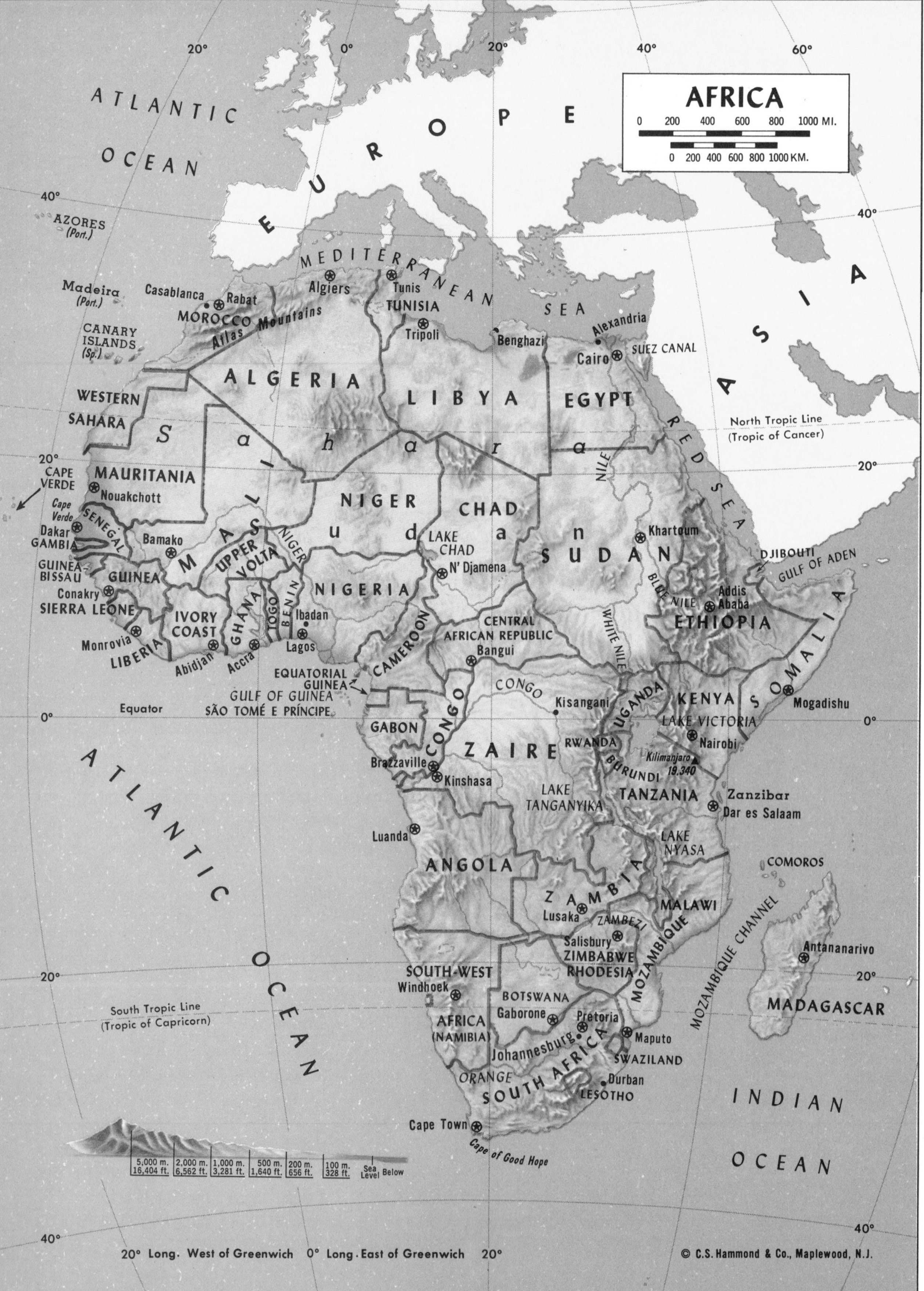

The capital of Somalia is now Muqdisho. Zimbabwe Rhodesia is now Zimbabwe. Central African Empire is now Central African Republic. South-West Africa is now Namibia.

AFRICA

Geographically Speaking

Africa is the second-largest continent in the world.

It's surrounded — by two oceans, the Atlantic Ocean and the Indian Ocean, and by two seas, the Mediterranean Sea and the Red Sea.

It's connected — to the continent of Asia, in Egypt, by the Sinai Peninsula.

Most of Africa is a giant plateau covered with deserts, forests, and grasslands.

Two-fifths of the African continent is desert. The Sahara in the north, the world's largest, is made up of smaller deserts like the Libyan Desert in Libya and Egypt, and the Nubian Desert in Sudan. The Kalahari and Great Karoo deserts are in the south in Botswana and South Africa.

Less than one-fifth of the continent is covered by forests, but there *are* dense tropical rain forests that extend from the Congo River basin in Zaire westward to Liberia.

Grasslands or *savannas* cover more than two-fifths of Africa. They are located in between the Sahara Desert and the rain forests on the eastern plateaus, and from the Congo River basin to southern Africa.

The Atlas Mountains in the northwest corner of Africa (Morocco and Algeria) are actually a continuation of the European Alpine Mountain System. The Drakensberg range in southeast Africa extends northward from South Africa and forms the highland plateaus of East Africa — all the way to Ethiopia.

How's the Weather?

Whew! Is it ever hot! Africa is one of the warmest continents in the world. In the deserts it's hot and dry. Near the equator it's hot and wet. But there is skiing in the Atlas Mountains in Morocco and snow covers the majestic Mount Kilimanjaro of Tanzania.

In the highland plateau countries along the eastern and southern coast, the weather, in fact, is quite nice.

Maptalk

A **desert** is a region that has little water and little vegetation.

A desert as big as the United States? Impossible, but true. The Sahara Desert, located in

North Central Africa, is estimated to be over 9,100,000 square kilometers (3.5 million square miles) — and growing!

The Sahara is no ordinary sandbox. Sand comes in many colors. There are many dunes over

300 meters (1,000 feet) high that have sand "waves" that go on for 4.8 kilometers (3 miles). There are desert mountains nearly 3,350 meters (11,000 feet) high.

When is the desert really cold? At night, when the sun goes down. Why? Because there is no water to retain the heat from the sun.

Maptalk

A **valley** is low land that lies between two areas of higher elevation, like hills or mountains.

The largest valley in the world begins in Syria, which is in Asia, and ends in Mozambique, in Africa. Its sides at their highest are 1.6 kilometers (1 mile) and it can be as wide as 32 kilometers to 48 kilometers (20 miles to 30 miles). The Great Rift Valley cuts through most of East Africa.

A **river** is a stream of water that generally flows into a larger stream, lake, or ocean.

In Africa the Nile River meets a sea, the Mediterranean. The Nile is the longest river in the world, roughly 6,738 kilometers (4,187 miles). Every year it floods its banks, fertilizing the land. Fortunately, unlike most, this flood is welcome and necessary.

"Looks like hieroglyphics to me!" Well, it is. Hieroglyphics are simple drawings that are the oldest known form of writing. They were developed by the Egyptians in 3000 BC and can be found today on ancient pyramids, temples, and tombs.

Is That a Fact?

	Africa
Area:	30,320,000 sq. km. (11,707,000 sq. mi.)
Total population:	431,900,000
Children aged 0–14:	181,595,000
High spot:	Mount Kilimanjaro, Tanzania 5,895 m. (19,340 ft.)
Low spot:	Qattara Depression, Egypt 133 m. (436 ft.) below sea level
Hot spot:	Libya, Sept. 13, 1922 58°C (136°F), a world record
Largest country:	Sudan 2,505,813 sq. km. (967,500 sq. mi.)
Smallest country:	Mayotte 374 sq. km. (144 sq. mi.)
City with most people:	Cairo, Egypt
Largest lake:	Lake Victoria 69,488 sq. km. (28,828 sq. mi.) second largest in the world
Longest river:	Nile River 6,738 km. (4,187 mi.), world's longest river

No Kidding!

Caravans crossing the desert often stop and rest at an *oasis,* a lush, green watering hole. This unique type of rest area owes its existence to the presence of a spring or underground stream.

Camels, with their humps serving as built-in food and energy sources and their heat-resistant footpads, are still the best means of transportation for desert travel.

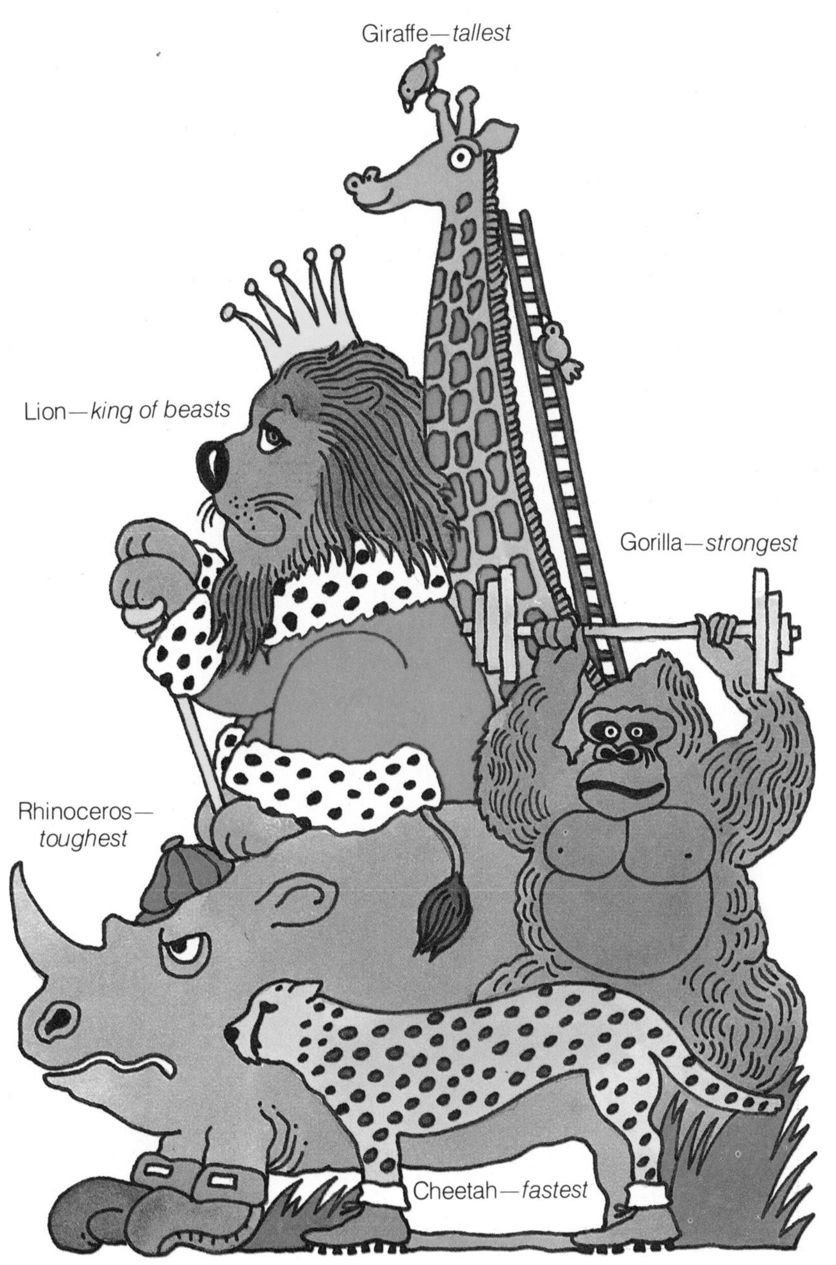
Giraffe—*tallest*
Lion—*king of beasts*
Gorilla—*strongest*
Rhinoceros—
toughest
Cheetah—*fastest*

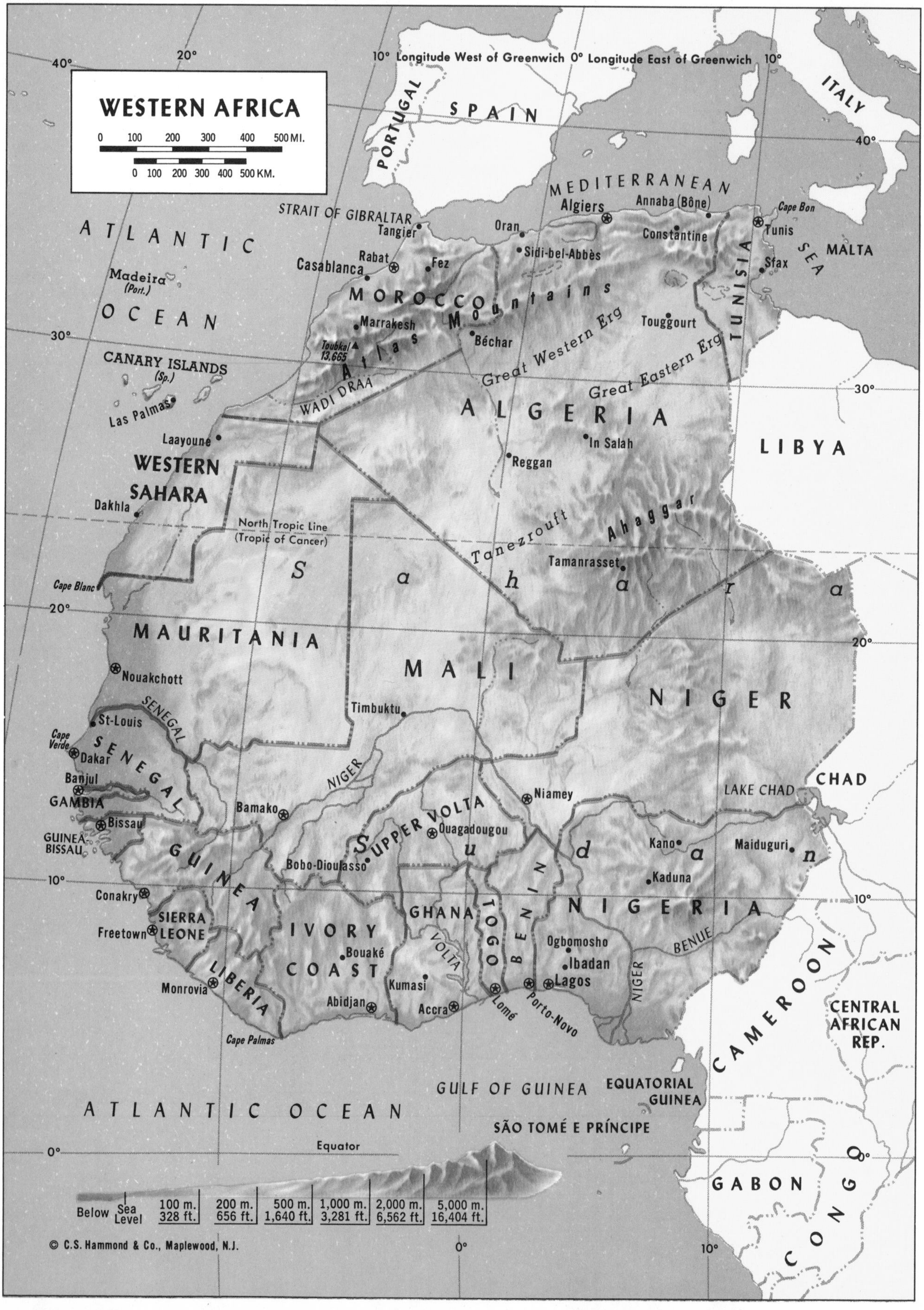

WESTERN AFRICA

0 100 200 300 400 500 MI.
0 100 200 300 400 500 KM.

10° Longitude West of Greenwich 0° Longitude East of Greenwich 10°

PORTUGAL
SPAIN
ITALY
MEDITERRANEAN SEA
STRAIT OF GIBRALTAR
Tangier
Algiers
Annaba (Bône)
Cape Bon
Tunis
Oran
Constantine
MALTA
Rabat
Fez
Sidi-bel-Abbès
Casablanca
Sfax
MOROCCO
Atlas Mountains
TUNISIA
Marrakesh
Touggourt
Toubkal 13,665
Béchar
Great Western Erg
Great Eastern Erg
WADI DRAA
ATLANTIC OCEAN
Madeira (Port.)
CANARY ISLANDS (Sp.)
Las Palmas
ALGERIA
Laayoune
In Salah
LIBYA
Reggan
WESTERN SAHARA
Dakhla
North Tropic Line (Tropic of Cancer)
Tanezrouft
Ahaggar
Tamanrasset
Sahara
Cape Blanc
MAURITANIA
MALI
Nouakchott
NIGER
Timbuktu
SENEGAL
St-Louis
Cape Verde
Dakar
Banjul
GAMBIA
NIGER
Niamey
CHAD
LAKE CHAD
Bamako
UPPER VOLTA
Ouagadougou
Bissau
GUINEA-BISSAU
GUINEA
Sudan
Kano
Maiduguri
Bobo-Dioulasso
Kaduna
Conakry
GHANA
TOGO
BENIN
NIGERIA
SIERRA LEONE
Freetown
IVORY COAST
Bouaké
VOLTA
Ogbomosho
Ibadan
BENUE
Lagos
Kumasi
Monrovia
LIBERIA
Abidjan
Accra
Lomé
Porto-Novo
NIGER
CAMEROON
CENTRAL AFRICAN REP.
Cape Palmas
GULF OF GUINEA
EQUATORIAL GUINEA
ATLANTIC OCEAN
SÃO TOMÉ E PRÍNCIPE
Equator
GABON
CONGO

40° 30° 20° 10° 0°

Below Sea Level | 100 m. 328 ft. | 200 m. 656 ft. | 500 m. 1,640 ft. | 1,000 m. 3,281 ft. | 2,000 m. 6,562 ft. | 5,000 m. 16,404 ft.

Status of Western Sahara, formerly Spanish Sahara, is undetermined. Laayoune (Western Sahara) is now El Aaiún. Timbuktu (Mali) is now Tombouctu.

Western Africa

"Big Blue Marble" Photograph

Geographically Speaking

The coastal areas of Morocco, Algeria, and Tunisia have a Mediterranean climate — warm, dry summers and mild, rainy winters. Do you know why? Besides being located on the Mediterranean Sea, the Atlas Mountains act as a windbreaker and keep the hot Saharan desert air away from the coasts.

Mali, Upper Volta, and Niger have something in common besides borders. All three countries are landlocked, that is, cut off from the sea.

Senegal is cut into and practically cut in two by the tiny country Gambia.

A Tale of Two Rivers. The Gambia River in Gambia is so deep that ocean-going ships can sail on it up to 241 kilometers (150 miles) inland.

The Niger River gets its start 241 kilometers (150 miles) inland from the Atlantic Ocean in Guinea.

Five countries and 4,180 kilometers (2,600 miles) later, from the Gulf of Guinea, the Niger River begins to fan out and form the Niger delta in Nigeria. This is the largest river delta in Africa.

The country of Benin has flat terrain, *naturally.* It is the coastal east-west crossroad between Nigeria and Ghana, and the north-south crossroad for landlocked Niger to the Gulf of Guinea.

Naturally

There are those who may wonder why you're playing in the pebbles, but in Sierra Leone it may be a brilliant idea. It is in the gravel of river beds and swamps on the east coast that half of Sierra Leone's gem and industrial diamonds are found. Sierra Leone is third in the world in the production of industrial diamonds.

It's none of your beeswax, it's Guinea-Bissau's. They make a lot of it.

Take the cocoa from Nigeria, the Ivory Coast, and Ghana. Take the peanuts from Senegal. Add coconut, pineapple, and banana, which all come from these countries, and you've got the fixings for a superdooper sundae.

It's rich in fish! The water off the coast of Mauritania is the site of one of the world's richest fishing grounds.

"The-great-Saharan-oasis-rest-stop-system" keeps on trucking! That's what nomadic herdsmen do with their cattle, sheep, goats, camels, donkeys, and horses as they cross the Great Sahara Desert. They keep going by making pit stops at the oases' watering holes.

No Kidding!

A tree that builds up land? Guinea has been called the Switzerland of West Africa because of its spectacular mountains and waterfalls. However, Guinea has something that Switzerland doesn't and that is mangrove swamps! A *mangrove* is a tropical tree that grows in still, shallow salt waters. It sends down roots that look like stilts forming a tropical thicket. The roots slow the flow of water, and this helps to settle the silt. The buildup of this silt, after quite some time, becomes dry land.

Ever since AD 1200 people have been going all the way to Timbuktu and back again. Its central location in Mali made it an ideal halfway meeting trading place for the camel caravans carrying goods from North Africa and its canoe counterparts from West Africa.

Come with me to the Casbah! Casbah is the name given to the old sections of towns in Algeria and Morocco. In the Casbah the streets are so narrow that if you stand in the middle and stretch your arms out, you can touch buildings on either side of the street at the same time!

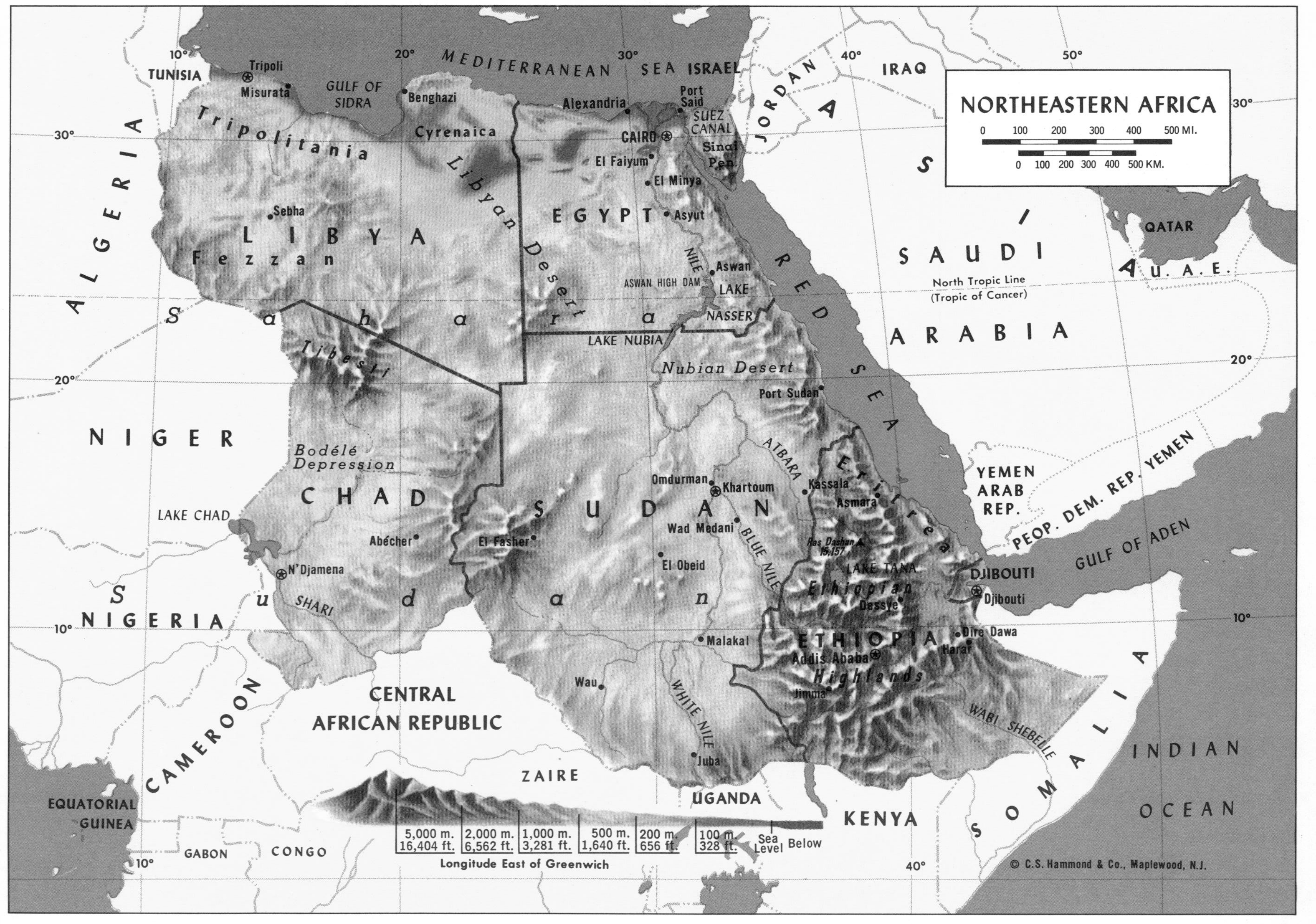
NORTHEASTERN AFRICA
0 100 200 300 400 500 MI.
0 100 200 300 400 500 KM.
MEDITERRANEAN SEA
ALGERIA
TUNISIA
Tripoli
Misurata
GULF OF SIDRA
Benghazi
Cyrenaica
Tripolitania
Sebha
LIBYA
Fezzan
Libyan Desert
Sahara
Tibesti
EGYPT
Alexandria
Port Said
SUEZ CANAL
CAIRO
Sinai Pen.
El Faiyum
El Minya
Asyut
NILE
Aswan
ASWAN HIGH DAM
LAKE NASSER
LAKE NUBIA
Nubian Desert
ISRAEL
JORDAN
IRAQ
SAUDI ARABIA
QATAR
U. A. E.
North Tropic Line
(Tropic of Cancer)
RED SEA
Port Sudan
ATBARA
NIGER
Bodélé Depression
CHAD
LAKE CHAD
Abécher
N'Djamena
SHARI
Sudan
NIGERIA
CAMEROON
EQUATORIAL GUINEA
GABON
CONGO
CENTRAL AFRICAN REPUBLIC
ZAIRE
SUDAN
El Fasher
Omdurman
Khartoum
Wad Medani
BLUE NILE
El Obeid
Malakal
Wau
WHITE NILE
Juba
UGANDA
KENYA
Kassala
Asmara
Eritrea
Ras Dashan
15,157
LAKE TANA
Ethiopian Highlands
Dessye
ETHIOPIA
Addis Ababa
Jimma
Dire Dawa
Harar
DJIBOUTI
Djibouti
YEMEN ARAB REP.
PEOP. DEM. REP. YEMEN
GULF OF ADEN
WABI SHEBELLE
SOMALIA
INDIAN OCEAN
5,000 m. 16,404 ft.
2,000 m. 6,562 ft.
1,000 m. 3,281 ft.
500 m. 1,640 ft.
200 m. 656 ft.
100 m. 328 ft.
Sea Level
Below
Longitude East of Greenwich
10°
20°
30°
40°
50°
© C.S. Hammond & Co., Maplewood, N.J.

Northeastern Africa

"Big Blue Marble" Photograph

Geographically Speaking

When it is hot, it's hot! For openers ("Get out your canteens!"), 90 percent of Libya is in the Sahara Desert. The hottest temperature ever recorded on Earth was here in Al' Azizyah on September 13, 1922. It was 58°C (136°F). Do you think that was in the shade?

Ethiopia has been known to boast about its Red Sea Coast, which is one of the hottest areas in the world. Luckily most of Ethiopia is way above sea level — 1,800 meters to 2,400 meters (6,000 feet to 8,000 feet) — so it's not that hot.

Just outside of Khartoum, in Sudan, south meets east and flows north, or more specifically, the White Nile, which gets its waters from Lake Victoria, Uganda, in the south, meets the Blue Nile, which gets its waters from Lake Tana, in Ethiopia, in the east. They meet in the Albara River. It is here that the White and Blue Niles become *the* Nile and flow over 6,738 kilometers (4,187 miles) north to the Mediterranean Sea. Its valley and delta, like a long green stripe across the desert land, is among the world's most fertile farmland.

You may only be up to your neck. Lake Chad is .9 meters to 1.2 meters (3 feet to 4 feet) deep. However shallow it may be, that doesn't stop it from being the source of Central Africa's major rivers.

Double time. Djibouti is a country on the Gulf of Aden. Djibouti is the capital of Djibouti.

Naturally

Life in the desert depends on finding water. In Sudan, they have come up with some unique ways to store it when they find it. The most outstanding way is in tree trunks.

Even though in Libya it may boil,
Libya's lucky — it is loaded with oil.

Sudan is the world's second-largest producer of Egyptian cotton. Three guesses as to which country is number one.

A Man-made W.O.W.

See the Pyramids along the Nile! The three pyramids at Giza, in Egypt, are the only wonder out of the seven ancient Wonders of the World that exist today. The dry desert air is one reason for their preservation. The other reason may very well be the Giant Sphinx, with the head of a man and the body of a lion, that has been standing guard for over 4,500 years. The Giant Sphinx is approximately 73 meters (240 feet) long and 20 meters (66 feet) high. The largest pyramid, made of over 2 million stone blocks, was originally 147 meters (481 feet) high and its base covers 5 hectares (13 acres).

To shed more light on the ancients, another ancient Wonder of the World was the 134-meter (440-feet)-high Lighthouse of Alexandria. It once stood on the island of Pharos, off Alexandria in the Mediterranean Sea. Fire was the source of the light, which burned all through the night.

It made the "Modern Wonders of the World" list. The Suez Canal links the Mediterranean Sea and the Red Sea, *artificially.* This man-made shortcut has reduced shipping time from west to east ever since 1869.

Central African Empire is now Central African Republic. Mogadishu (Somalia) is now Muqdisho. Seychelles (Aldabra Island group) is now an independent nation. Macras Nguema Biyogo (Equatorial Guinea) is now Bioko.

Central Africa

"Big Blue Marble" Photograph

Geographically Speaking

It is the official headwaters of the White Nile. It is in three countries at the same time — Uganda, Kenya, and Tanzania. It is the second-largest freshwater lake in the world. It is Lake Victoria.

It isn't so unusual to find lakes in a valley. In Central Africa there are Lake Albert, Lake Edward, and Lake Nyasa. But a lake, the likes of Lake Tanganyika, is not only one of the world's longest, 676 kilometers (420 miles), but is also one of the world's deepest, 1,435 meters (4,708 feet). It is in the Great Rift Valley, the largest in the world.

To the east of the Great Rift Valley in Tanzania is the highest mountain in all of Africa, a snow-capped volcano called Mount Kilimanjaro, 5,895 meters (19,340 feet).

The climate in Uganda, Rwanda, Burundi, Kenya, and Tanzania is not so hot. In fact, it's quite nice. Not what you'd expect in countries located on and near the equator! The cooler climate is due to the highland plateaus. If it were not for these plateaus, the climate would be typically tropical, like that of their neighbors to the west.

The Central African Republic may be landlocked, but it is the important transportation crossroad, or more accurately "cross-river" between western Africa and central Africa. Rivers flow north to the Lake Chad basin and south to the Congo River basin.

Safaris. The scene of the game is Kenya and Tanzania, in the wide-open spaces of the savanna. And it's wild! Wild animals are being stalked in their natural habitat. Animals are being shot — but the hunters are armed with cameras and rolls of film. Snap! Click! Hooray for preservation!

For another kind of safari, the scene changes to Zaire to some of the world's deepest, darkest, thickest tropical rain forests. Here the leaves are so dense that sunlight may never reach the forest's floor. To take pictures here you had better remember your flash bulbs.

Equatorial Guinea is a two-part country: one is the volcanic island of Fernando Po; the other is on the mainland, Rio Muni.

Tanzania is a three-part country: mainland Tanganyika and the islands of Zanzibar and Pemba.

Seventy-five percent of the people in Somalia are nomads. They roam the countryside herding their camels, cattle, goats, and sheep.

Naturally

That's a Hill of Beans! Cocoa (hot chocolate) comes from the cacao bean, which comes from Cameroon. Coffee beans come from Kenya.

Instant coffee comes from the *robusta* bean, which grows in Rwanda and Burundi. Do you drink only tea? It thrives in most African countries abundantly.

Industrial diamonds are mined in Zaire and Tanzania.

The copper mines in Zaire and Uganda are worth a pretty penny. They are among the world's richest!

Aluminum is supplied by Cameroon.

The Congo, along with Gabon, is where many ebony and mahogany trees grow.

Ships by the droves go to Zanzibar to load up with cloves — from the world's greatest supplier.

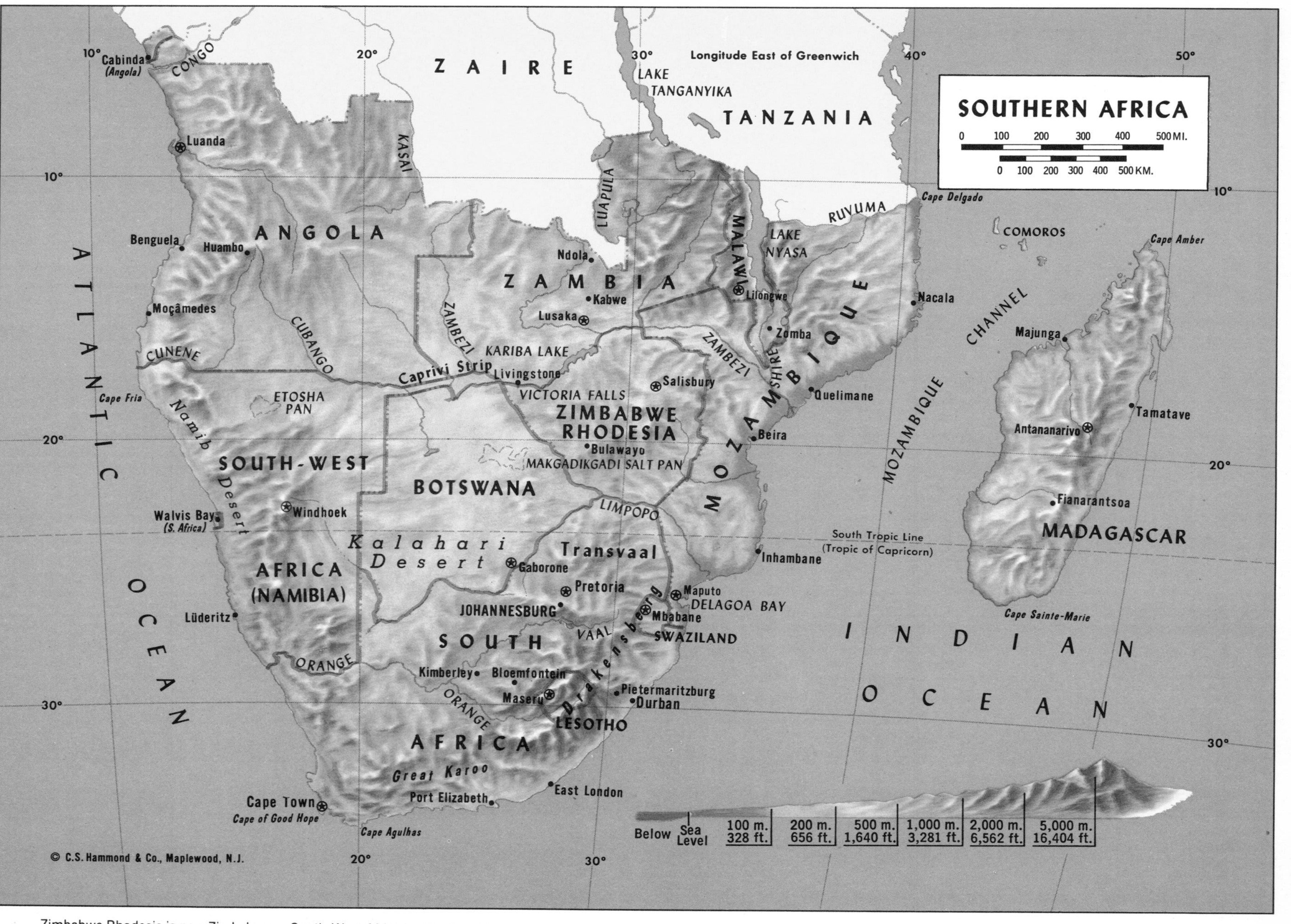

Zimbabwe Rhodesia is now Zimbabwe. . South-West Africa is now Namibia.

Southern Africa

"Big Blue Marble" Photograph

Geographically Speaking

Do you know a country that has water borders on three sides and is not a peninsula? It's Namibia, a country once called South-West Africa. On the north is the Cunene River, on the west is the Atlantic Ocean, and on the south is the Orange River. On the east? It's the sandy red soil of the Kalahari Desert.

The western part of Botswana is in the Kalahari Desert and it is hardly deserted. It is home to the huge herds of wild animals that roam around.

It's *R. & R.—rivers and railroads!* In the west Angola gets no rest, even though it's "catchin' zzzs"—Zambia and Zaire. Angola acts as their access to the Atlantic. In the east it's Mozambique. With its deep-water harbors in the Indian Ocean, Mozambique keeps ships from Zambia, South Africa, Malawi, and Zimbabwe, once called Rhodesia, in perpetual motion.

A Natural W.O.W.

One of the world's natural wonders is the waterfall on the Zambezi River that borders on Zambia and Zimbabwe. Victoria Falls rises to 108 kilometers (355 feet) at the center before it falls.

It's electrifying! The Kariba Dam forms the Kariba Lake, 5,200 square kilometers (2,000 square miles) on the Zambia-Zimbabwe border. It's the site of one of the world's largest hydroelectric plants.

Two countries within a country? Swaziland and Lesotho are completely surrounded by South Africa.

Maptalk

A **cape,** or point, is a piece of land that extends into a body of water.

Last Exit to the East. The cape known as Good Hope (South Africa) was first reached in 1488 by Vasco da Gama, a Portuguese explorer. He called it Cape of Storms. It must have been raining the day he got there! The king of Portugal, undoubtedly an optimist and obviously not on the trip, changed the name to the Cape of Good Hope, hoping it was in fact the sea route to India and the Far East. Nine years later they discovered it to be the route they were seeking.

Naturally

Sugar and spice make food taste nice. In the island country of Mauritius, you have rocks in your head if you don't clear the volcanic rocks out of your field before you plant your sugar cane.

When it comes to desserts, think of Madagascar and its vanilla, which is more than just a flavor. Did you know vanilla is in chocolate and all other sweet things? It is an essential ingredient.

Southern Africa is a real gold mine! Angola's got oil and Botswana's got manganese. Zambia has enough copper to make it one of the richest countries in Africa.

Gold comes from Mozambique and Zimbabwe. But from South Africa comes more gold than from any other country in the world! South Africa is also a gem, when it comes to diamonds. South Africa mines more diamonds than any other country in the world.

If you love coconut, the Seychelles, a country of islands off the central and southeastern coast of Africa in the Indian Ocean, is the place to go. There are double coconuts called *coco de mer* that can weigh almost 23 kilos (50 pounds).

Mozambique Channel, an important shipping lane, is more than 1,600 kilometers (1,000 miles) long and varies from 402 kilometers to 970 kilometers (250 miles to 600 miles) wide.

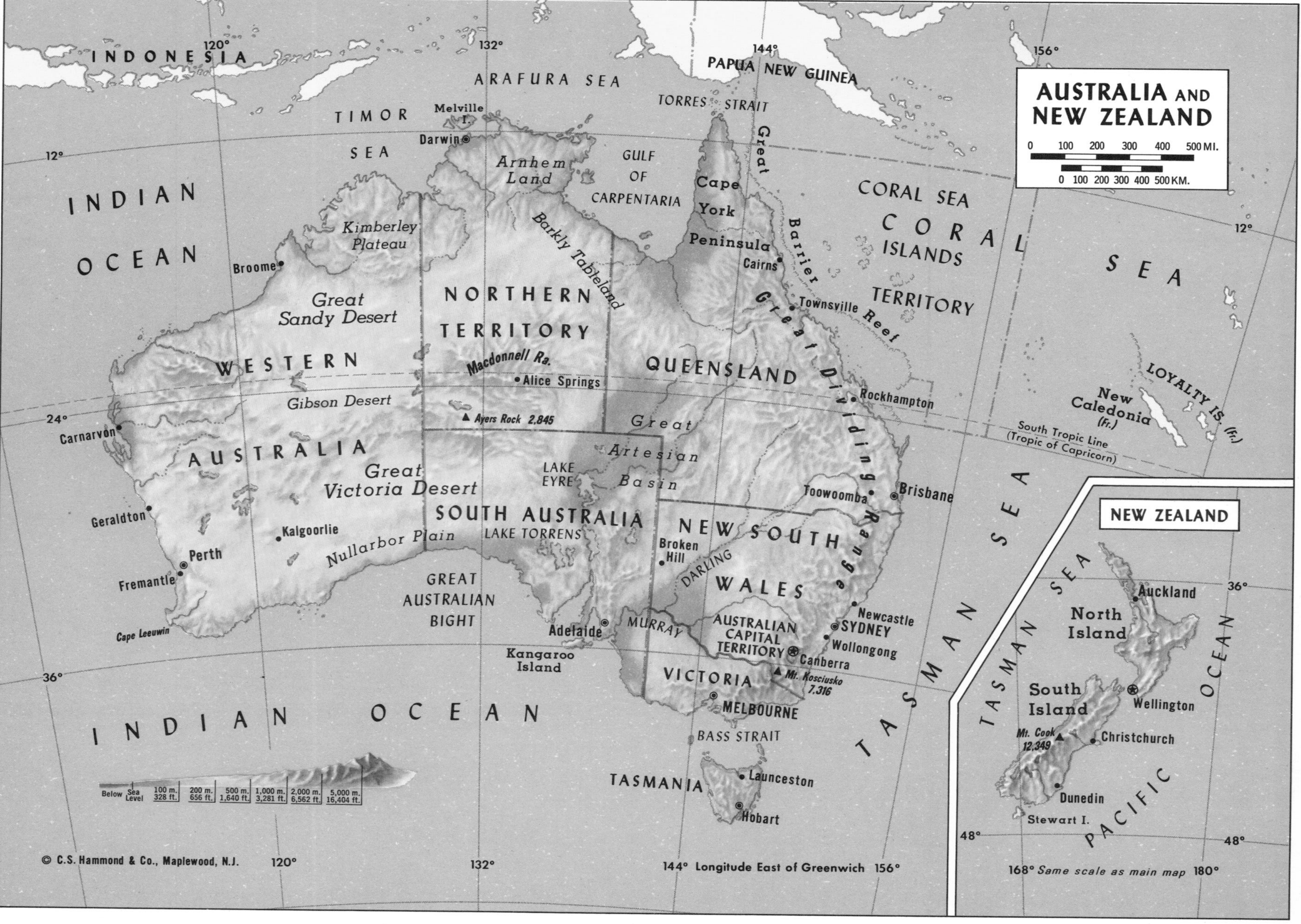

AUSTRALIA AND NEW ZEALAND
0 100 200 300 400 500 MI.
0 100 200 300 400 500 KM.
INDONESIA
ARAFURA SEA
PAPUA NEW GUINEA
TIMOR SEA
Melville I.
Darwin
TORRES STRAIT
GULF OF CARPENTARIA
Arnhem Land
Cape York Peninsula
Cairns
Great Barrier Reef
Townsville
CORAL SEA
CORAL SEA ISLANDS TERRITORY
INDIAN OCEAN
Kimberley Plateau
Broome
Barkly Tableland
NORTHERN TERRITORY
Great Sandy Desert
WESTERN AUSTRALIA
Macdonnell Ra.
Alice Springs
QUEENSLAND
Great Dividing Range
Rockhampton
LOYALTY IS. (Fr.)
New Caledonia (Fr.)
Gibson Desert
Ayers Rock 2,845
Carnarvon
Great Artesian Basin
South Tropic Line (Tropic of Capricorn)
Great Victoria Desert
LAKE EYRE
Toowoomba
Brisbane
Geraldton
SOUTH AUSTRALIA
Kalgoorlie
LAKE TORRENS
NEW SOUTH WALES
Broken Hill
DARLING
Nullarbor Plain
Perth
Fremantle
GREAT AUSTRALIAN BIGHT
Cape Leeuwin
Adelaide
MURRAY
AUSTRALIAN CAPITAL TERRITORY
Canberra
Newcastle
SYDNEY
Wollongong
Kangaroo Island
VICTORIA
Mt. Kosciusko 7,316
MELBOURNE
TASMAN SEA
BASS STRAIT
TASMANIA
Launceston
Hobart
INDIAN OCEAN
Below Sea Level 100 m. 328 ft. 200 m. 656 ft. 500 m. 1,640 ft. 1,000 m. 3,281 ft. 2,000 m. 6,562 ft. 5,000 m. 16,404 ft.
NEW ZEALAND
Auckland
North Island
South Island
Wellington
Mt. Cook 12,349
Christchurch
Dunedin
Stewart I.
PACIFIC OCEAN
Same scale as main map
12° 24° 36° 48°
120° 132° 144° 156° 168° 180°
144° Longitude East of Greenwich

AUSTRALIA AND NEW ZEALAND

Geographically Speaking

Australia Comes in Sixth and Seventh! Australia is the only continent comprised of just one country. Australia is the sixth largest country and the seventh largest continent in the world. Since there are only seven continents in the world, you know what that means — Australia is the smallest!

The name "Australia" comes from the Latin word *australis,* meaning "southern." It is the "down under" country because it is entirely south of the equator. However, Australia is not alone in the Southern Hemisphere. The country of New Zealand is Australia's nearest neighbor, located only 1,930 kilometers (1,200 miles) to the southeast.

The Great Sandy Desert in Australia is sandy! Isn't that great!

The Great Dividing Range stretches from Queensland through New South Wales, Victoria, and under the Bass Strait to the island of Tasmania. The Snowy Mountain Range (and it is snowy), located in the Australian Alps, includes Australia's highest mountain, Mount Kosciusko, 2,228 meters (7,316 feet).

Maptalk

A **watershed** is generally elevated land that is located between and divides two drainage areas. Water (rivers) at this point flows to either side of a ridge, hills, or mountains.

The Great Dividing Range does just that. Rivers that originate here flow either east to the Pacific Ocean or west to the central lowlands and the Indian Ocean.

Murray is the name of the main river system of Australia. Starting in the Snowy Mountains of the Great Dividing Range, the Murray flows westward 2,570 kilometers (1,600 miles) to the Indian Ocean, south of Adelaide.

The Darling River is Australia's "not-so-little" Darling. It is the longest river in Australia, beating the Murray River by 100 miles . It is 2,740 kilometers (1,700 miles) long!

Nullarbor, the coastal plain in Western Australia and South Australia is plain all right. There isn't a tree in sight. The name Nullarbor comes from the Latin *nulla,* meaning "no," and *arbor,* meaning "tree."

No Kidding!

Did you know that both Australia and New Zealand have more sheep than people? In Australia there are approximately 155 million sheep and only 14 million people. Where there are sheep, there is wool!

The continent-country of Australia has some unusual geographic features!

The Incredible Disappearing Lake! It was last seen evaporating near Canberra in New South Wales, Australia. Named Lake George, this lake is not shy; in fact, it's quite fresh — fresh water, that is! Its disappearance and reappearance have a lot to do with rainfall. When it rains, it pours, and presto — Lake George. Lake George covers 151,580 hectares (38,500 acres) and is 6 meters to 7.6 meters (20 feet to 25 feet) deep. During dry weather, it disappears again.

A dry lake! It is dry Lake Eyre, located in South Australia and Australia's largest lake (wet or dry). It measures 9,580 square kilometers (3,700 square miles). It is the lowest spot in Australia at 16 meters (52 feet) below sea level. After rain, Lake Eyre is approximately 3.7 meters (12 feet) deep. However, most of the time it is a huge, dry mud flat covered by a crust of salt.

An **artesian well** is formed when water that is trapped underground rises and reaches the surface of the land.

Well! Well! Well! The Great Artesian Basin — all 1,740,000 square kilometers (670,000 square miles of it) — is overflowing with artesian wells. Don't drink the water! It is for sheep and cattle only in this Great "grazing" Artesian Basin.

It took small primitive organisms that secrete a skeletonlike material, called *coral,* over a million years to form the largest coral reef in the world — the Great Barrier Reef. It stretches 2,012 kilometers (1,250 miles) off the northeast coast of Australia.

A giant clam, weighing 268.9 kilograms (579.5 pounds), was found in these waters.

Kangaroos and koalas are related. They both are members of the marsupial family. All marsupials have pouches in which they carry their young. There is only one marsupial native to the United States. Can you name it? You are right if you said opossum.

Is That a Fact?

	Australia
Area:	7,686,848 sq. km. (2,967,909 sq. mi.)
Total population:	13,993,000
Children aged 0–14:	3,818,000
High spot:	Mount Kosciusko 2,228 m. (7,316 ft.)
Low spot:	Lake Eyre 16 m. (52 ft.) below sea level
City with most people:	Sydney

The country of New Zealand is made up of two islands: one in the north called North Island and one in the south called—you guessed it—South Island.

New Zealand belongs to a group of Pacific Ocean islands known as *Polynesia* (which means many islands). New Zealand is the southernmost boundary of Polynesia.

How's the Weather... in Australia?

Extreme Northern Australia is typically tropical because it is not too far from the equator! The rest of Australia is warm and dry.

... in New Zealand?

It's "m" and "m," moist and mild, or moistly mild, just like the United States' Pacific Northwest (Washington State and Oregon). It is warmer on North Island because it is closer to the equator than South Island.

An island with a peninsula? It is North Island and it's warm, with just the right climate and soil conditions for citrus-tree groves. South Island is covered by snowcapped mountains called the Southern Alps.

Naturally

"Baa, Baa, All You Australian Sheep. Do You Have Any Wool?" How about a bag 790 million kilograms (1.75 billion pounds) full each year!

Australia is a world leader when it comes to growing wheat!

Australia is chock full of minerals. It is a world-leading producer of bauxite, iron, lead, nickel, tin, and zinc!

Australia gets good mileage from its own fuel. It has one of the largest reserves of coal, and oil and natural gas, too.

Australia, having been isolated from other continents, has some of the most unusual animals in the world.

New Zealand is known to let off steam in and around the volcanic areas of North Island. This is "power potential."

Located on South Island is the fifth-highest waterfall in the world, Sutherland Falls—580 meters (1,904 feet) tall!

Mount Cook, the highest in New Zealand, pierces the clouds with its 3,764 meter (12,349 feet) height.

One-third of New Zealand has fertile soil.

One-third of New Zealand is covered with trees—"timber."

One-third of New Zealand is mountains, rivers, and lakes—you can imagine how much hydroelectricity that much water can generate.

Australians speak English that has been spiced up with words borrowed from the Aborigines, the original Australians.

Once upon a time, there was a bloke[1] and his cobber[2], both jackeroos[3], who were bringing a mob[4] of sheep in from the bush[5] to the ranch. It was dinkum[6] yacker[7] because they had to cross a billabong[8]. With the help of a digger[9] they made it, not losing a single jumbuck[10]. Whacko[11]!

1 *Man*
2 *Friend*
3 *Ranch workers*
4 *Flock, herd*
5 *Interior region*
6 *True, real*
7 *Hard work*
8 *A branch of a river*
9 *Australian soldier*
10 *Sheep with thick fleece*
11 *Hurrah!*

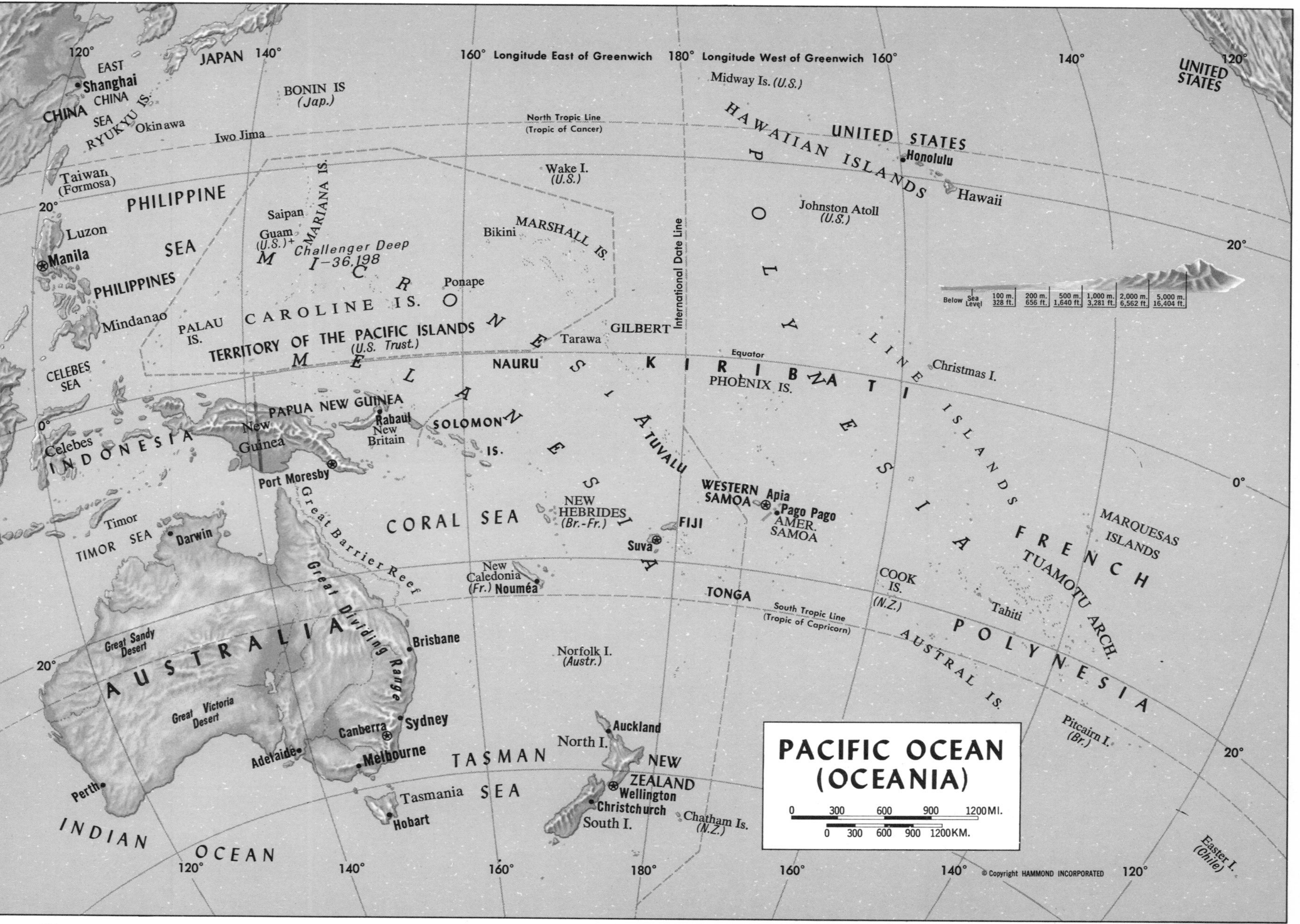

Gilbert Island group is now an independent nation called Republic of Kiribati. New Hebrides Island group is now an independent nation called Vanuatu.

OCEANIA

"Big Blue Marble" Photograph

Geographically Speaking

Oceania is the name given to the thousands of Pacific Islands located in — where else? — the Pacific Ocean.

The Pacific Ocean is an ocean of an ocean! It's the world's largest, covering one-third of the Earth's surface. Put together, all the continents plus another landmass the size of Asia could just about cover this ocean! The amount of land of all the Pacific Islands is only about the size of the state of Alaska!

These "lost island paradises" didn't know they were "lost" until they were "found." Until the 1500s people living on these islands didn't know the rest of the world existed. And the rest of the world didn't know these islands existed.

These thousands of islands — roughly 20,000 to 30,000, no one knows the exact number — are either high islands or low islands.

- The high islands are mountainous, volcanic islands like Hawaii, Fiji, Samoa, the Solomons, and the "new" group — New Hebrides, New Caledonia, New Guinea, New Zealand, and New Britain.
- The low islands are a few feet above sea level. These islands are actually atolls. An **atoll** is a coral reef that surrounds a shallow area of water that is called a **lagoon.**

Maptalk

A **lagoon** is a shallow area of water separated from an ocean or lake by a sand bank, a strip of land, or a coral reef.

There are three groups of islands that make up Oceania:

- Melanesia is located in the southwestern Pacific.
- Micronesia is located in the central Pacific, north of Melanesia and south of Japan.
- Polynesia is located in the eastern Pacific. Midway Island is the northernmost, New Zealand is the southernmost, and Easter Island is the easternmost boundary of Polynesia.

How's the Weather?

It's in the tropics, so it could be *too* hot. However, ocean breezes gently cool the islands, making them heavenly. In the Pacific there are *typhoons* that are more than breezes. They are big-winded tropical storms that blow in all too frequently, bringing with them heavy rains.

Because of the long, warm growing season, tropical coconuts, sugar cane, bananas, coffee, and cacao grow in this typically tropical island region.

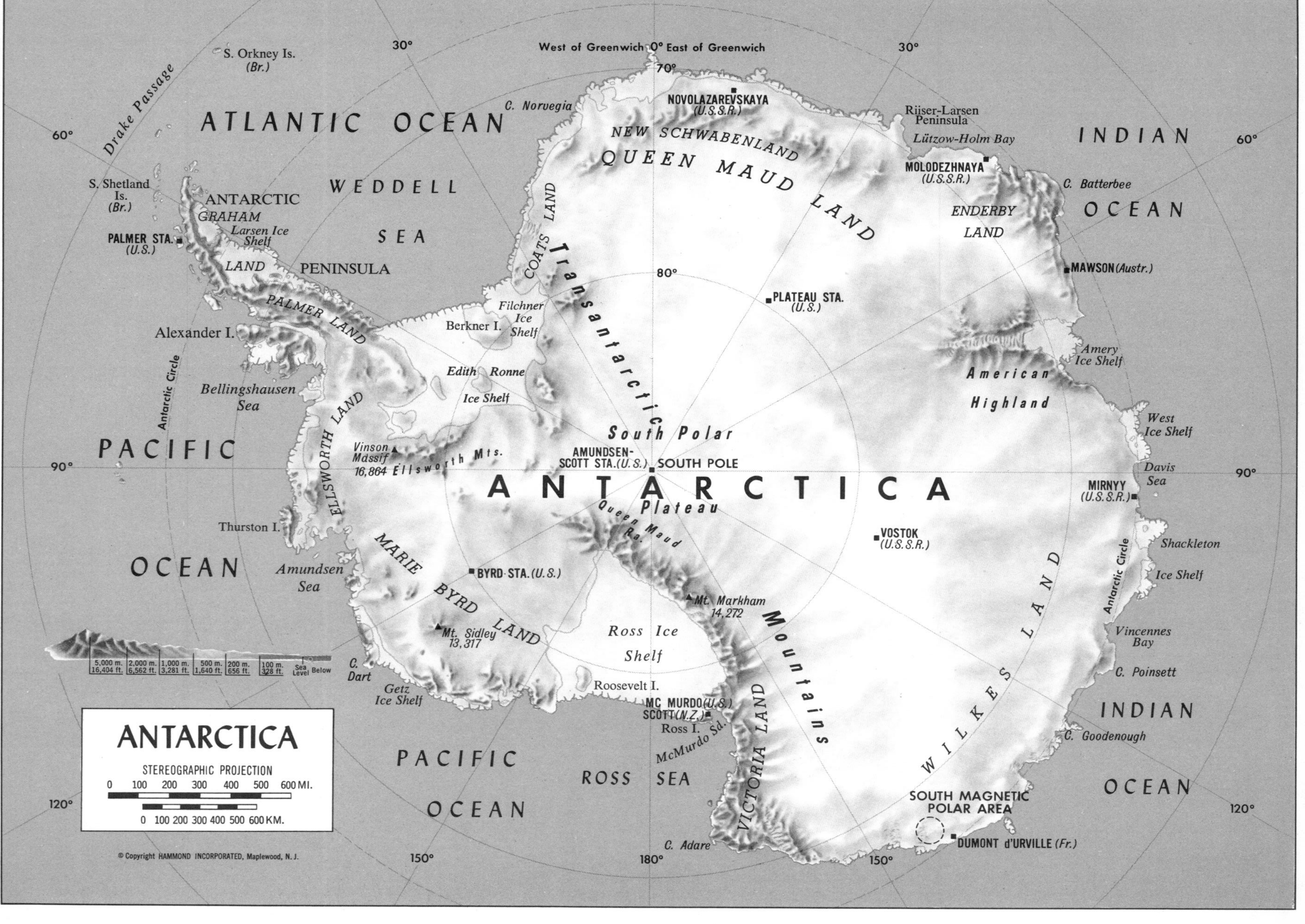
ANTARCTICA
STEREOGRAPHIC PROJECTION
0 100 200 300 400 500 600 MI.
0 100 200 300 400 500 600 KM.
5,000 m. 16,404 ft.
2,000 m. 6,562 ft.
1,000 m. 3,281 ft.
500 m. 1,640 ft.
200 m. 656 ft.
100 m. 328 ft.
Sea Level
Below
West of Greenwich 0° East of Greenwich
ATLANTIC OCEAN
INDIAN OCEAN
PACIFIC OCEAN
WEDDELL SEA
ROSS SEA
Drake Passage
S. Orkney Is. (Br.)
S. Shetland Is. (Br.)
PALMER STA. (U.S.)
ANTARCTIC PENINSULA
GRAHAM LAND
Larsen Ice Shelf
PALMER LAND
Alexander I.
Bellingshausen Sea
Antarctic Circle
ELLSWORTH LAND
Thurston I.
Amundsen Sea
C. Dart
Getz Ice Shelf
MARIE BYRD LAND
Mt. Sidley 13,317
BYRD STA. (U.S.)
Vinson Massif 16,864
Ellsworth Mts.
Edith Ronne Ice Shelf
Berkner I.
Filchner Ice Shelf
COATS LAND
C. Norvegia
NOVOLAZAREVSKAYA (U.S.S.R.)
NEW SCHWABENLAND
QUEEN MAUD LAND
Riiser-Larsen Peninsula
Lützow-Holm Bay
MOLODEZHNAYA (U.S.S.R.)
C. Batterbee
ENDERBY LAND
MAWSON (Austr.)
PLATEAU STA. (U.S.)
Amery Ice Shelf
American Highland
West Ice Shelf
Davis Sea
MIRNYY (U.S.S.R.)
Shackleton Ice Shelf
Vincennes Bay
C. Poinsett
C. Goodenough
VOSTOK (U.S.S.R.)
WILKES LAND
SOUTH MAGNETIC POLAR AREA
DUMONT d'URVILLE (Fr.)
Transantarctic Mountains
South Polar Plateau
AMUNDSEN-SCOTT STA. (U.S.)
SOUTH POLE
ANTARCTICA
Queen Maud Ra.
Mt. Markham 14,272
Ross Ice Shelf
Roosevelt I.
MC MURDO (U.S.)
SCOTT (N.Z.)
Ross I.
McMurdo Sd.
VICTORIA LAND
C. Adare
30°
60°
70°
80°
90°
120°
150°
180°
© Copyright HAMMOND INCORPORATED, Maplewood, N. J.

ANTARCTICA

Antarctica, the fifth-largest continent in the world, is located at the South Pole. But don't let the word "south" fool you. The air conditioning here is on all the time, *naturally.*

Antarctica's surface is made up of ice and snow — 29 million cubic kilometers (7 million cubic miles). In the interior and along the coast, mountains manage to poke through this incredible icecap.

There are rivers here, but they are made of ice, better known as *glaciers.* They flow very slowly from the mountains to the sea.

What's underneath this mile-thick skating rink almost completely surrounded by mountains and glaciers? Real land — hills, valleys, lowlands, and fiords — just like on any other continent.

The Antarctic icecap, if melted, would yield more fresh water than is found in all of the rest of the world.

Scientists believe that it was once warm in Antarctica! Fossils have been found that prove plants and animals lived here. There are also deposits of fossil fuels like coal, oil, and natural gas.

How's the Weather?

It was here at Vostok Station on August 24, 1960, that the world's coldest-ever temperature was recorded, minus 88°C (127°F below zero)! Can you imagine what the wind-chill factor was — especially when you consider that Antarctica is the hub of the world's wind circulation and that it even influences weather in the Northern Hemisphere!

Antarctica's largest land creature is an insect! Related to the housefly, it is wingless and less than 2.5 millimeters (.1 inch) long. That is short!

Antarctica's waters are packed with fish. These waters are home for the largest mammal that ever lived — the blue whale — weighing about 90 metric (100 short) tons, with a length of about 30 meters (100 feet).

How did Antarctica happen? This and many other questions as to the formation of the Earth and the beginnings of life are being researched in Antarctica by international groups of scientists.

In 1959 a treaty was signed stating that for a 30-year period, no nation could make any territorial claims on Antarctica. You may ask "What about the native Antarcticans, isn't it their land? " Yes, but Antarctica is uninhabited by people.

Geographically Speaking

The Transantarctic Mountains do just what their name implies. They cross the entire continent and are as high as 4,900 meters (16,000 feet). They divide Antarctica into two regions: East Antarctica, which faces Africa, the Indian Ocean, and Australia, and West Antarctica, which faces the Pacific Ocean and South America.

The east is a plateau covered by 2,700 meters (9,000 feet) of ice, with an elevation anywhere from 1,800 meters to 3,660 meters (6,000 feet to 12,000 feet). The west is thousands of feet below sea level. Here the icecap can be as much as 4,270 meters (14,000 feet) thick — that's nearly three miles! Scientists believe that if this icecap were to melt, there would be a series of mountainous islands underneath.

The Antarctic Peninsula, reaching northward from West Antarctica, comes within 970 kilometers (600 miles) of South America! This peninsula is 2,250 kilometers (1,400 miles) long. The mountains that cover it are a continuation of the Andean mountain chain of South America.

Is That a Fact?

	Antarctica
Size:	13,209,000 sq. km. (5,100,000 sq. mi.)
High spot:	Vinson Massif 5,140 m. (16,864 ft.)
Low spot:	Sea level

PACIFIC OCEAN
ALEUTIAN IS. (U.S.)
BERING SEA
Longitude 160° East of Greenwich
Petropavlovsk-Kamchatskiy
Sakhalin I.
SEA OF OKHOTSK
UNITED STATES
Anchorage
Mt. McKinley 20,320
Yukon
Nome
Bering Str.
Anadyr
Arctic Circle
Whitehorse
Rocky Mts.
ALASKA
International Date Line
Ambarchik
Siberia
UNION
Barrow
Pt. Barrow
EAST SIBERIAN SEA
Mackenzie
Inuvik
BEAUFORT SEA
NEW SIBERIAN ISLANDS
Lena
Tiksi
Approximate Limit of Pack Ice in September
Banks I.
LAPTEV SEA
OF
CANADA
Victoria I.
QUEEN ELIZABETH ISLANDS
ARCTIC OCEAN
Nordvik
SEVERNAYA ZEMLYA
NORTH POLE
Dudinka
Yenisey
Ellesmere I.
KARA SEA
SOVIET
FRANZ JOSEF LAND
Baffin I.
BAFFIN BAY
Thule
NOVAYA ZEMLYA
BARENTS SEA
Ob
GREENLAND (Den.)
GREENLAND SEA
SVALBARD (Nor.)
Ural Mts.
Davis Strait
Bear I. (Nor.)
Naryan-Mar
SOCIALIST
Godthaab
North Cape
Murmansk
Archangel
Jan Mayen (Nor.)
Denmark Strait
NORWEGIAN SEA
NORWAY
SWEDEN
FINLAND
C. Farewell
ICELAND
Reykjavík
Leningrad
Moscow
16,000 ft. 6,500 ft. 3,200 ft. 1,600 ft. 600 ft. 300 ft. Sea Level Below
FAEROE IS. (Den.)
Helsinki
Oslo
Stockholm
REPUBLICS
ARCTIC REGIONS
Scale of Miles
0 200 400 600 800 1000
NORTH SEA
DEN.
UNITED KINGDOM
IRE.
W. GER.
E. GER.
POLAND
Longitude West of 20° Greenwich
© Copyright HAMMOND INCORPORATED

ARCTIC

Geographically Speaking

The Arctic region is sitting on top of the world. It is located in the northernmost area of Earth.

The Arctic Circle is a select circle! Continents in the Southern Hemisphere need not bother to apply for membership. (You know why!) As for Europe, Asia, and North America, they are — continentally speaking — eligible, because they are located in the Northern Hemisphere.

To get into this select circle, the True Arctic, say the secret words, "Ten degrees Centigrade, fifty degrees Fahrenheit, summer isotherm." Congratulations, Norway, Sweden, Finland, USSR, United States (Alaska), and Canada — your northern portions are in! Going full circle around the globe, these areas are located above the 66° 30′ north latitude — roughly 2,623 kilometers (1,630 miles) from the geographic North Pole, and they all have an average summer temperature of 10°C (50°F).

Not all of the Arctic is frozen year round. Ten degrees Centigrade (50°F) is warm enough to melt the ice and snow of nine-tenths of the Arctic region. During the short summer, wild berries and wild flowers grow

Greenland lies almost entirely within the Arctic Circle, and holds many distinctions. It is the winner of the largest island in the world contest— 2,175,600 square kilometers (840,000 square miles). It is the only land within the Arctic Circle that remains covered with ice and snow all year round. Greenland is hardly green. The southwest coast, where most of the people live, is the only green area.

How, then, did Greenland get its name? It happened nearly 1,000 years ago when this great island was first sighted by the Vikings. Trying to attract settlers, the Vikings named this island Greenland. With a name like that who would suspect it to be permanently frozen all year?

If it were possible to pull up Greenland's 1.6 kilometers to 3.2 kilometers (1 mile to 2 miles) thick sheet of ice, you'd find a lowland plateau, surrounded by coastal mountains hiding underneath.

Glaciers (ice lakes) make icebergs (ice mountains) that can make great waves and rock boats as they float and drift through Baffin Bay. Greenland's glaciers flow gradually from the coastal highlands to the shore. Once a glacier reaches the water's edge, it is on the brink of becoming an iceberg as it snaps, crackles, and plops into the sea. Only one-eighth to one-tenth of an iceberg is above water, like the top of a gigantic floating pyramid. Many of Greenland's icebergs drift southward from Baffin Bay, through the Davis Strait, and float eastward all the way to Labrador on Canada's Atlantic shore.

Naturally

The Arctic is a real cold mine! There's plenty of gold, copper, nickel, and tin. There's also coal, iron ore, and oil. The Arctic waters are some of the best fishing areas in the world.

The countries in the polar region bear many similarities. Rudolph and his reindeer and caribou friends roam the vast tundra land. Fur-coated animals like ermines, sables, foxes, squirrels, hares, and bears are naturally warm enough to live there. Falcons, gulls, geese, sandpipers, and snowbirds are not *loony* when they take *terns* calling the Arctic "home, sweet home."

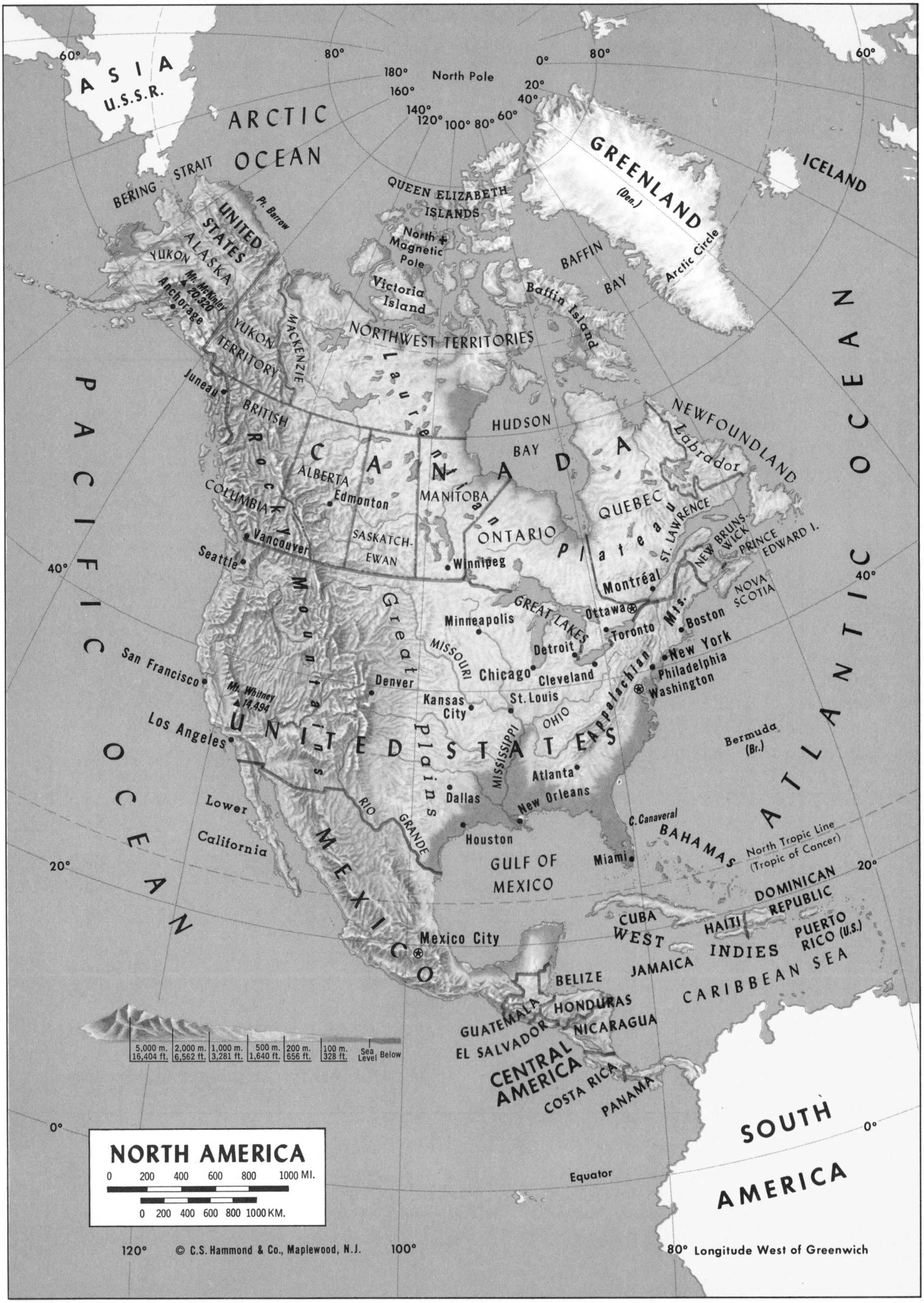

NORTH AMERICA

0 200 400 600 800 1000 MI.

0 200 400 600 800 1000 KM.

ASIA
U.S.S.R.
ARCTIC OCEAN
BERING STRAIT
North Pole
Pt. Barrow
UNITED STATES
ALASKA
YUKON
Mt. McKinley 20,320
Anchorage
QUEEN ELIZABETH ISLANDS
North Magnetic Pole
Victoria Island
GREENLAND (Den.)
ICELAND
BAFFIN BAY
Arctic Circle
Baffin Island
NORTHWEST TERRITORIES
YUKON TERRITORY
MACKENZIE
Laurentian Plateau
Juneau
BRITISH COLUMBIA
Rocky Mountains
HUDSON BAY
CANADA
NEWFOUNDLAND
Labrador
ALBERTA
Edmonton
MANITOBA
SASKATCHEWAN
QUEBEC
ONTARIO
ST. LAWRENCE
NEW BRUNSWICK
PRINCE EDWARD I.
NOVA SCOTIA
Vancouver
Seattle
Winnipeg
Montréal
Ottawa
GREAT LAKES
Toronto
Boston
New York
Philadelphia
Washington
Appalachian Mts.
Minneapolis
MISSOURI
Detroit
Chicago
Cleveland
Great Plains
PACIFIC OCEAN
ATLANTIC OCEAN
San Francisco
Mt. Whitney 14,494
Denver
Kansas City
St. Louis
OHIO
Los Angeles
UNITED STATES
MISSISSIPPI
Atlanta
Bermuda (Br.)
Dallas
New Orleans
Lower California
RIO GRANDE
Houston
C. Canaveral
BAHAMAS
North Tropic Line (Tropic of Cancer)
Miami
GULF OF MEXICO
MEXICO
DOMINICAN REPUBLIC
CUBA
HAITI
WEST INDIES
PUERTO RICO (U.S.)
JAMAICA
Mexico City
BELIZE
CARIBBEAN SEA
HONDURAS
GUATEMALA
NICARAGUA
EL SALVADOR
CENTRAL AMERICA
COSTA RICA
PANAMA
SOUTH AMERICA
Equator
80° Longitude West of Greenwich

60° 80° 180° 160° 140° 120° 100° 80° 60° 0° 80° 20° 40° 60° 40° 40° 20° 20° 0° 0° 120° 100°

5,000 m. 16,404 ft. | 2,000 m. 6,562 ft. | 1,000 m. 3,281 ft. | 500 m. 1,640 ft. | 200 m. 656 ft. | 100 m. 328 ft. | Sea Level | Below

Panama Canal Zone, built and operated by the United States, was granted to Panama in October 1979.

NORTH AMERICA

North America is the third-largest continent in the world. It extends from the cold Arctic regions of the North Pole to the hot tropics of Central America.

Mexico, Central America, and the West Indies are often referred to as Latin America. Latin America is a cultural region where Latin-based languages like Spanish are spoken.

North America is surrounded by oceans of oceans! The Pacific to the west, the Arctic to the north, the Atlantic to the east, and the Pacific to the south.

North America is attached to South America, another continent, by the Central American country of Panama. Central America is the southernmost part of North America.

How's the Weather? A multiple-choice test

a) The winters are long and cold; the summers are short and cool.

b) The summers are long and hot; the winters are short and warm.

c) Spring is warm; summer is hot; fall is cool; winter is cold.

d) It rains. It snows. It's cloudy.

e) It doesn't rain. It doesn't snow. It's sunny.

All of these? None of these? Another combination of any of these? When it comes to weather, North America has got it all, in just about any combination. There is the frozen desert in Alaska's and northern Canada's Arctic tundra regions. Close by is Greenland, whose name would be more appropriate if it were "Whiteland." This island, the largest in the world, is a desert of snow and ice.

There are *hot* deserts like the Mojave and Death valleys in southeastern California. Mexico has its fair share: the Chihuahua, the Sonora, and the Colorado deserts get their start in the United States' most southern part. There are the *hot,* rainy, tropical rain forests of Central America. There is the *cold* rain forest of Washington State's Olympic Peninsula in the northwestern United States.

Seasonally speaking, however, the southern portion of Canada and much of the United States generally have the regular four-season variety of weather: spring, summer, fall, winter.

North America has eight peninsulas:

- The Alaskan Peninsula is in the northwestern United States; geographically it extends northwest from Canada.
- The Gaspé Peninsula is in Québec, Canada.
- The Upper and the Lower peninsulas are *both* in Michigan.
- The Olympic Peninsula is in Washington.
- The state of Florida is a peninsula.
- The Lower California Peninsula is in Mexico.
- So is the Yucatán Peninsula.

Maptalk

An **inland waterway** generally connects two distant bodies of water through rivers, lakes, canals, channels, or locks, *naturally* or *artificially.*

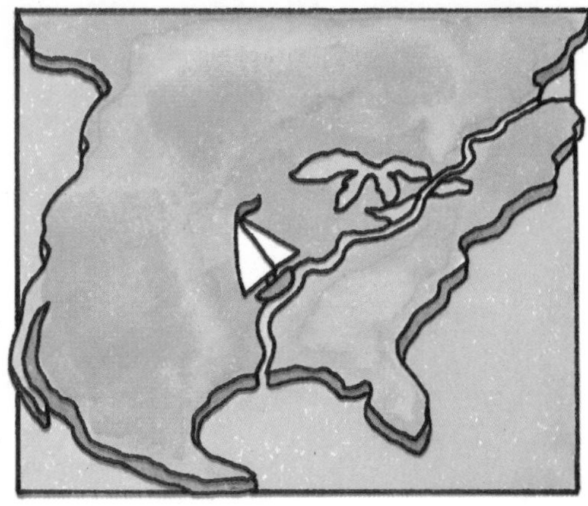

Did you know you can travel on water from the Atlantic Ocean all the way to the Gulf of Mexico by taking a scenic inland route?

Climb aboard a boat up north where the St. Lawrence Seaway meets the Atlantic. Take it south through the Great Lakes to Chicago, pick up the Illinois River, join the Mississippi, and sail on down to the Gulf of Mexico.

The Panama Canal connects the Atlantic Ocean and the Pacific Ocean.

The Sault Ste. Marie Canal, popularly referred to as the "Soo" Locks, connects Lake Superior and Lake Huron, making Duluth, Minnesota, accessible to the Atlantic Ocean. It is water all the way!

The Mackenzie River is central Canada's roving river connection to the Arctic Ocean.

Geographically Speaking

The North American continent has seven distinct land regions:

- The Pacific Coastland Mountains start in Alaska and go all the way down to Mexico. They are two chains that are parallel to each other: The outer chain is made up of the Olympic Mountains in Washington and the Coastal Mountains in Oregon and California.

In the inner chain are the Alaska Range, the Coast Mountains in Canada, the Cascade Range in Washington and Oregon, the Sierra Nevadas in California, and the Sierra Madre Occidental in Mexico.

- The Intermountain region is in between the Pacific Coastland Mountains and the Rocky Mountains. It has highland plateaus like the Interior Plateau of British Colombia, the Colorado Plateau, and the Mexican Plateau. It is dotted with great river basins like the Yukon River basin in Alaska and Canada and the Great Basin in Nevada. The Grand Canyon is in the Great Basin. Death Valley, the lowest point in North America, 86 meters (282 feet) below sea level, is in there too.
- The Rocky Mountains are the backbone of North America. This chain begins in northern Alaska and extends down to Mexico, where the range continues but its name is changed to Sierra Madre Oriental.
- The Interior Plain begins in the west where the Rocky Mountains end and stretches east to where the Appalachian Mountain System begins. The Interior Plain is interior all right; centrally located on the continent, it reaches north into Canada and down into the central areas of the United States.
- The Canadian Shield stretches north and east across half of Canada and southward into the northern parts of Minnesota, Wisconsin, Michigan, and New York.
- The Appalachian Mountain System begins along the St. Lawrence River in Canada. It continues south along the Atlantic coast, where it ends in northern Alabama.
- The Coastal Plain is called the Atlantic Coastal Plain when it lies along the ocean of the same name. It is called the Gulf Coastal Plain when it lies along the Gulf of Mexico. It has its start in Cape Cod, Massachusetts, runs all along the east coast, around the Gulf of Mexico to the Yucatán Peninsula in Mexico, and then into Central America.

To the American Indian, as well as to many other peoples, all living things in nature are of equal importance and must be respected. This principle gave rise to the awareness and necessity of conservation, a great contribution to modern civilization.

When the glaciers of the ice age receded, they gouged out large holes in the land. The ice melted and filled the holes with water — fresh water. The most spectacular result was the five Great Lakes. One, Lake Superior, is the largest freshwater lake in the world. It is about the size of South Carolina.

Is That a Fact?

North America	
Area:	24,399,000 sq. km. (9,420,000 sq. mi.)
Total population:	355,200,000
Children aged 0–14:	106,782,000
High spot:	Mount McKinley, Alaska 6,194 m. (20,320 ft.)
Low spot:	Death Valley, California 86 m. (282 ft.) below sea level
City with most people:	Mexico City, Mexico
Largest country:	Canada 9,976,200 sq. km. (3,851,800 sq. mi.)
Smallest country:	Grenada 344 sq. km. (133 sq. mi.)
Largest island:	Greenland 2,175,600 sq. km. (840,000 sq. mi.)
Deepest gorge:	Hell's Canyon, Idaho 2,400 m. (7,900 ft.), the world's deepest
World's strongest surface wind ever recorded:	231 m.p.h. at Mount Washington, New Hampshire (1934)

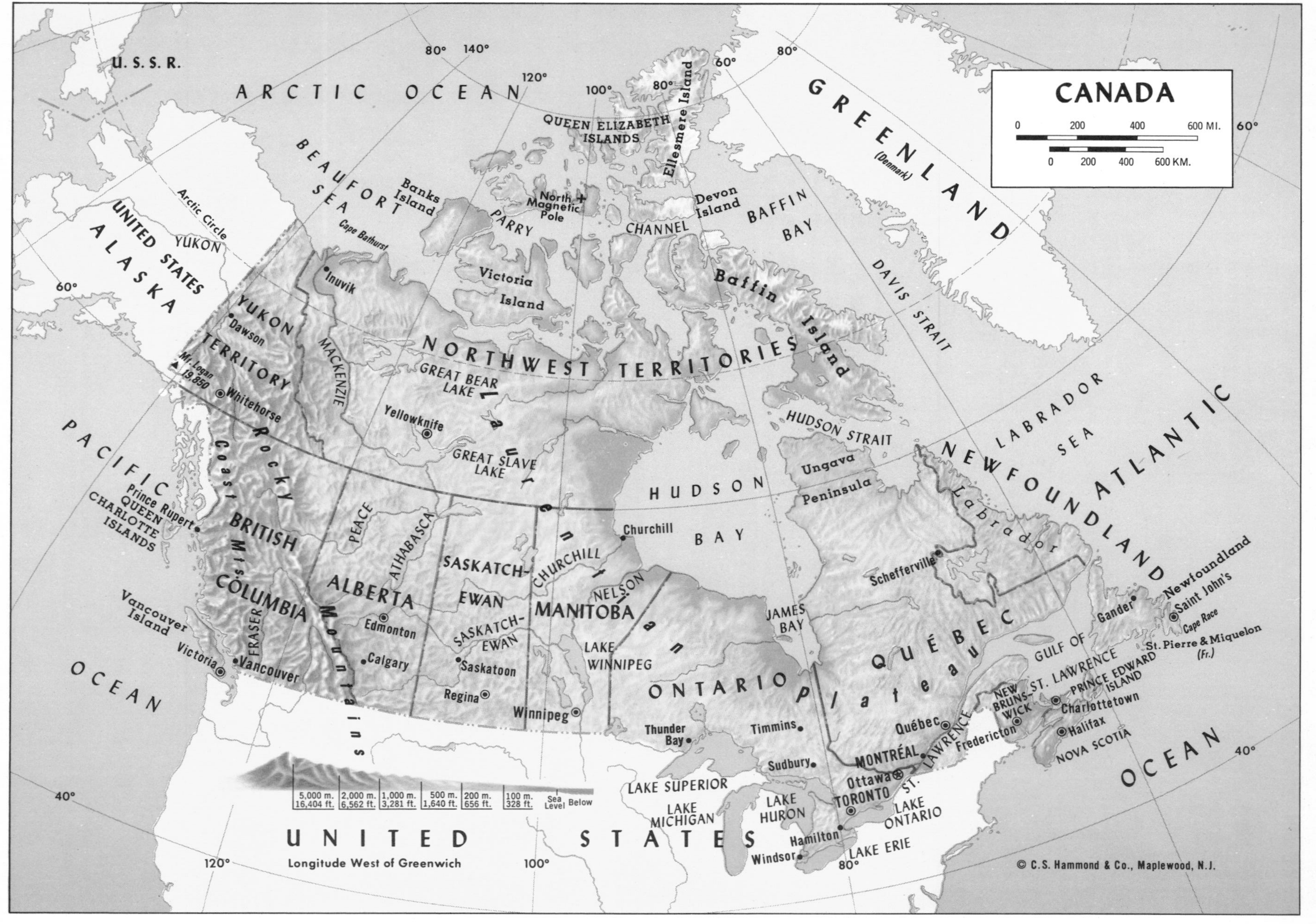

CANADA
0 200 400 600 MI.
0 200 400 600 KM.
U. S. S. R.
ARCTIC OCEAN
GREENLAND
(Denmark)
QUEEN ELIZABETH ISLANDS
Ellesmere Island
BEAUFORT SEA
Banks Island
North Magnetic Pole
PARRY
CHANNEL
Devon Island
BAFFIN BAY
Cape Bathurst
Arctic Circle
YUKON
UNITED STATES
ALASKA
Inuvik
Victoria Island
Baffin Island
DAVIS STRAIT
YUKON TERRITORY
Dawson
MACKENZIE
NORTHWEST TERRITORIES
GREAT BEAR LAKE
Mt. Logan 19,850
Whitehorse
Yellowknife
HUDSON STRAIT
LABRADOR SEA
PACIFIC
Coast Mts.
Rocky Mountains
GREAT SLAVE LAKE
Ungava Peninsula
NEWFOUNDLAND
ATLANTIC
HUDSON BAY
Labrador
Prince Rupert
QUEEN CHARLOTTE ISLANDS
BRITISH COLUMBIA
PEACE
ATHABASCA
SASKATCHEWAN
CHURCHILL
Churchill
Schefferville
ALBERTA
NELSON
MANITOBA
Laurentian Plateau
Newfoundland
Saint John's
Gander
Cape Race
Vancouver Island
Edmonton
SASKATCHEWAN
JAMES BAY
QUÉBEC
St. Pierre & Miquelon (Fr.)
FRASER
Calgary
Saskatoon
LAKE WINNIPEG
GULF OF ST. LAWRENCE
Victoria
Vancouver
ONTARIO
PRINCE EDWARD ISLAND
OCEAN
NEW BRUNSWICK
Charlottetown
Regina
Winnipeg
Thunder Bay
Timmins
Québec
Halifax
Fredericton
NOVA SCOTIA
MONTRÉAL
ST. LAWRENCE
Sudbury
Ottawa
OCEAN
LAKE SUPERIOR
TORONTO
5,000 m. 16,404 ft.
2,000 m. 6,562 ft.
1,000 m. 3,281 ft.
500 m. 1,640 ft.
200 m. 656 ft.
100 m. 328 ft.
Sea Level
Below
LAKE MICHIGAN
LAKE HURON
LAKE ONTARIO
UNITED STATES
Hamilton
LAKE ERIE
Windsor
Longitude West of Greenwich
120°
100°
80°
60°
40°
140°
© C.S. Hammond & Co., Maplewood, N.J.

Canada

Geographically Speaking

Canada is the second-largest country in the world. Both English and French are the official languages of Canada.

Maptalk

A **bay** is any indentation of the land that borders on a body of water such as a sea, a lake, or an ocean.

The Hudson Bay lies within the northern portion of Canada. It is practically a little sea. It is four times larger than all five of the great Great Lakes put together. Over 30 rivers empty into the Hudson Bay. Two of the largest are the Churchill and the Nelson. Through the Hudson Bay the traffic is two-way, connecting the Arctic Ocean and the Atlantic Ocean — but for only half of the year. The other half? Well, the route is frozen.

The Bay of Fundy is out in the North Atlantic Ocean, located at the southern end of Canada, in between Nova Scotia and New Brunswick. The Bay of Fundy is famous for not being too much fun at high tide. It is here that there are some of the world's highest tides — like 15 meters (50 feet) high.

It's for the birds; they deserve a hand. Fishermen should give them thanks, for their help at Grand Banks. Grand Banks is a huge underwater plateau located 160 kilometers (100 miles) off the southeast coast of the island of Newfoundland. These shallow waters are some of the world's richest fishing grounds. Fishermen watch for the "fisherbirds" that act like "bird scouts" by circling the schools of fish. That's how the fishermen know exactly where to go for a big catch.

*What's new? New*foundland, which is a two-part province made up of the island of Newfoundland and the mainland of Labrador. *New* Brunswick and *Nova* Scotia (New Scotland), along with Prince Edward Island, make up the Canadian Maritime Provinces.

The Maritime Provinces profit most from their jagged coasts, which play host to tremendous fishing opportunities. There are great harbors here: St. John in Newfoundland, Charlottetown in New Brunswick, and Halifax in Nova Scotia.

Newfoundland is really an old-found land. Vikings are said to have "found" it as early as the year 1000 — a long time ago.

The Maritime Provinces' highlands, plus the southeast part of Québec's mountains and hills, belong to the good old North American continent's Appalachian Mountain System.

In this mountainous region many minerals

abound. In Newfoundland, for example, iron ore, lead, and zinc are found. Nova Scotia and New Brunswick are thick with coal. In the Gaspé Peninsula of Québec, all is fitting and proper, they've got copper. *Good, better, best,* here's the topper! Southeastern Québec does better than as best as it can. The Western Hemisphere's largest deposits of asbestos are found here!

The St. Lawrence River and the Great Lakes make the greatest inland waterway in North America. It is also here, along the Lake Huron, Lake Erie, and Lake Ontario lowland coast, that over half of Canada's population lives.

An area of land called the Canadian Shield is horseshoe shaped. It covers most of the Northwest Territories, the northeast corner of Alberta, the top half of Saskatchewan, three-quarters of Manitoba, three-quarters of Ontario, and all the way north to Québec's northern coast. In other words, the Canadian Shield "shields" roughly half of Canada.

In the eastern part of the shield — the Laurentian uplands — it's hilly. The western part is overflowing with lakes, not to mention the famous horseshoe-shaped Niagara Falls, which is located there. In addition to the five Great Lakes at the southern boundary (Ontario, Erie, Huron, Michigan, and Superior), there are three "great lakes" in the province of Manitoba. Lake Winnipeg is the largest at 24,341 square kilometers (9,398 square miles).

In the Northwest Territories there are two large lakes — the Great Slave Lake and the Great Bear Lake. The Great Bear Lake is the largest inland lake in Canada at 31,792 square kilometers (12,275 square miles). Hold on to your fishing and swimming gear for this! The province of Ontario alone has about a quarter of a million lakes (250,000).

The Canadian Shield is made up of the oldest and hardest rock on Earth. Geologists believe every mineral under the sun, except bauxite, can be found there. This is an inventory of existing "stock." Canada has more than a nickel's worth of nickel. It leads the world in its production. In the two provinces of Ontario and Manitoba, there are platinum and copper. In fact, one of the world's largest copper mines is at Timmons, Ontario. In Sudbury and Hamilton, Ontario, there are large steel works. Québec and Labrador both have iron ore. Western Québec, north-central Ontario, and the Northwest Territories are all aglitter with gold. Ontario has the richest reserve of uranium. Not to be outdone, Saskatchewan has a city named Uranium City. You'll never guess what is mined there!

Lakes are a source for rivers, of course. The Canadian Shield is anywhere from 180 meters to 366 meters (600 feet to 1,200 feet) above sea level. So as the rivers flow to the sea, bays, and lakes that are more or less at sea level, the rivers fall rapidly, forming rapids or waterfalls. It's water power all the way. Canada is the third most water-powerful country in the world. This water supplies the power necessary to make aluminum, and Canada happens to be one of the world's leading aluminum-manufacturing countries.

Maptalk

A **prairie** is a plain by another name. It varies from wide and flat terrain to rolling hills, with both covered by grassland.

The Canadian Western Interior Plains are part of the great Interior Plains of North America. They're the northern extension of the Great Plains of the United States. Canada's Prairie Provinces are (from east to west): Manitoba, Saskatchewan, Alberta, and the northeast corner of British Columbia. In the summer there's just the right amount of rain here on the Canadian plain to grow an essential grain — wheat.

In this prairie land there's something called bituminous sand. It is sand mixed by nature with oil. The fuel potential is real because underground, along Lake Athabasca, the world's largest deposit of bituminous sand, consisting of 49,200 square kilometers (19,000 square miles), can be found. Add more fuel to this rich land; there's coal here too.

The Canadian Western Rocky Mountain region, sometimes called the Cordilleran region, starts up north in the Yukon and extends into British Columbia and Alberta. This region gives rise to many mighty rivers. The Peace and Athabasca rivers originate here in the Canadian Rockies. They flow their separate ways and make peace at the Great Slave Lake, where they join up and meet the Mackenzie River. Then they go with the flow to the Arctic Ocean. On the North American continent, only the Mississippi-Missouri river system is longer than the Mackenzie River system.

The Canadian Rockies are breathtakingly majestic. They reach 2,100 to 3,660 meters (7,000 to 12,000 feet) above sea level. Some mountains are covered with trees; some are topped with glaciers. There are many glacier lakes in the valleys below. Salts from the glaciers, not pollution, give these waters most unusual colors. For example, Lake Louise is famous for its turquoise-colored water.

A **glacier** is a large mass of ice that moves slowly down a valley from the highlands to sea level.

It's down from the valley! The Columbia Ice Fields, 260 square kilometers (100 square miles), are located in the Canadian Rockies. This area is made up of glaciers left over from the last ice age. These glaciers are still slowly flowing.

On the other side of the Rockies, to the west, is the Rocky Mountain trench. On the other side of the trench there are plateaus, valleys, basins, and mountains that are low. Still farther to the west rise the steep Coast Mountains. In the Coast Mountain range in the Yukon is Mount Logan, the highest peak in Canada at 6,050 meters (19,850 feet). The Coast Mountains, as you might expect, follow the Pacific Coast and therefore the Pacific Ocean, of course. But there's another range of mountains, one that is underwater and surfaces to form Vancouver Island and Queen Charlotte Island.

Naturally

This region is rich. It has not only gold and silver, but iron ore and coal for steel as well. There is also lead and zinc, of course. And that's not all. Have you read that Canada is the largest producer of newsprint in the world? That means timber. There is tungsten here too — an essential element in light bulbs.

Canada is hard to beat when it comes to the production of barley, flaxseed, oats, rye, and wheat.

Canada leads the world in the production of nickel, silver, and zinc.

The Arctic Islands are in the Arctic Circle (where else?), which is at 66°30′ north latitude. The islands are (from east to west): Baffin, Devon, Ellesmere, Victoria, and Banks. Brrrrr. It's barren and cold, and covered with tundra (frozen soil).

This area is not without people, though. Here and in the Northwest Territories Inuits and Indians live. They travel in kayak boats, which are lightweight canoes covered with animal skins that waterproof the boats for travel on the rivers and lakes. Overland, or over snow or over ice, transportation is mainly by means of sleds pulled by teams of dogs. Inuits, the preferred name of Eskimos, do a lot of hunting and mining too.

Isn't it interesting that the buffalo and the whooping crane, animals that have both made the endangered species list, roam and nest in the Canadian National Park named Wood Buffalo? This park is located along the border shared by Alberta and the Northwest Territories.

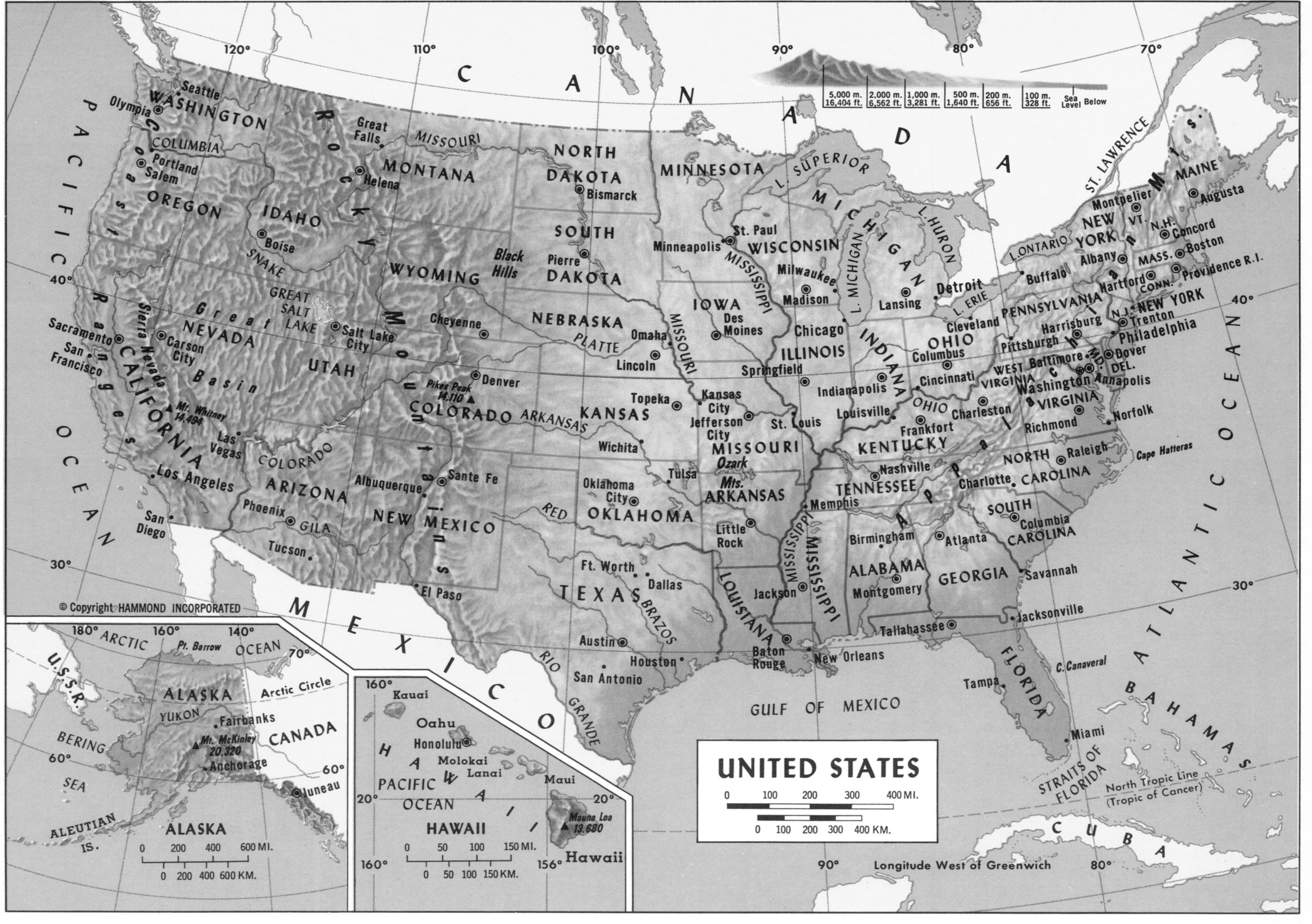
UNITED STATES
0 100 200 300 400 MI.
0 100 200 300 400 KM.
5,000 m. 16,404 ft.
2,000 m. 6,562 ft.
1,000 m. 3,281 ft.
500 m. 1,640 ft.
200 m. 656 ft.
100 m. 328 ft.
Sea Level Below
CANADA
MEXICO
PACIFIC OCEAN
ATLANTIC OCEAN
GULF OF MEXICO
BAHAMAS
CUBA
STRAITS OF FLORIDA
North Tropic Line (Tropic of Cancer)
Longitude West of Greenwich
Rocky Mountains
Coast Ranges
Great Basin
Sierra Nevada
Appalachian Mts.
Black Hills
Ozark Mts.
Pikes Peak 14,110
Mt. Whitney 14,494
Cape Hatteras
C. Canaveral
WASHINGTON
OREGON
CALIFORNIA
NEVADA
IDAHO
MONTANA
WYOMING
UTAH
ARIZONA
NEW MEXICO
COLORADO
NORTH DAKOTA
SOUTH DAKOTA
NEBRASKA
KANSAS
OKLAHOMA
TEXAS
MINNESOTA
IOWA
MISSOURI
ARKANSAS
LOUISIANA
WISCONSIN
ILLINOIS
MICHIGAN
INDIANA
OHIO
KENTUCKY
TENNESSEE
MISSISSIPPI
ALABAMA
GEORGIA
FLORIDA
SOUTH CAROLINA
NORTH CAROLINA
VIRGINIA
WEST VIRGINIA
PENNSYLVANIA
NEW YORK
VT.
N.H.
MAINE
MASS.
CONN.
R.I.
N.J.
DEL.
MD.
L. SUPERIOR
L. MICHIGAN
L. HURON
L. ERIE
L. ONTARIO
GREAT SALT LAKE
ST. LAWRENCE
COLUMBIA
SNAKE
MISSOURI
PLATTE
ARKANSAS
RED
BRAZOS
RIO GRANDE
COLORADO
GILA
MISSISSIPPI
OHIO
Seattle
Olympia
Portland
Salem
Boise
Great Falls
Helena
Bismarck
Pierre
Sacramento
San Francisco
Carson City
Los Angeles
San Diego
Las Vegas
Salt Lake City
Cheyenne
Denver
Phoenix
Tucson
Albuquerque
Sante Fe
El Paso
Omaha
Lincoln
Topeka
Wichita
Kansas City
Jefferson City
St. Louis
Oklahoma City
Tulsa
Little Rock
Ft. Worth
Dallas
Austin
San Antonio
Houston
Baton Rouge
New Orleans
Jackson
Memphis
Minneapolis
St. Paul
Des Moines
Milwaukee
Madison
Chicago
Springfield
Indianapolis
Louisville
Frankfort
Nashville
Birmingham
Montgomery
Atlanta
Tallahassee
Jacksonville
Tampa
Miami
Savannah
Columbia
Charlotte
Raleigh
Norfolk
Richmond
Charleston
Cincinnati
Columbus
Cleveland
Detroit
Lansing
Pittsburgh
Harrisburg
Washington
Baltimore
Annapolis
Dover
Philadelphia
Trenton
Buffalo
Albany
Hartford
Providence
Boston
Concord
Montpelier
Augusta
© Copyright HAMMOND INCORPORATED
ALASKA
ARCTIC OCEAN
Pt. Barrow
Arctic Circle
YUKON
Fairbanks
Mt. McKinley 20,320
Anchorage
Juneau
CANADA
U.S.S.R.
BERING SEA
ALEUTIAN IS.
0 200 400 600 MI.
0 200 400 600 KM.
HAWAII
Kauai
Oahu
Honolulu
Molokai
Lanai
Maui
Hawaii
Mauna Loa 13,680
PACIFIC OCEAN
0 50 100 150 MI.
0 50 100 150 KM.

United States

Geographically Speaking

The United States is the fourth-largest country in the world. There are fifty states in this country.

The United States can be divided into the following geographic regions:

- New England States
- Middle Atlantic States
- Southeastern States
- North Central States
- South Central States
- Northwestern States
- Southwestern States

The Appalachian Highlands and the Central Lowland Plains are in the New England, the Middle Atlantic, and the Southeastern states.

The Interior Plains are in most of the North Central States. In the western part of the South Central States and the eastern part of the Northwestern and Southwestern states, the Interior Plains become the Great Plains in the United States.

The southern part of the North Central States and the northern part of the South Central States are in a region called the Ozark-Ouachita Highlands.

The Rocky Mountains, the western plateaus, basins, ranges, and the Pacific ranges and lowlands go north and south from east to west respectively in the Northwestern and Southwestern states.

Naturally

The United States has three world-record-winning trees, *naturally!*

In northern California and Oregon you must look up to your elders: Methuselah, a bristlecone pine tree, is 4,600 years old. It is the oldest known living thing and it can be found here.

Sequoiadendron giganteum — the General Sherman — is 83 meters (272 feet) high, with a circumference of about 24 meters (79 feet). It is the world's largest tree. Look up to the sky!

The Sequoia Redwoods are the world's tallest trees. At maturity they average over 91 meters (300 feet) high — almost twice as high as Niagara Falls, which is 51 meters (167 feet) high.

Three World-Record-Winning Trees

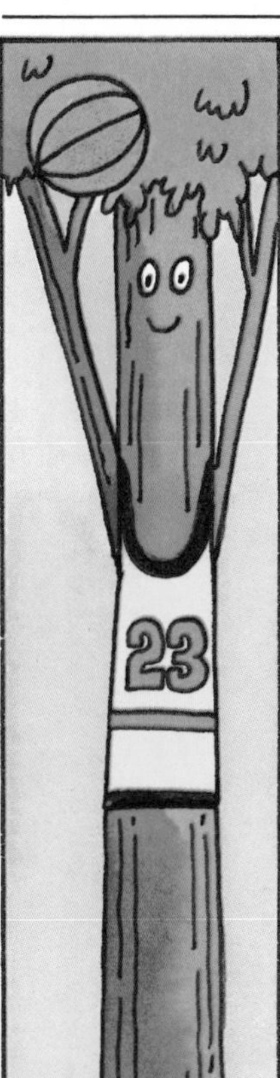

Redwood — *World's tallest!*

Bristlecone Pine — *World's oldest!*

General Sherman Sequoia — *World's largest!*

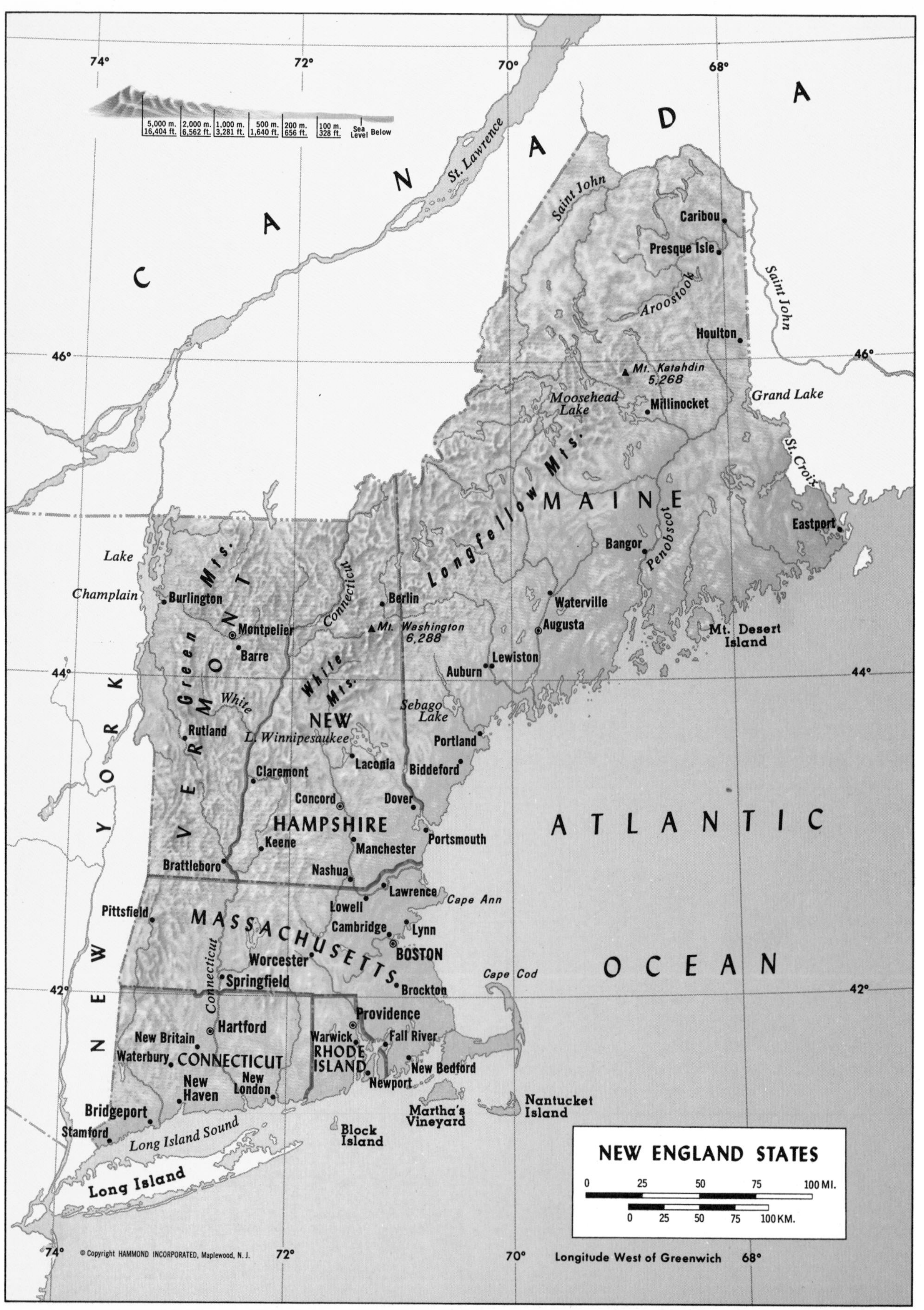
NEW ENGLAND STATES
0 25 50 75 100 MI.
0 25 50 75 100 KM.
5,000 m. 16,404 ft.
2,000 m. 6,562 ft.
1,000 m. 3,281 ft.
500 m. 1,640 ft.
200 m. 656 ft.
100 m. 328 ft.
Sea Level
Below
74°
72°
70°
68°
46°
44°
42°
Longitude West of Greenwich
C A N A D A
St. Lawrence
Saint John
Caribou
Presque Isle
Aroostook
Saint John
Houlton
Mt. Katahdin 5,268
Grand Lake
Moosehead Lake
Millinocket
St. Croix
Longfellow Mts.
MAINE
Penobscot
Eastport
Bangor
Waterville
Augusta
Mt. Desert Island
Lewiston
Auburn
Sebago Lake
Portland
Biddeford
Lake Champlain
Burlington
Green Mts.
VERMONT
Montpelier
Barre
White
Rutland
Connecticut
Berlin
Mt. Washington 6,288
White Mts.
NEW HAMPSHIRE
L. Winnipesaukee
Laconia
Claremont
Concord
Dover
Portsmouth
Keene
Manchester
Brattleboro
Nashua
ATLANTIC OCEAN
NEW YORK
Pittsfield
MASSACHUSETTS
Lawrence
Cape Ann
Lowell
Cambridge
Lynn
BOSTON
Worcester
Springfield
Brockton
Cape Cod
Providence
Hartford
New Britain
Waterbury
CONNECTICUT
Warwick
RHODE ISLAND
Fall River
New Bedford
Newport
New Haven
New London
Bridgeport
Stamford
Long Island Sound
Long Island
Block Island
Martha's Vineyard
Nantucket Island
© Copyright HAMMOND INCORPORATED, Maplewood, N. J.

New England States

Geographically Speaking

In New England the mountain scene is blue made up of white and green! The Blue Ridge Mountains are the northern extension of the great-granddad of all the North American mountain systems, the oldest on the continent, the Appalachians. The White Mountains of New Hampshire and the Green Mountains of Vermont are part of the Blue Ridge Mountains, which are part of the Appalachian Mountain System. The White Mountains are not really white, they just look that way because of the reflection of sunlight. The Green Mountains get their name and "color" because they are covered with evergreen trees.

The *monadnocks* are rocks as hard and as strong as the hardest kind of rocks. They did not give in to water and to wind while the land around them did. As a matter of fact, some of the White Mountains are monadnocks formed by nature's erosion of the land surrounding them.

Hold on to your hats! On Mount Washington, the tallest mountain (1,917 meters/6,288 feet) in the White Mountains, the highest windspeed ever recorded on Earth was 231 m.p.h., recorded on April 12, 1934. That's 372 k.p.h. Swoosh!

Rhode Island is the smallest state in the Union. Where is the "island" part of Rhode Island? Actually, there are 36 little ones that make up this state known as "Little Rhody."

New England can boast about its jagged Atlantic coast. Do you know why? Jagged coasts form great bays. Great bays mean great harbors. It's a natural for fishing and shipping. Three deepwater harbors are Portland in Maine and Boston and Cape Cod, both in Massachusetts.

Cape Cod gets it name from the native inhabitants of its nearby waters — none other than the codfish.

Cape Cod looks like a hooked-arm peninsula that is motioning ships to come on over to it. Maybe that is one reason, besides looking for a shortcut to and from the Boston and New York harbors, that the Cape Cod Canal was built. It is the world's widest artificial two-way canal. It is 146 meters (480 feet) wide.

Naturally

The time: Late winter or early spring
The place: Vermont

It's open sapping-season on the sugar-maple trees! The sapping-season is short; it usually lasts only a few weeks. When the nights are cold and the days are warm, the change in temperature starts the sap flowing. The sap is tapped by inserting a spout in the tree and hanging a bucket on it to catch the sap that drips out. Then it is off to a sugarhouse to cook it and make it into syrup. Get out your pancakes and waffles, the eating season is long!

The cranberry connection? What do you think? The first New England Thanksgiving was celebrated in 1621 in Massachusetts, which today is a leading cranberry-producing state.

MIDDLE ATLANTIC STATES
0 25 50 75 100 MI.
0 25 50 75 100 KM.
CANADA
LAKE ONTARIO
LAKE ERIE
St. Lawrence
Ogdensburg
Plattsburgh
Lake Champlain
Mt. Marcy 5,344
VERMONT
NEW HAMPSHIRE
Adirondack Mts.
Hudson
Watertown
L. Oneida
Rome
Utica
Mohawk
Niagara Falls
Rochester
Syracuse
Auburn
Buffalo
Finger Lakes
Schenectady
Troy
Albany
NEW YORK
Ithaca
MASSACHUSETTS
Erie
Jamestown
Elmira
Binghamton
Catskill Mts.
Allegheny Plateau
Mountains
Delaware
Poughkeepsie
CONNECTICUT
Allegheny
PENNSYLVANIA
Scranton
Sharon
New Castle
Williamsport
Wilkes-Barre
OHIO
Ohio
Long Island Sound
Montauk Pt.
Paterson
Newark
Elizabeth
Yonkers
NEW YORK
Long Island
Pittsburgh
McKeesport
Altoona
Johnstown
Allegheny Mts.
Appalachian
Bethlehem
Allentown
Reading
Harrisburg
Susquehanna
NEW JERSEY
Trenton
Sandy Hook
Long Branch
Lancaster
PHILADELPHIA
Camden
York
Chester
Wilmington
Cumberland
Hagerstown
Potomac
Baltimore
Atlantic City
WEST VIRGINIA
Rockville
Washington
DISTRICT OF COLUMBIA
Annapolis
MARYLAND
Dover
DELAWARE
Delaware Bay
Cape May
Salisbury
ATLANTIC OCEAN
VIRGINIA
Chesapeake Bay
Cape Charles
5,000 m. 16,404 ft.
2,000 m. 6,562 ft.
1,000 m. 3,281 ft.
500 m. 1,640 ft.
200 m. 656 ft.
100 m. 328 ft.
Sea Level
Below
80° 78° 76° 74° 72°
44° 42° 40° 38°
© Copyright HAMMOND INCORPORATED, Maplewood, N. J.

Middle Atlantic States

Geographically Speaking

Slowly it flows, mile by mile, foot by foot, to Niagara Falls! The Niagara River is short, only 56 kilometers (35 miles) long, and slow, even though four of the Great Lakes empty into it. The Niagara River flows north to Lake Ontario.

Maptalk

A **waterfall** occurs when there is a sudden drop of a river from a high level to a much lower one.

The Niagara River is higher than Lake Ontario, 99 meters (326 feet) higher! So over the top and down a steep-walled gorge the Niagara River falls, in two places: the horseshoe-shaped falls on the Canadian side and the higher falls on the American side. Did you know that the walls of the gorge are wearing away at approximately 30 centimeters (1 foot) a year — a result of water erosion?

AAA, Triple A, from east to west! It's the Atlantic Coastal Plain, the Appalachian Mountains, and the Appalachian Plateau.

AAA, Triple A, again! The Adirondack Mountains in New York and the Allegheny Mountains in Pennsylvania are part of the Appalachian Mountain System.

It seems that the Allegheny Mountains have some of the greatest seams of coal in the world. In these mountains of Pennsylvania are the only anthracite (hard coal) deposits in the United States. Hard coal gives off hardly any smoke when it burns.

Also in these mountains are major deposits of bituminous coal, which makes coke. Coke, not cola, is used to stoke the great furnaces that melt down iron ore. It goes without saying that steel steals the show in Pittsburgh, Pennsylvania.

The Adirondack Mountains in northern New York are the source of the Hudson River. As the Hudson flows south it meets the Mohawk River, which happens to give the state of New York a "Mohawk" haircut by cutting across its center from west to east. These two rivers form a major inland waterway linking the Great Lakes to the Atlantic Ocean in New York Harbor, one of the world's largest and busiest ports.

A **gap** is a notch or an opening in the crest of a mountain that has been formed by wind or water.

The mountains were so wide, rivers couldn't go around them. So after thousands of years, the rivers flowing over them succeeded in cutting through them, creating steep-sided valleys. As an example, the Delaware River formed the Delaware Water Gap. The Mohawk-Hudson Valley is considered a gap. These are only two of many found in the central Appalachian region.

Great bays! Great harbors! New York Bay — New York Harbor! Delaware Bay — Philadelphia Harbor! Chesapeake Bay — Baltimore Harbor!

The Chesapeake Bay goes a long way, 320 kilometers (200 miles), inland. It narrowly misses dividing the state of Maryland in half. The Susquehanna River, flowing from Pennsylvania, and the Potomac River on Maryland's western border empty here, too.

Naturally

Thirsty? Juice! Wine! It's apples and grapes from New York State.

Chicken? Delaware, one of the largest raisers of chickens in the United States, was brave enough to be the first state to join the Union in 1787.

SOUTHEASTERN UNITED STATES
0 50 100 150 200 MI.
0 50 100 150 200 KM.
5,000 m. 16,404 ft.
2,000 m. 6,562 ft.
1,000 m. 3,281 ft.
500 m. 1,640 ft.
200 m. 656 ft.
100 m. 328 ft.
Sea Level
Below
92°
88°
84°
80°
76°
40°
36°
32°
28°
24°
IOWA
PENNSYLVANIA
OHIO
Wheeling
N.J.
MD.
Washington
DEL.
ILLINOIS
INDIANA
Parkersburg
Ohio
WEST VIRGINIA
Covington
Alexandria
Charleston
MISSOURI
Louisville
Frankfort
Lexington
Huntington
VIRGINIA
Richmond
Chesapeake Bay
Owensboro
KENTUCKY
James
Lynchburg
Ohio
Paducah
Lake Barkley
Bowling Green
Roanoke
Newport News
Norfolk
Cumberland
Appalachian Mountains
Blue Ridge
Piedmont Plateau
Atlantic Coastal Plain
Kentucky Lake
Oak Ridge
Knoxville
Winston-Salem
Greensboro
Jackson
Nashville
Durham
Raleigh
Roanoke
ARKANSAS
TENNESSEE
Mt. Mitchell 6,684
Asheville
NORTH CAROLINA
C. Hatteras
Memphis
Chattanooga
Charlotte
Mississippi
Tennessee
Huntsville
Greenville
Spartanburg
Tombigbee
Rome
SOUTH CAROLINA
Wilmington
Gadsden
Chattahoochee
Athens
Columbia
Cape Fear
Greenville
Birmingham
Atlanta
Augusta
Savannah
MISSISSIPPI
Tuscaloosa
ALABAMA
Macon
Charleston
Vicksburg
Jackson
Meridian
Columbus
Montgomery
GEORGIA
Savannah
Natchez
Hattiesburg
Alabama
Albany
Dothan
ATLANTIC OCEAN
LOUISIANA
Biloxi
Mobile
Pensacola
Valdosta
FLORIDA
Tallahassee
Jacksonville
Panama City
Cape San Blas
Gainesville
Daytona Beach
GULF OF MEXICO
Cape Canaveral
Orlando
Tampa
Lakeland
St. Petersburg
Lake Okeechobee
West Palm Beach
Ft. Myers
The Everglades
Ft. Lauderdale
Miami
BAHAMAS
Cape Sable
Key West
FLORIDA KEYS
Straits of Florida
North Tropic Line (Tropic of Cancer)
CUBA
Longitude West of Greenwich
© Copyright HAMMOND INCORPORATED, Maplewood, N. J.

Southeastern States

"Big Blue Marble" Photograph

Geographically Speaking

Richmond, Virginia, and Raleigh, North Carolina, are located on the "fall line." This is where rivers fall rapidly to form waterfalls and rapids. The rivers provide water power as they flow from the Appalachian Mountains to the Atlantic Ocean.

The Atlantic Coastal Plain widens on these southeastern shores. It extends inland 800 kilometers (500 miles) and more.

From north to north! The Blue Ridge Mountains stretch from northern Virginia to northern Georgia.

Before the Appalachian Mountain System ends geographically and officially in Georgia, it surfaces rich in coal in West Virginia. Along the same vein further south in Alabama there's coal, iron ore, and limestone, almost everything needed to make steel efficiently. Did you know that Birmingham, Alabama, is the Pittsburgh, Pennsylvania, of the South?

On top of old misty, it is all covered with haze, and that is why the Great Smoky Mountains look "smokey." They are the most rugged range in the Appalachians and form the border between Tennessee and North Carolina, *naturally.*

Why do you think they call the cape off the coast of North Carolina Cape Fear? Because of storms? Because spooky Cape Hatteras is near? Cape Hatteras, like Cape Fear, has its fair share of hurricanes to be sure, but beware of the shallow waters surrounding it. They are dangerous for ocean-going ships. Cape Hatteras is the site of many shipwrecks and it is called the Graveyard of the Atlantic.

From 1775 to 1800 the Cumberland Gap in Kentucky and Tennessee was the main gateway to the West, *naturally!*

Maptalk

A **swamp** is a low area of wet, spongy ground, usually containing reedlike vegetation.

The southern part of the Florida peninsula is swamped by one of the world's largest swamps, the Florida Everglades. This region was once at the bottom of the sea, and it is one of the few subtropic areas in the United States. There are mangroves, cypresses, palms, and all kinds of exotic trees there. Orchids grow wild. Did you ever see sawgrass? It can grow 3.7 meters (12 feet) high. And you had better watch out for the turtles, crocodiles, and alligators that may be hiding out in the tall grass.

Naturally

Did you know that Virginia, North Carolina, South Carolina, Georgia, Florida, Tennessee, and Kentucky grow tobacco?

And let it not be forgotten that along these two coastal plains the soil and weather are right for planting cotton in Georgia, Alabama, Mississippi, and Tennessee.

Besides being peachy, Georgia is no peanut. It is the biggest state east of the Mississippi River and it is number one in peanut production. Georgia also produces plenty of pecans.

Do Tennessee Walking horses run in Kentucky's Derby or do they just graze on its "blue grass?"

There is gold in those hills. Georgia was the site of the first American gold rush. However, prospectors dropped their pans and rushed westward in 1849, hoping for the golden opportunity to strike it rich in California!

NORTH CENTRAL
UNITED STATES
0 50 100 150 200 MI.
0 50 100 150 200 KM.
CANADA
MONTANA
WYOMING
COLORADO
TEXAS
OKLAHOMA
ARKANSAS
TENN.
KENTUCKY
VIRGINIA
WEST VIRGINIA
PA.
NORTH DAKOTA
SOUTH DAKOTA
NEBRASKA
KANSAS
MINNESOTA
IOWA
MISSOURI
WISCONSIN
ILLINOIS
MICHIGAN
INDIANA
OHIO
LAKE SUPERIOR
LAKE MICHIGAN
LAKE HURON
LAKE ERIE
Georgian Bay
Isle Royale
Lake of the Woods
Great Plains
Black Hills
Ozark Mts.
Missouri
Lake Sakakawea
Lake Oahe
Red River of the North
James
Cheyenne
Niobrara
N. Platte
S. Platte
Platte
Republican
Kansas
Arkansas
Minnesota
Mississippi
St. Croix
Wisconsin
Des Moines
Wabash
Ohio
Minot
Grand Forks
Bismarck
Jamestown
Fargo
Aberdeen
Rapid City
Pierre
Huron
Sioux Falls
Scottsbluff
North Platte
Grand Island
Norfolk
Omaha
Lincoln
Hastings
Salina
Dodge City
Hutchinson
Wichita
Topeka
Kansas City
Hibbing
Duluth
Superior
St. Cloud
Minneapolis
St. Paul
Rochester
Sioux City
Council Bluffs
Des Moines
Waterloo
Cedar Rapids
Dubuque
Davenport
St. Joseph
Kansas City
Jefferson City
Columbia
Joplin
Springfield
St. Louis
Cape Girardeau
Eau Claire
La Crosse
Madison
Appleton
Oshkosh
Green Bay
Milwaukee
Racine
Rockford
CHICAGO
Joliet
Rock Island
Peoria
Quincy
Springfield
Decatur
Alton
Marquette
Sault Ste. Marie
Traverse City
Saginaw
Flint
Pontiac
Grand Rapids
Lansing
Ann Arbor
Kalamazoo
DETROIT
Gary
South Bend
Fort Wayne
Muncie
Indianapolis
Terre Haute
Evansville
New Albany
Toledo
Cleveland
Akron
Canton
Lima
Springfield
Columbus
Dayton
Cincinnati
104° 100° 96° 92° 88° 84° 80°
48° 44° 40° 36°
5,000 m. 16,404 ft.
2,000 m. 6,562 ft.
1,000 m. 3,281 ft.
500 m. 1,640 ft.
200 m. 656 ft.
100 m. 328 ft.
Sea Level
Below
Longitude West of Greenwich
© Copyright HAMMOND INCORPORATED, Maplewood, N. J.

North Central States

Geographically Speaking

The North Central States are central all right! North Dakota is at the center of the North American continent. South Dakota is the center of attention, too. It is at the center of the United States.

It's really great . . . plains and lakes! The Great Plains are the western part of the Interior Plains. The exterior boundaries are the Appalachians on the east and the Rockies on the west. The Great Plains states are North Dakota, South Dakota, Nebraska, and Kansas. This is where America's wheat for cereals, bread, and — are you ready? — for spaghetti is grown.

Did you know that Nebraska was once part of the Great American Desert, a term used by pioneers to describe the Great Plains? How can that be when Nebraska is the number-one producer of hay and one of the nation's most fertile farm- and pasture lands? Ever hear of irrigation?

It's the mighty Mississippi River's headwaters, or source. It's a lake. Its name is Itasca. It's in north-central Minnesota.

Make no mistake about it. Lake Superior (one of the five greats) is the largest freshwater lake in the world!

Naturally

Michigan is a large producer of iodine in the United States.

Illinois, Indiana, Iowa, Kansas, Minnesota, Missouri, Nebraska, Ohio, South Dakota, and Wisconsin all hog the title of largest U.S. corn producers. And, wouldn't you know it? All these states with the exception of Wisconsin hog the title of largest U.S. hog producers.

Pop goes the corn, especially in Iowa, where the world's largest popcorn processing plant is found.

Iowa, Kansas, Missouri, Nebraska, and South Dakota have a lot to beef about. They are among the nation's leading producers of beef cattle — and Iowa, Michigan, Minnesota, Missouri, Ohio, and Wisconsin milk them for all they're worth. Their cows are dairy cattle.

Missouri leads the nation in the production of lead. Where there's lead there's zinc, so Missouri is a leader in the production of zinc too.

North Dakota and Illinois have some of the nation's largest reserves of coal.

North Dakota has oil!

Michigan and Ohio are worth their salt. These two states have the nation's largest deposits of salt and are the largest producers of it.

The Lake Superior region of Minnesota, Wisconsin, and Michigan once supplied three-quarters of this nation's iron ore. Iron ore is a nonrenewable mineral. Unfortunately, in this region there isn't too much more.

Michigan is a bowl of cherries because it is the nation's number-one producer.

South Dakota is a gold mine! It is the Western Hemisphere's largest gold producer!

A Man-made W.O.W.

George Washington, Thomas Jefferson, Abraham Lincoln, and Theodore Roosevelt meet face to face, regardless of time and space. The place is Mount Rushmore in South Dakota.

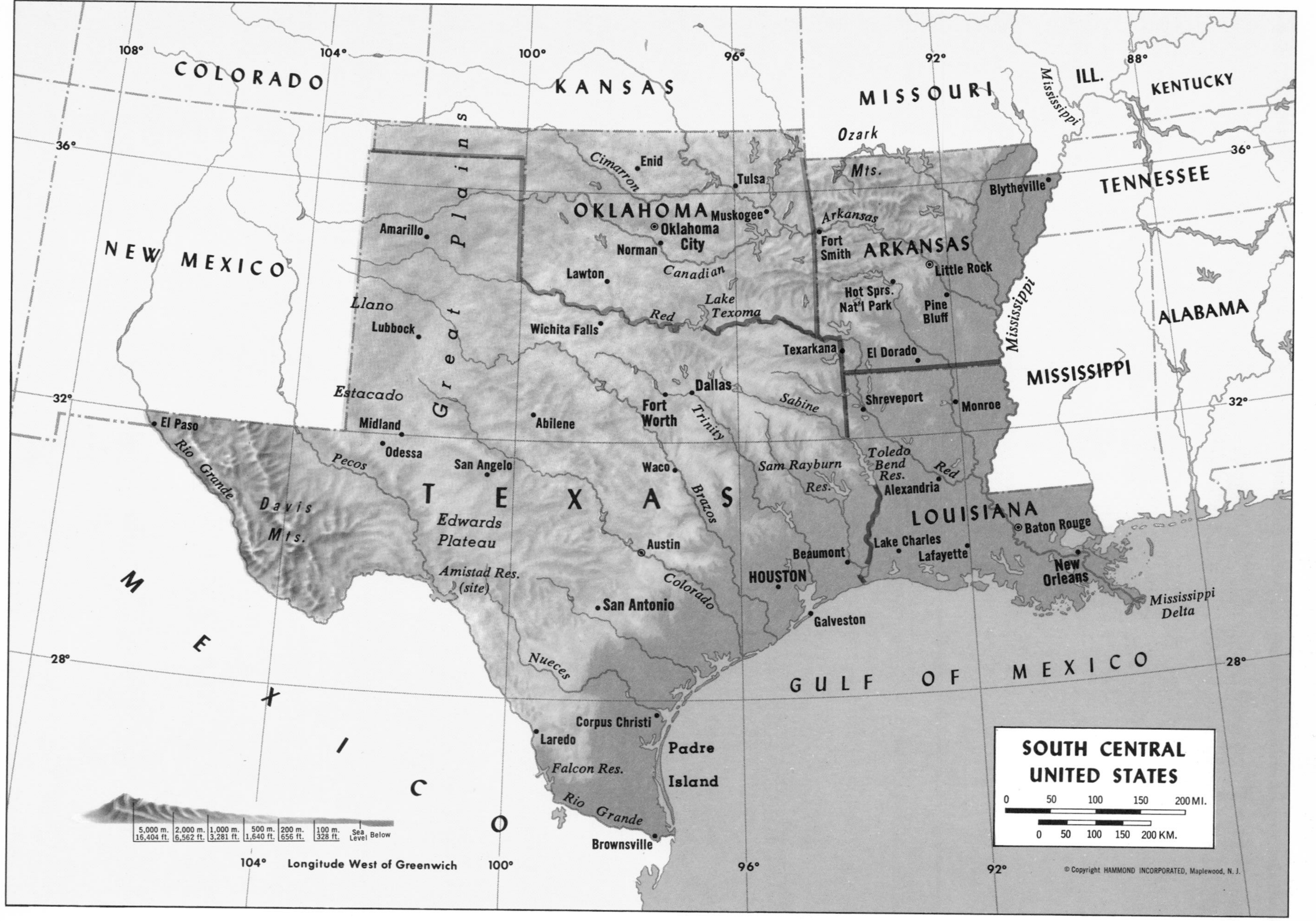
SOUTH CENTRAL
UNITED STATES
0 50 100 150 200 MI.
0 50 100 150 200 KM.
COLORADO
KANSAS
MISSOURI
ILL.
KENTUCKY
TENNESSEE
ALABAMA
MISSISSIPPI
NEW MEXICO
OKLAHOMA
ARKANSAS
LOUISIANA
TEXAS
MEXICO
GULF OF MEXICO
Great Plains
Llano
Estacado
Ozark
Mts.
Davis
Mts.
Edwards
Plateau
Amistad Res.
(site)
Falcon Res.
Sam Rayburn
Res.
Toledo
Bend
Res.
Lake
Texoma
Padre
Island
Mississippi
Delta
Mississippi
Arkansas
Cimarron
Canadian
Red
Sabine
Trinity
Brazos
Colorado
Pecos
Nueces
Rio Grande
Enid
Tulsa
Muskogee
Oklahoma
City
Norman
Lawton
Amarillo
Lubbock
Wichita Falls
Fort
Smith
Little Rock
Hot Sprs.
Nat'l Park
Pine
Bluff
Blytheville
El Dorado
Texarkana
Shreveport
Monroe
Alexandria
Lake Charles
Lafayette
Baton Rouge
New
Orleans
Dallas
Fort
Worth
Abilene
Midland
Odessa
El Paso
San Angelo
Waco
Austin
San Antonio
Beaumont
HOUSTON
Galveston
Corpus Christi
Laredo
Brownsville
108°
104°
100°
96°
92°
88°
36°
32°
28°
5,000 m. 16,404 ft.
2,000 m. 6,562 ft.
1,000 m. 3,281 ft.
500 m. 1,640 ft.
200 m. 656 ft.
100 m. 328 ft.
Sea Level
Below
Longitude West of Greenwich
© Copyright HAMMOND INCORPORATED, Maplewood, N. J.

South Central States

Geographically Speaking

The Mississippi River has been called "old man river" for good reason. It was formed about 1¾ million years ago at the beginning of the last ice age and is the longest river in the United States.

By the time the Mississippi flows 3,779 kilometers (2,348 miles) to the Gulf of Mexico, it no longer is the clear stream it was at its source in Minnesota. Once it meets the muddy Missouri, it becomes the muddy Mississippi.

It's a grand ole river, the Río Grande, Texas' largest river, one of the United States' largest, and one of North America's largest. It is 3,034 kilometers (1,885 miles) long. It forms part of the international border between the United States (Texas) and Mexico.

Hot Springs, Arkansas. Is it ever! The water in the springs, which bubbles continually and constantly, is 62°C (143°F) — not just in the spring, but all year!

Arkansas is all aglitter. It has the only diamond field in North America.

The Gulf Coastal Plain is in Louisiana, about half of Arkansas, and a Texas-sized portion of Texas.

Naturally

No state can complain if it is located on the Gulf Coastal Plain; its rich soil and water make it right for beef cattle, rice, and sugar cane.

When it comes to sweet potatoes and strawberries, Louisiana is no shrimp. Yes, it has shrimp too. It is number one in producing all three.

Guess which state has 95 percent of the United States' bauxite. Arkansas, that's right. There is no bluffing at Chalk Bluff, Arkansas. You can chalk it up to reality, *naturally.* There's enough chalk here for the next several hundred years. So the next time your teacher runs out of chalk, this is the place to go.

Texas has nothing to beef about. It is the number-one producer of beef cattle in the country. . . . And of sheep, too.

Materially Texas does well: from its sheep comes wool and they grow loads of cotton, the most in the United States.

Fuel for thought . . . or how about fuel for transportation, heat, and industry? In Texas, Oklahoma, and Louisiana there is natural gas and oil. There's some mighty fancy cooking going on in the Texas Panhandle. That is the location of the largest known natural gas reservoirs in the world.

Up, up, and away! Whether a weather balloon, a fun balloon, or even a rocket, all have something in common, and that is helium, the lighter-than-air element. It comes from Texas and Oklahoma.

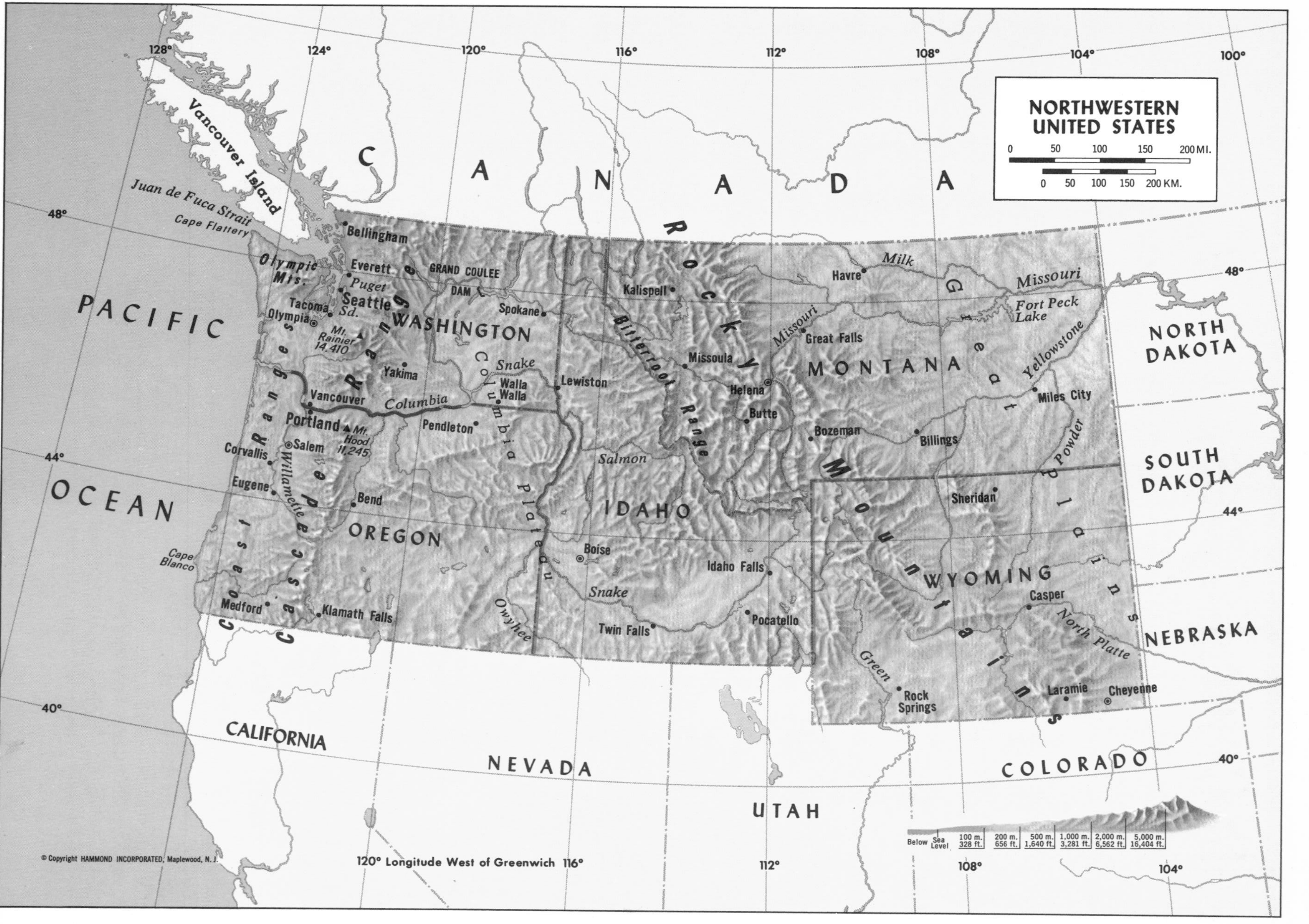

NORTHWESTERN UNITED STATES
0 50 100 150 200 MI.
0 50 100 150 200 KM.
CANADA
PACIFIC OCEAN
Vancouver Island
Juan de Fuca Strait
Cape Flattery
Cape Blanco
Olympic Mts.
Bellingham
Everett
Puget Sd.
Seattle
Tacoma
Olympia
Mt. Rainier 14,410
GRAND COULEE DAM
Spokane
WASHINGTON
Yakima
Snake
Walla Walla
Vancouver
Columbia
Portland
Mt. Hood 11,245
Pendleton
Columbia Plateau
Salem
Corvallis
Eugene
Willamette
Bend
OREGON
Medford
Klamath Falls
Owyhee
Coast Ranges
Cascade Range
Rocky Mountains
Great Plains
Kalispell
Bitterroot Range
Missoula
Lewiston
Salmon
IDAHO
Boise
Snake
Twin Falls
Idaho Falls
Pocatello
Helena
Butte
Missouri
Great Falls
Havre
Milk
Fort Peck Lake
MONTANA
Yellowstone
Miles City
Bozeman
Billings
Powder
Sheridan
WYOMING
Casper
North Platte
Green
Rock Springs
Laramie
Cheyenne
NORTH DAKOTA
SOUTH DAKOTA
NEBRASKA
CALIFORNIA
NEVADA
UTAH
COLORADO
128° 124° 120° 116° 112° 108° 104° 100°
48° 44° 40°
120° Longitude West of Greenwich 116°
Below Sea Level 100 m. 328 ft. 200 m. 656 ft. 500 m. 1,640 ft. 1,000 m. 3,281 ft. 2,000 m. 6,562 ft. 5,000 m. 16,404 ft.

Northwestern States

Geographically Speaking

It's one of the rainiest places in the world. As a result, it is covered by a junglelike forest. It's mountainous. It's misty. There are seagulls. It is in the northern and westernmost portion of the "lower forty-eight." It is the Olympic Peninsula of the state of Washington.

The Rocky Mountains form the continental divide from which all rivers either flow to the east or the west side. For example, the Missouri River flows east from the Rockies to the Mississippi and the Columbia River flows west from the Rockies to the Pacific Ocean.

Mount Rainier, the highest mountain in the state of Washington, is an old volcano. It still fusses, frets, and fumes. But Mount St. Helens blew!

Naturally

Beware of states dressed in sheep's clothing —like Idaho, Montana, and Wyoming.

There's silver in Idaho! That is where the United States' largest silver mines are located. Idaho also produces lead and zinc, which are often found together.

Montana is big sky and vast mineral deposit country: gold, silver, magnesium, and copper. In fact, it's quite a beaut! Butte Hill is the site of one of the largest copper mines in the world.

"No fueling," there's great fuel potential in Alaska, Washington, Montana, and Wyoming. There is coal, oil, and natural gas. Uranium is found in Alaska and Idaho!

You can hardly see Washington, Oregon, Idaho, and Montana for all the trees! Just about half of each of these states is wooded. Idaho has some of the largest white pine forests in the world. Timber! Lumber! Paper! *Naturally!*

Any way you like them—fried, baked, boiled —Idaho is the number-one potato producer in the United States.

State mint. The state is Oregon; the mint is peppermint. Oregon is the largest U.S. producer of peppermint.

Apples are the apple of Washington's eye. This state is America's number-one apple producer.

It would be in a lot of hot water if it wasn't dependable. It is the only hot spring you can rely on. Every 65 minutes, this faithful spring spurts out 10,000 gallons of near-boiling hot water, approximately 93° C (220° F), more than 30 meters (100 feet) into the air! It's Old Faithful, a regular attraction in Yellowstone National Park, Wyoming—the oldest and largest national park in the United States, established in 1872.

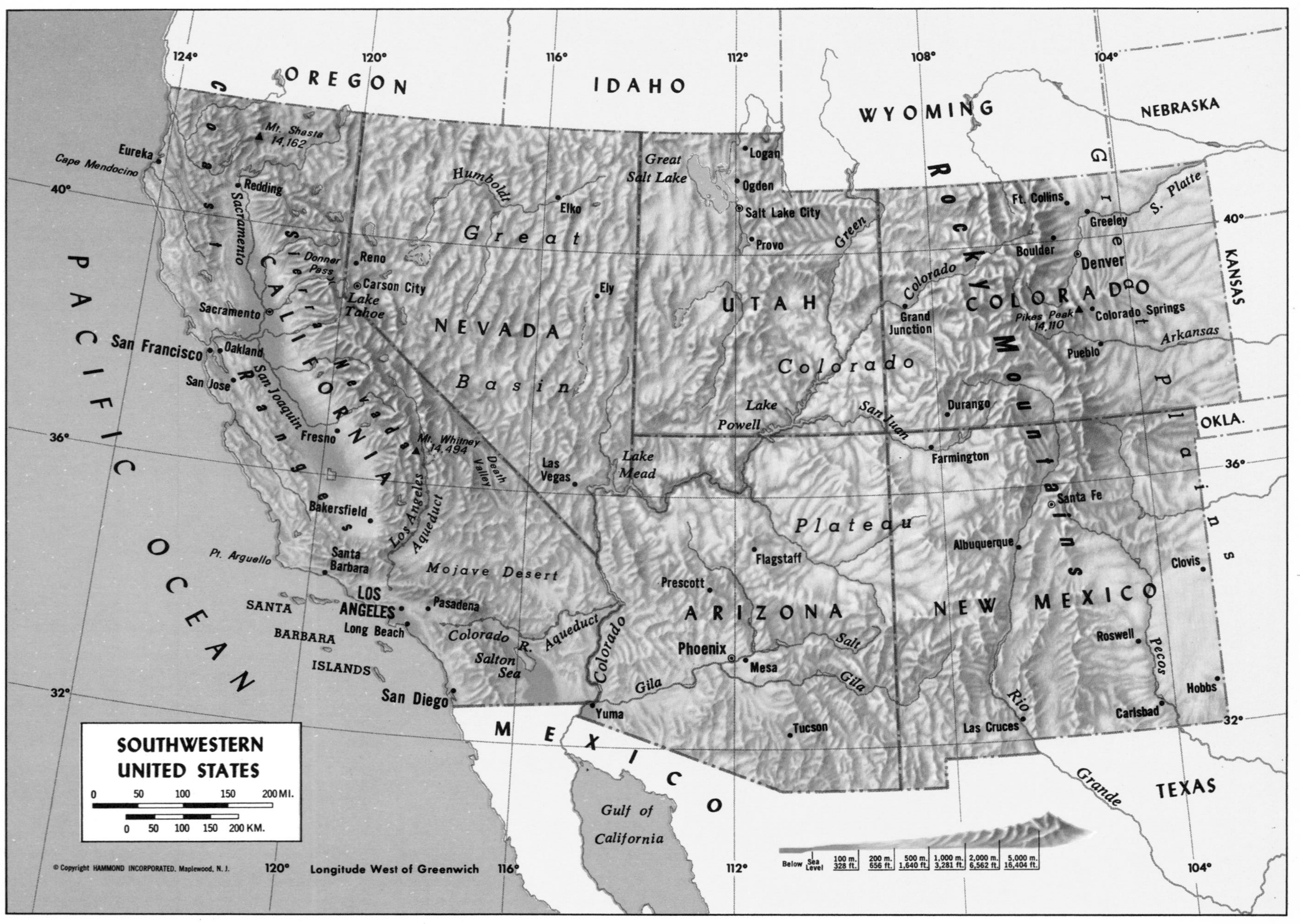
SOUTHWESTERN
UNITED STATES
0 50 100 150 200 MI.
0 50 100 150 200 KM.
OREGON
IDAHO
WYOMING
NEBRASKA
KANSAS
OKLA.
TEXAS
MEXICO
NEVADA
UTAH
COLORADO
CALIFORNIA
ARIZONA
NEW MEXICO
PACIFIC OCEAN
Gulf of California
Great Basin
Colorado Plateau
Rocky Mountains
Great Plains
Coast Ranges
Sierra Nevada
Mojave Desert
Death Valley
Mt. Shasta 14,162
Mt. Whitney 14,494
Pikes Peak 14,110
Donner Pass
Eureka
Cape Mendocino
Redding
Sacramento
San Francisco
Oakland
San Jose
Fresno
Bakersfield
Santa Barbara
Pt. Arguello
LOS ANGELES
Pasadena
Long Beach
SANTA BARBARA ISLANDS
San Diego
Reno
Carson City
Lake Tahoe
Elko
Ely
Las Vegas
Lake Mead
Humboldt
Great Salt Lake
Logan
Ogden
Salt Lake City
Provo
Green
Lake Powell
San Juan
Colorado
Grand Junction
Durango
Farmington
Ft. Collins
Greeley
Boulder
Denver
Colorado Springs
Pueblo
S. Platte
Arkansas
Santa Fe
Albuquerque
Clovis
Roswell
Pecos
Hobbs
Carlsbad
Las Cruces
Rio Grande
Flagstaff
Prescott
Phoenix
Mesa
Salt
Gila
Tucson
Yuma
Salton Sea
Colorado R. Aqueduct
Los Angeles Aqueduct
Sacramento
San Joaquin
124°
120°
116°
112°
108°
104°
40°
36°
32°
Longitude West of Greenwich
Below Sea Level
100 m. 328 ft.
200 m. 656 ft.
500 m. 1,640 ft.
1,000 m. 3,281 ft.
2,000 m. 6,562 ft.
5,000 m. 16,404 ft.

Southwestern States

Geographically Speaking

The only place in the whole United States where four states actually touch each other is the "Four Corners," located where Utah, Arizona, New Mexico, and Colorado meet.

It is only the beginning. The Rocky Mountains in Colorado are sometimes called the roof of North America because there are fifty to sixty mountains that peak over 4,270 meters (14,000 feet). It is here that many great rivers, like the Arkansas, the South Platte, the Rio Grande, and the Colorado, originate.

Dams are essential for harnessing waterpower. Some are presidential — like Coolidge, Hoover, and Roosevelt. The Hoover Dam forms Lake Mead on the Arizona-Nevada border. The waterpower from here electrifies Arizona, California, and Nevada.

In the Great Basin is the Great Salt Lake in the desert salt flats of Utah. It is the largest lake west of the Mississippi River. It is 121 kilometers (75 miles) long and 80 kilometers (50 miles) wide.

Boo! It took a lot to "petrify" a forest enough to actually turn its trees to stone. It took mud, sand, and volcanic ash to cover the trees and bury them for about 150 million years. These stone trees can be seen lying on their sides in the Petrified Forest in northern Arizona.

A Natural W.O.W.

In a cavern called Carlsbad, in New Mexico, 60 million years ago, water began hollowing out the limestone rock. Limestone icicles called stalactites hang from the top of the cavern and stalagmites grow up from the bottom of these caves. It didn't happen overnight! They are quite a fantastic sight!

The Carlsbad Cavern is some bat cave! Millions of bats call it home. They come out at dusk in the warm night air looking for delicious insects to eat! By the time it's morning, they return to the cavern to sleep.

Naturally

The two central valleys in California are the San Joaquin and Sacramento River valleys. These valleys are among the most productive farming areas in the country! Crops include *nuts,* like all the almonds and walnuts in the United States; *tutti-frutti,* or most of the fruits like apricots, boysenberries, cantaloupes, dates, figs, grapes, honeydew melons, lemons, nectarines, peaches, pears, plums, and prunes in the United States; and *mixed salads* with all the fixings, like lettuce, tomatoes, celery, olives, artichokes, avocados, and garlic for dressing. Don't forget to eat your California vegetables either: asparagus, broccoli, brussel sprouts, carrots, and cauliflower.

Any way you slice it, it tastes good. Pineapple comes from Hawaii.

Half of the nation's copper comes from Arizona. California, Nevada, New Mexico, and Utah have quite a bit, too.

This area is a real powerhouse! There is oil and natural gas in California and New Mexico.

There's uranium in Colorado, Utah, and California, but by itself New Mexico has half of the nation's uranium reserves.

When the mercury begins to rise, in New Mexico it's no surprise. There's lots of mercury here!

Prospectors rushed to California in 1849 looking for gold. They found it! But they could have struck it rich in Arizona, Colorado, Nevada, and Utah, too.

Hi, ho! There's silver in Arizona, California, Colorado, and Utah. The lead-zinc link is unbroken here.

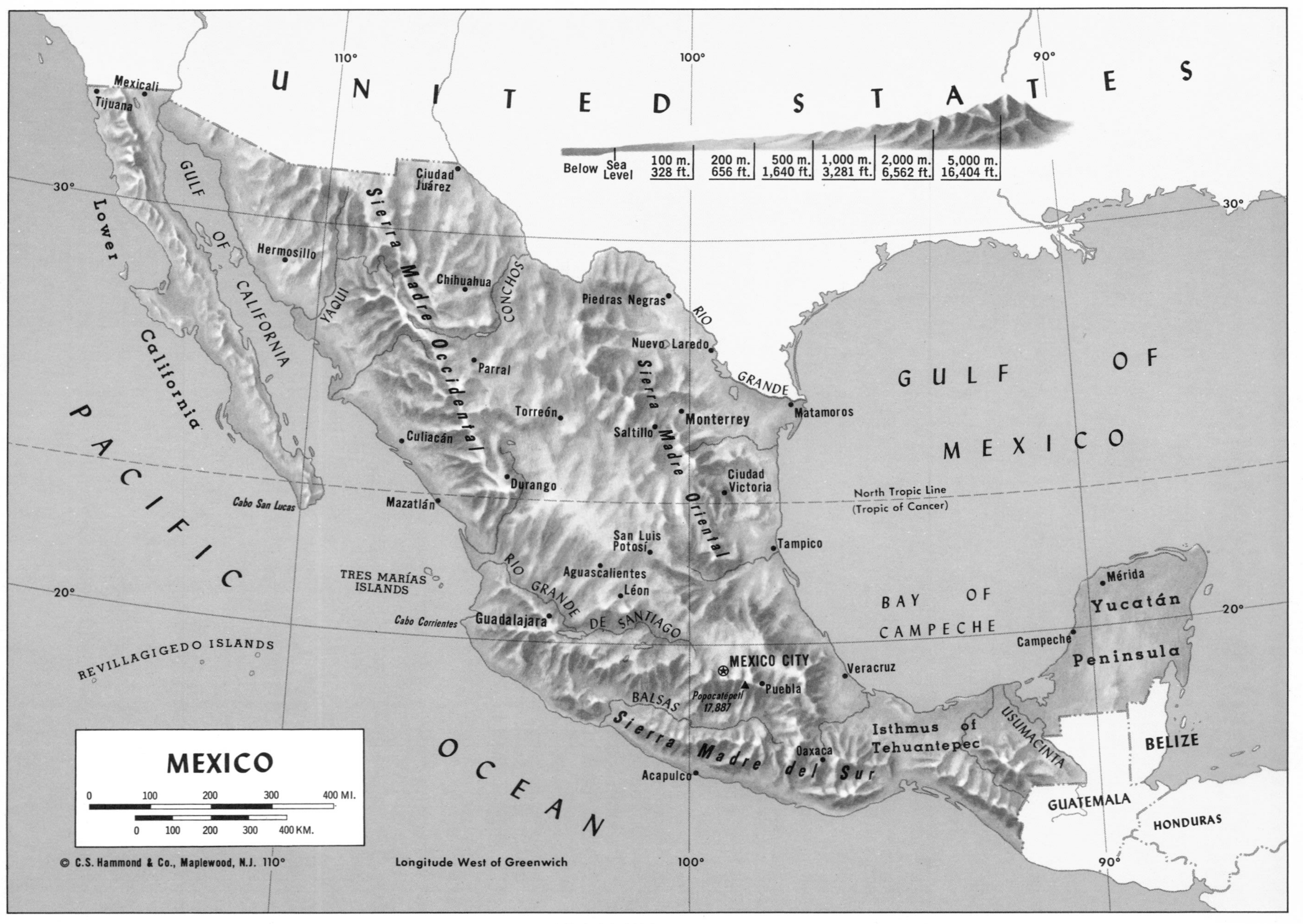

In Mexico, the Rio Grande is called the Rio Bravo del Norte. Mexico City is called Ciudad de México.

Mexico

"Big Blue Marble" Photograph

Geographically Speaking

Mexico is south of the border! What border? The United States' border, two-thirds of which is the Rio Grande.

Most of Mexico is a plateau, below which is volcano row. Actually, it is called the volcanic axis and it crosses Mexico in an east-west direction, south of Mexico City. Two of Mexico's most famous volcanoes are Ixtacihuatl and Popocatépetl. Ixtacihuatl has three snow-covered peaks and looks like a woman fast asleep. In fact, it has been "dormant," or inactive, for years. Popocatépetl, just 17.6 kilometers (11 miles) away, is a different story. It lets off steam occasionally. Both volcanoes are approximately 5,180 meters (17,000 feet) high.

The northern plateau of Mexico has tons of silver — in the richest silver mines in the world.

On the northern plateau between Chihuahua and Durango, *vacqueros,* the original North American *cowboys,* are armed with lassos and lariats. They herd cows on this range.

It's not accidental that the Sierra Madre Occidental, which is part of the Pacific Coastal Mountain System, is in *western* Mexico. The Sierra Madre Oriental is across the country in *eastern* Mexico. (*Occidental* means western; *oriental* means eastern.) This range is an extension of the Rocky Mountain System. On the other side of these mountains, near coal and iron ore deposits, is Monterrey, the center of Mexico's steel industry.

In the south, just below the volcanic axis, is one more Sierra Madre mountain range, the Sierra Madre del Sur, which means "south."

Maptalk

A **gulf** is an extensive indentation of a shore line bordering a lake, bay, or ocean.

How about a little gulf? The Gulf of California is 1,100 kilometers (700 miles) long and 48 kilometers to 241 kilometers (30 miles to 150 miles) wide. It lies between two parts of Mexico. Don't forget that Baja California, the Lower California peninsula, is part of Mexico.

How about a big gulf? Of course, it is the Gulf of Mexico, which is actually a part of the Atlantic Ocean. It forms a huge ocean basin nearly 1,800,000 square kilometers (700,000 square miles). From north to south it is 1,300 kilometers (800 miles) long and from west to east it is 1,770 kilometers (1,100 square miles) wide.

Spanning hemispheres in a constant flow, the Gulf Stream is the wonderful warm-water ocean current that originates in the Gulf of Mexico. The Gulf Stream travels up the east coast of the North American continent and then crosses the Atlantic Ocean, continuing to win friends and influence the weather in Europe all the way north and east to Norway.

The Yucatán Peninsula juts into the Gulf of Mexico. It is a low limestone plateau that has no rivers. Did you know that limestone dissolves in water? Just because there are no rivers doesn't mean there is no water. Over thousands of years enormous deep pits have been formed by rainwater in the limestone of Yucatán. These Great Pits were the sacred wells of the ancient Maya Indians.

Naturally

Commercial fishermen are well rewarded with abalone, oysters, sardines, shrimp, and tuna, which are all found in Mexican waters.

It is a milky, gumlike juice that comes from the Sapodilla tree. It is called *chicle* and you'll never guess what it is "chewed" for. Gum, of course.

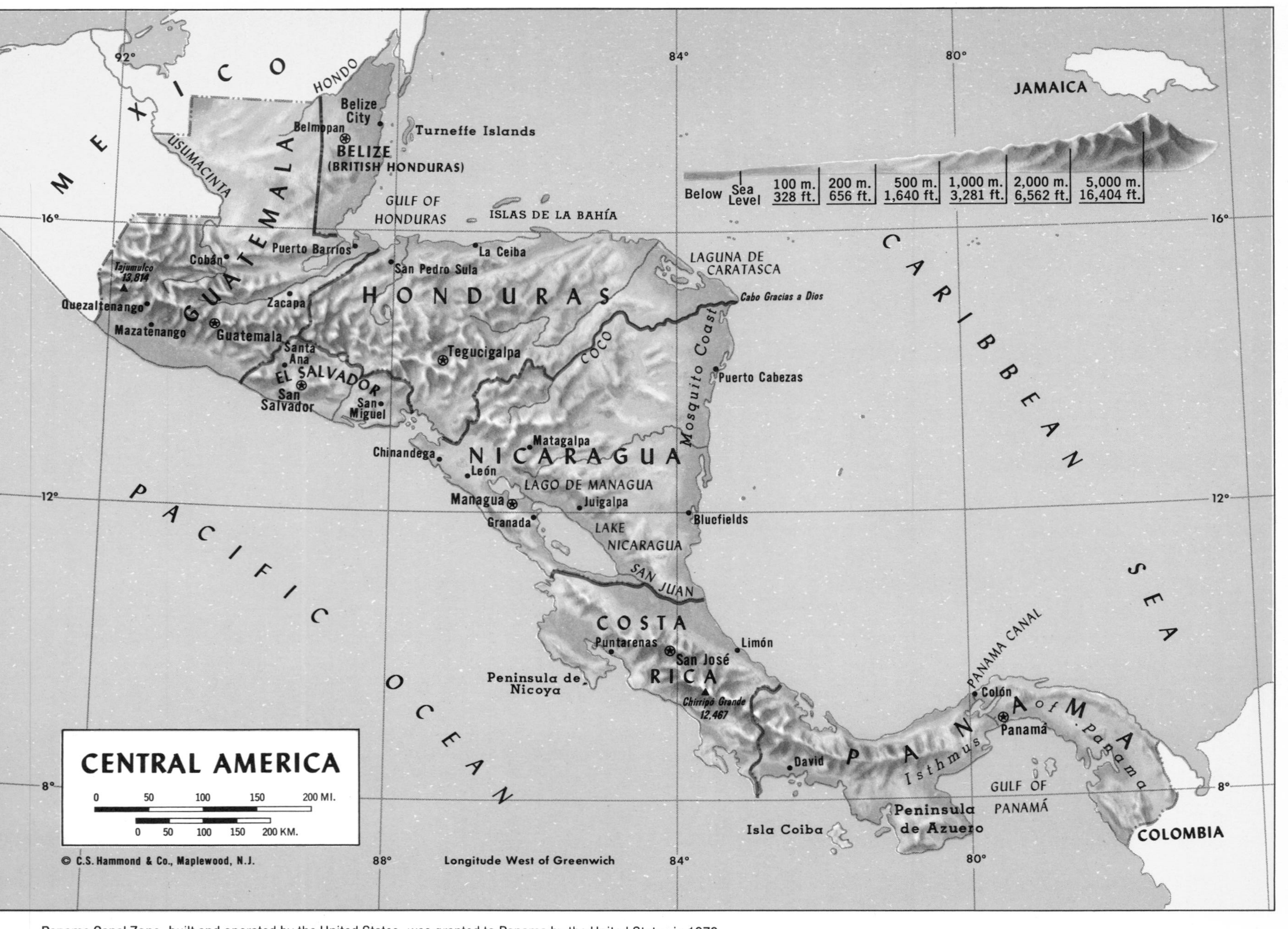

Panama Canal Zone, built and operated by the United States, was granted to Panama by the United States in 1979.

Central America

Geographically Speaking

It is not unusual for land formations, such as mountains, and bodies of water, such as rivers, to serve as boundaries between countries. Central America happens to be a boundary! It separates oceans — the Atlantic and the Pacific oceans, *naturally.*

Cross over the bridge. Central America, the central character in the great American land-link, forms the bridge between North America and South America. The connection is at the Isthmus of Panama. All seven countries that make up Central America cover less area than the state of Texas.

A strange twist of geography: The Atlantic Ocean is to the west and the Pacific Ocean is to the east where Panama twists to make the great continental connection. So, a ship sailing from the Atlantic to the Pacific through the canal actually leaves 43 kilometers (27 miles) farther east!

Nicaragua is the largest country in Central America, so it seems natural that Lake Nicaragua would be the largest lake in Nicaragua *and* in Central America.

Volcán Tajumulco in Guatemala is the highest peak in Central America, 4,144 meters (13,814 feet).

Maptalk

An **isthmus** is a narrow strip of land, located between two bodies of water, connecting two larger land areas.

The Panama Canal, which is only 81.63 kilometers (50.72 miles) long, saves 12,530 kilometers (7,800 miles) of water travel/shipping distance from New York City to San Francisco, California. The distance is now only 8,370 kilometers (5,200 miles).

The key to the Panama Canal is three sets of locks and a man-made body of water, Gatun Lake, which takes up one-third of the distance of the Panama Canal.

Naturally

Chocolate fiends could go wild with the abundance of cacao beans. The Coco of Central America is liquid, but it is hardly a hearty chocolate drink. The Coco is a major river on the Honduras-Nicaragua border. Like all major rivers in Central America, it begins in Central America's central mountainous highlands and flows to the sea. In this case, it empties into the Caribbean.

The lowlands are covered with trees that supply about 10 percent of the world's coffee beans.

The mountains have minerals like silver, gold, copper, lead, and manganese just to mention a few.

Hats off to Panama, maker of the world-famous Panama hat!

For 300 years Belize has been one of the world's great suppliers of mahogany.

Guess which country produces the world's most Balsam of Peru, a cough suppressant syrup. Cough . . . cough . . . it's El Salvador.

El Salvador's active volcano, Izalco, has been called the Lighthouse of the Pacific.

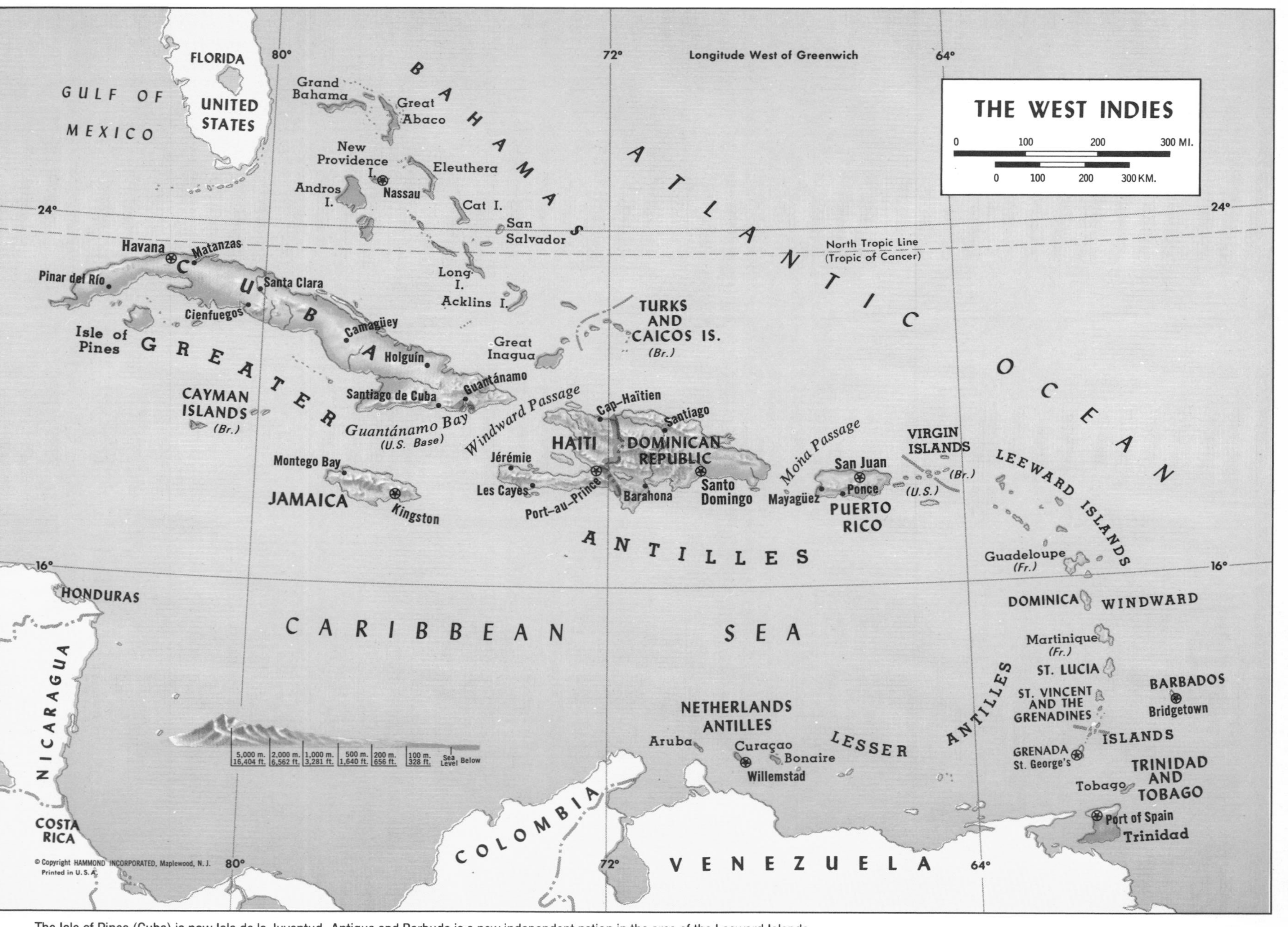

The Isle of Pines (Cuba) is now Isla de la Juventud. Antigua and Barbuda is a new independent nation in the area of the Leeward Islands.

West Indies

Geographically Speaking

The missing link is underwater! The Caribbean Andes is an underwater mountain range. It's a geographical "peak-a-boo." The Caribbean Andes mountain peaks do surface. They form the islands known as the West Indies.

The West Indies stretch from the southern tip of Florida to Mexico's Yucatán Peninsula in North America to Venezuela in South America.

Before they went underwater ages ago, the Caribbean Andes are thought to have been a land chainlike link between the North and South American continents.

Maptalk

An **atoll** is a reef made of a chain of rocks, sand, or coral, generally located below sea level but with some dry areas above the water.

The West Indies islands are mostly volcanic, although some are atolls.

The West Indies separate the Atlantic Ocean and the Caribbean Sea.

This 3,200-kilometer (2000-mile) long curve of islands was named by Christopher Columbus in 1492 when he landed on the island of San Salvador in the Bahamas. Columbus, looking for a short water route to the Spice Islands of Asia, wound up finding America.

A real sweet mistake! These islands, plus Cuba, are the leaders in the production of sugar cane, which when refined can become sugar, molasses, or rum.

A silly question: Do you know where there are a lot of Antilles? The Greater and Lesser Antilles are two major island chains that, along with the Bahamas, make up the West Indies.

Cuba is often called the Pearl of the Antilles. Cuba is one major island, plus 1,600 smaller ones.

Puerto Rico, in the Greater Antilles, is believed to be the only place in the United States where Columbus landed in the year 1493.

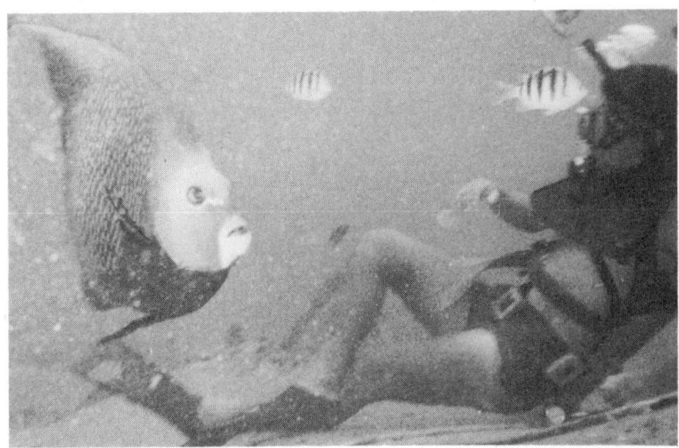

"Big Blue Marble" Photograph

Naturally

Jamaica is one of the world-leading producers of bauxite. That's right!

Trinidad's Pitch Lake is asphalt. It's not a road, but a lake. And asphalt is found there.

Tobago is a petroleum producer.

In both Central America and the West Indies the natural resource — soil — isn't good, it's great!

Honduras is known for bananas, Cuba for sugar, and Guatemala for coffee. It is safe to say that in Central America and the West Indies not only bananas, sugar, and coffee, but also cacao, citrus fruits, cotton, and tobacco are grown. These countries are also known for being rubber producers and as providers of trees like mahogany and ebony. Finally, in these waters there are fish galore.

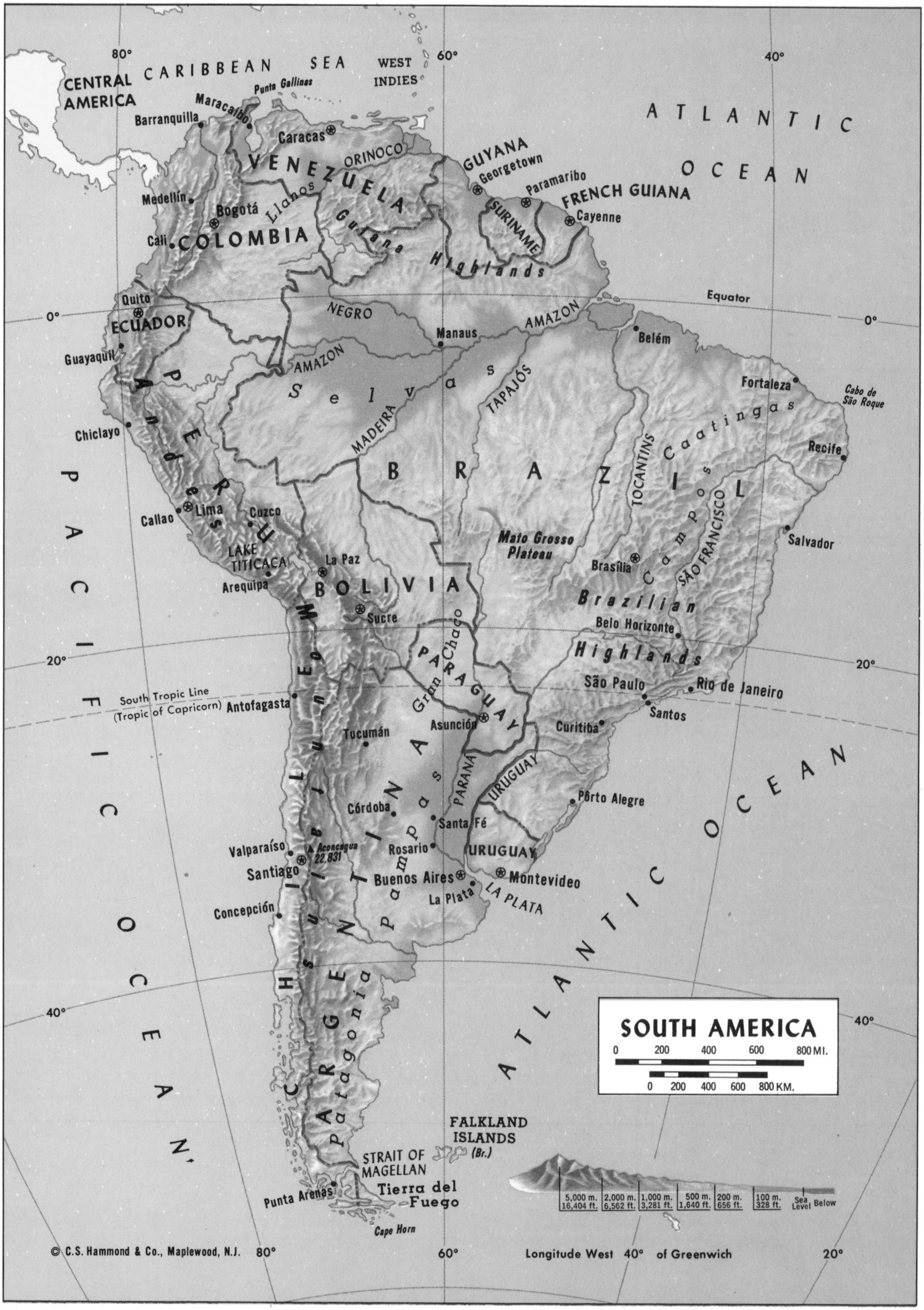

SOUTH AMERICA

0 200 400 600 800 MI.

0 200 400 600 800 KM.

CENTRAL AMERICA
CARIBBEAN SEA
WEST INDIES
Punta Gallinas
Maracaibo
Barranquilla
Caracas
VENEZUELA
ORINOCO
Llanos
Guiana Highlands
GUYANA
Georgetown
Paramaribo
SURINAME
FRENCH GUIANA
Cayenne
ATLANTIC OCEAN
Medellín
Bogotá
Cali
COLOMBIA
Quito
ECUADOR
Guayaquil
Equator
NEGRO
Manaus
AMAZON
Belém
Selvas
MADEIRA
TAPAJÓS
Fortaleza
Cabo de São Roque
Caatingas
Recife
TOCANTINS
BRAZIL
Campos
SÃO FRANCISCO
Salvador
Chiclayo
PERU
Andes
Callao
Lima
Cuzco
LAKE TITICACA
Arequipa
La Paz
BOLIVIA
Sucre
Mato Grosso Plateau
Brasília
Brazilian Highlands
Belo Horizonte
PACIFIC OCEAN
PARAGUAY
Gran Chaco
São Paulo
Rio de Janeiro
Santos
South Tropic Line (Tropic of Capricorn)
Antofagasta
Asunción
Curitiba
Tucumán
PARANA
URUGUAY
Pôrto Alegre
Córdoba
Santa Fé
Pampas
Valparaíso
Aconcagua 22,831
Rosario
Santiago
URUGUAY
Buenos Aires
Montevideo
La Plata
LA PLATA
Concepción
ARGENTINA
CHILE
Patagonia
ATLANTIC OCEAN
FALKLAND ISLANDS (Br.)
STRAIT OF MAGELLAN
Punta Arenas
Tierra del Fuego
Cape Horn

80° 60° 40° 20°
0° 20° 40°

5,000 m. 16,404 ft. | 2,000 m. 6,562 ft. | 1,000 m. 3,281 ft. | 500 m. 1,640 ft. | 200 m. 656 ft. | 100 m. 328 ft. | Sea Level | Below

Longitude West 40° of Greenwich

Falkland Islands are also called Malvinas, an Argentinian name.

SOUTH AMERICA

South America is the fourth-largest continent, double the size of the United States. It is completely surrounded — well, almost — by water. On the west, it is the Pacific, and on the east, the Atlantic. To the north, it is the Atlantic again, along with the Caribbean Sea. In the south, in the Magellan Strait, east meets west as the Atlantic Ocean meets the Pacific Ocean for the only time.

Barely attached to North America, South America's connection with its northern continental neighbor is made at and by the eastern border of Panama.

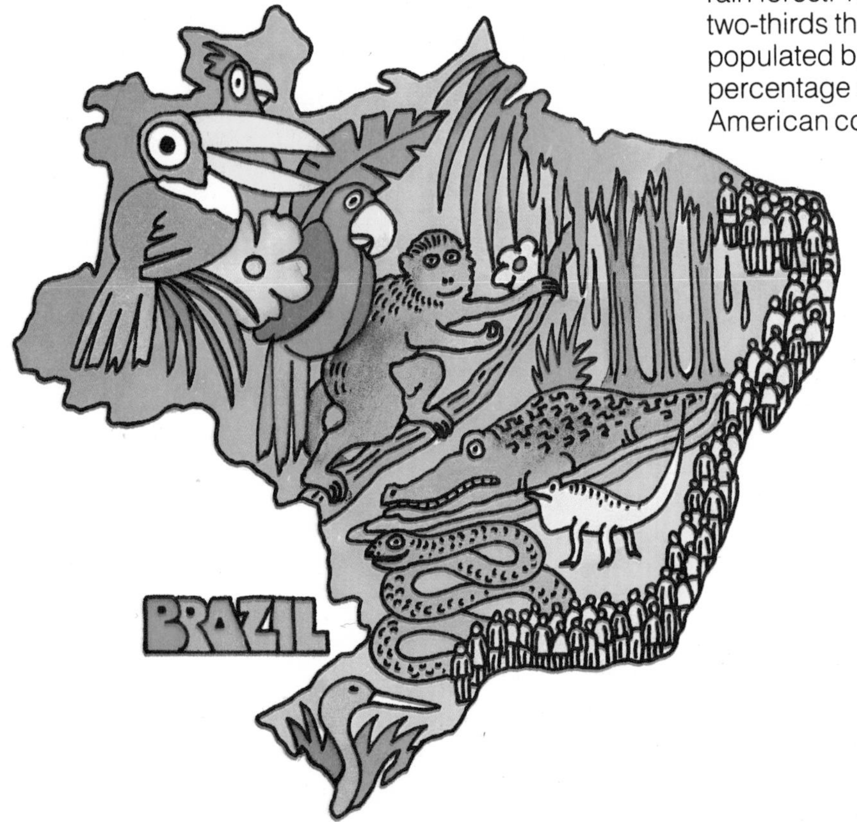

Maptalk

A **river basin** is a large, low-lying area that is drained by a river and its tributaries.

A **jungle** is an area that is thickly covered with tropical vegetation.

A **tropical rain forest,** or **selva,** is one of many forms of tropical vegetation. It is made up of tall, broad-leaved evergreen trees whose tops touch and form a "natural roof."

Along the Amazon River in Brazil is the Amazon River basin, home of the world's largest tropical rain forest. The rain forest covers an area equal to two-thirds the size of the United States and is populated by exotic birds and reptiles. A large percentage of the people of Brazil and other South American countries live along the coasts and rivers.

How would you like to go waterskiing on a lake that is as high as some of the Rocky Mountains? You can. Lake Titicaca, on the Peru-Bolivia border, is the highest lake in the world, roughly 3,812 meters (12,507 feet) above sea level! Lake Titicaca measures 8,446 square kilometers (3,261 square miles).

How's the Weather?

Much of South America is warm most of the year since 75 percent of it is in the tropics. The equator crosses South America's widest part — right through the Amazon River basin's heart. This area is the continent's most continuously humid and hot spot.

The weather gets better at the continent's narrower part, where the cool summers and mild winters start.

It is cold way down south around Cape Horn, the southernmost point of South America. Less than 970 kilometers (600 miles) from the permanent ice of Antarctica, it is only 3,760 kilometers (2,350 miles) from the South Pole.

It is cold way up there where the Andes mountaintops meet the thin air!

The Incan empire, the oldest civilization in South America, was advanced in many ways — from human rights to highly developed farming techniques. To maintain communication in this vast empire, which stretched from the Pacific coast to the inland jungles (Peru, Ecuador, Bolivia, parts of Argentina, and Chile), a sophisticated network of roads was built. The Incas set up a 24-hour messenger service in which relay runners, specially trained youths, carried reports from one end of the empire to the other.

Geographically Speaking

There are four major land regions in South America, seemingly corresponding to North America's regions. There is a narrow Pacific coast, a western high, rugged mountain system, central plains, and eastern "low" highlands.

- The Pacific coastlands are narrow — 80 kilometers to 8 kilometers (50 miles to 5 miles). Their terrain ranges from the swampy, tropical forests of the north in Colombia and Ecuador to southern Peru and northern Chile, where the land is desert dry, to central Chile where good farming and grazing land is abundant, and finally to southern Chile, the coastland of which is dotted with chilly, rainy islands.

• The Andes are the longest "land" mountain chain in the world. The system is 7,240 kilometers (4,500 miles) long, with 50 mountain peaks over 6,100 meters (20,000 feet) high. The Andes are widest in Bolivia, 724 kilometers (450 miles), and narrowest in Chile, 32 kilometers (20 miles). In the Andean region of Colombia and Venezuela, there are many grassy plateaus and valleys. In Bolivia the Andean Plateau is way up there, 3,810 meters (12,500 feet) above sea level.

• The central plains are centrally located. The terrain is flat but the ground cover is not at all the same. In the north, in Colombia and Venezuela, the *Llanos* is a grassy plain. In Brazil it is the *selva,* or tropical rain forest, that covers the Amazon River basin's plain. To the south, in Argentina and Paraguay, it's plain to see the Gran Chaco region is partly forested, "scrub-brush" land. The *pampas* of Argentina are some of the most productive farm- and ranch-lands in South America.

• The eastern highlands begin in the northeast. In Venezuela, Guyana, Suriname, French Guiana, and northern Brazil are the thickly tropical rain forests covering the Guiana Highlands. Brazil has highlands of its own, none other than the Brazilian Highlands, not to mention the inland Mato Grosso Plateau. The southernmost area of this eastern highland region is the Patagonian Plateau — high, flat, and rocky — located in Argentina.

Is That a Fact?

	South America
Area:	17,830,000 sq. km. (6,884,000 sq. mi.)
Total population:	236,000,000
Children aged 0–14:	86,886,000
High spot:	Mount Aconcagua, Argentina 6,960 m. (22,834 ft.)
Low spot:	Peninsula Valdes, Argentina 40 m. (131 ft.) below sea level
City with the most people:	São Paulo, Brazil
Largest country:	Brazil 8,511,965 sq. km. (3,286,488 sq. mi.)
Smallest country:	French Guiana 91,000 sq. km. (35,135 sq. mi.)
World's driest spot:	Atacama Desert, Chile
World's second-longest river:	Amazon River 6,437 km. (4,000 mi.)
World's longest "land mountain" chain:	Andes Mountains 7,240 km. (4,500 mi.)

La Paz, the capital of Bolivia, is the highest capital city in the world.

If you stand three Empire State buildings one on top of the other, Angel Falls, the world's highest waterfall, located in Venezuela, will still be a little higher—979 meters (3,212 feet) high.

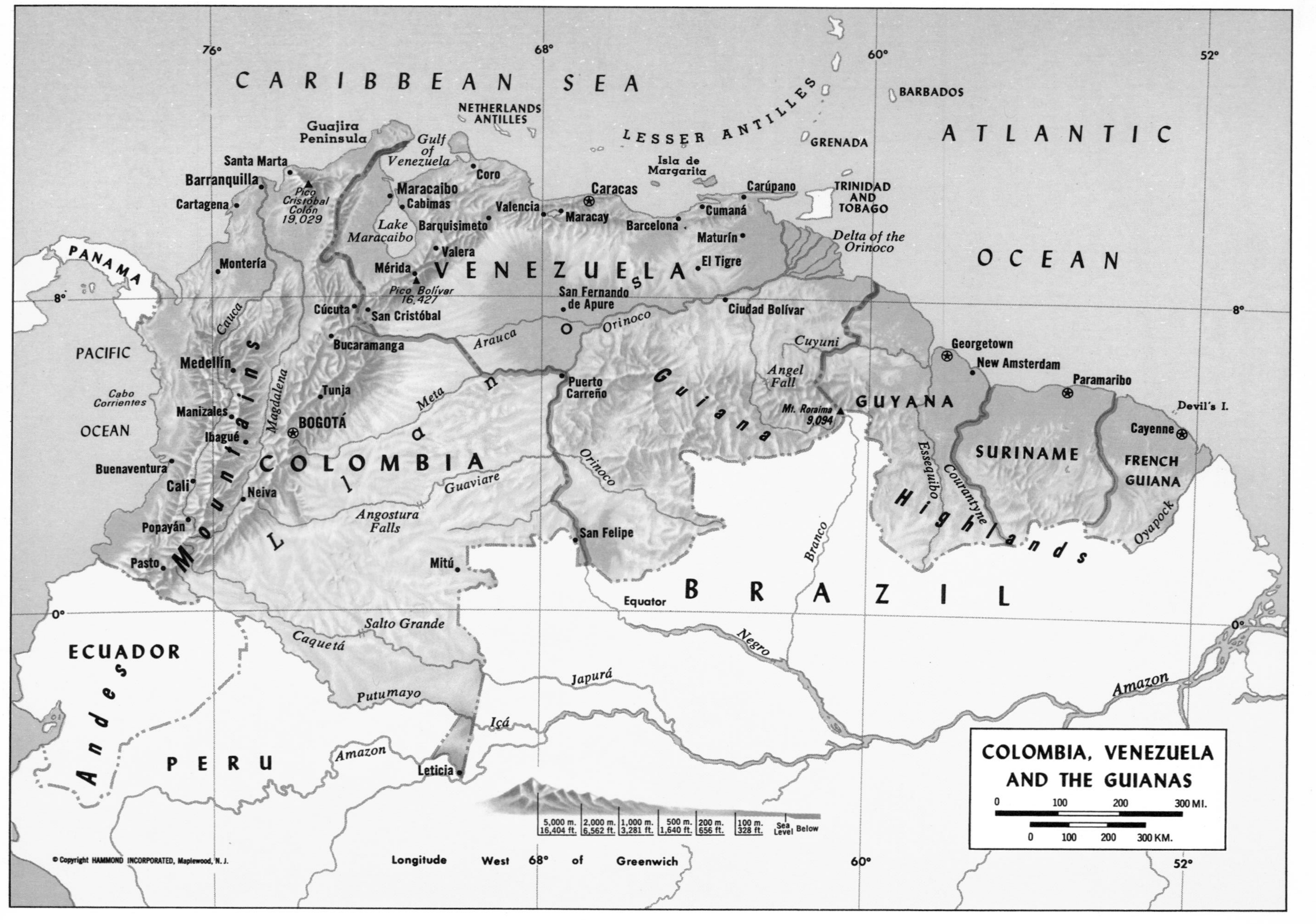
COLOMBIA, VENEZUELA AND THE GUIANAS
0 100 200 300 MI.
0 100 200 300 KM.
CARIBBEAN SEA
ATLANTIC OCEAN
PACIFIC OCEAN
NETHERLANDS ANTILLES
LESSER ANTILLES
BARBADOS
GRENADA
TRINIDAD AND TOBAGO
Isla de Margarita
Guajira Peninsula
Gulf of Venezuela
Lake Maracaibo
Delta of the Orinoco
Santa Marta
Barranquilla
Cartagena
Pico Cristóbal Colón 19,029
Maracaibo
Cabimas
Coro
Barquisimeto
Valencia
Maracay
Caracas
Barcelona
Cumaná
Carúpano
Maturín
El Tigre
Valera
Mérida
Pico Bolívar 16,427
VENEZUELA
Cúcuta
San Cristóbal
San Fernando de Apure
Ciudad Bolívar
Bucaramanga
Tunja
BOGOTÁ
COLOMBIA
Montería
Medellín
Manizales
Ibagué
Buenaventura
Cali
Neiva
Popayán
Pasto
Mitú
Leticia
Puerto Carreño
San Felipe
Cabo Corrientes
PANAMA
ECUADOR
PERU
BRAZIL
GUYANA
SURINAME
FRENCH GUIANA
Georgetown
New Amsterdam
Paramaribo
Cayenne
Devil's I.
Mt. Roraima 9,094
Angel Fall
Cuyuni
Essequibo
Courantyne
Oyapock
Guiana Highlands
Mountains
Andes
Llanos
Cauca
Magdalena
Meta
Arauca
Orinoco
Guaviare
Angostura Falls
Salto Grande
Caquetá
Putumayo
Amazon
Içá
Japurá
Negro
Branco
Equator
5,000 m. 16,404 ft.
2,000 m. 6,562 ft.
1,000 m. 3,281 ft.
500 m. 1,640 ft.
200 m. 656 ft.
100 m. 328 ft.
Sea Level
Below
76°
68°
60°
52°
8°
0°
Longitude West 68° of Greenwich

Colombia, Venezuela, Guyana, Suriname, and French Guiana

Venezuelan Tourist Information

Geographically Speaking

Colombia is the only country in South America whose borders border on the Pacific Ocean and the Caribbean Sea.

The rugged Andes are in the western part of Colombia. The three ranges — Cordillera Occidental, Cordillera Central, and Cordillera Oriental — range from north to south.

Colombia's Pacific coastlands are swamped. They are one of the rainiest places in all the Americas. The land is swampy, covered with thick tropical rain forest.

Lake Maracaibo, in Venezuela, the largest lake in South America, is roughly the same size as New Jersey, 16,300 square kilometers (6,300 square miles).

The grassy plains, *Llanos,* of the Orinoco River basin in northwest Colombia and central Venezuela, are about the size of Texas.

Four hundred tributaries flow into the Orinoco River as it winds its way from Colombia, through Venezuela, to the Atlantic Ocean.

The Guiana Highlands are about 1,500 meters (5,000 feet) high. They are located in the north and the east of the South American continent in parts of Venezuela, Guyana, Suriname, and French Guiana. These high eastern highlands resemble their eastern counterparts in North America, the Appalachian Mountains. Both are gently sloped, rounded hills. The difference is the type of trees that grow on the slopes. Near the equator there are typically tropical forests. These highlands, especially in Suriname and Guyana, are loaded with minerals. The amount of bauxite is out of sight. Both countries are leading world producers. In fact, in Guyana the mountains are covered with such a wild and thick rain forest (85 percent of the country) that much has not yet even been explored!

The sloped mountain edges are steep, causing the water in the many rivers to run over and down the sides. These great falls of water offer great water-power potential.

Naturally

The highlands are ideal for growing coffee, especially in Colombia, the second-largest coffee producer in the world.

Venezuela has oil — enough to provide the world with almost 10 percent of its total supply.

Catch this: Lake Guanoco in Venezuela, that covers nearly 400 hectares (1,000 acres), is no ordinary lake. It is the world's largest deposit of asphalt.

Scientists believe the world's largest deposits of iron ore are in Venezuela. And you know what that's good for.

PERU and ECUADOR
0 50 100 200 300 MI.
0 50 100 200 300 KM.
5,000 m. 16,404 ft.
2,000 m. 6,562 ft.
1,000 m. 3,281 ft.
500 m. 1,640 ft.
200 m. 656 ft.
100 m. 328 ft.
Sea Level
Below
80°
76°
72°
68°
0°
4°
8°
12°
16°
Equator
Longitude West of Greenwich
ECUADOR
COLOMBIA
BRAZIL
PERU
BOLIVIA
CHILE
PACIFIC OCEAN
Andes Mountains
Esmeraldas
Tulcán
Ibarra
Quito
Cotopaxi 19,347
Cabo San Lorenzo
Manta
Chimborazo 20,561
Ambato
Riobamba
Guayaquil
Gulf of Guayaquil
Cuenca
Tumbes
Machala
Loja
Talara
Chira
Piura
Punta Aguja
Napo
Putumayo
Pastaza
Içá
Iquitos
Amazon
Marañón
Yavarí
Yurimaguas
Tarapoto
Ucayali
Juruá
Chiclayo
Cajamarca
Trujillo
Huascarán 22,205
Chimbote
Huarás
Purus
Huánuco
Cerro de Pasco
Huacho
La Oroya
LIMA
Callao
Huancayo
Huancavelica
Ayacucho
Madre de Dios
Puerto Maldonado
Apurímac
Cuzco
Pisco
Ica
Sicuani
Vilcanota 17,999
Juliaca
Lake Titicaca
Puno
El Misti 19,199
Arequipa
Altiplano
Tacna

Peru and Ecuador

"Big Blue Marble" Photograph

Geographically Speaking

Ecuador, one of the smallest countries in South America, and Peru, the third-largest country in South America, have a lot in common — they share borders, mountains, and jungles.

Ecuador's coastal lowland is a low plain located along the Pacific coast. The terrain is flat, but it isn't "plain!" In the north the land is wet, muddy, and swampy. In the middle it is typically tropical — covered by rain forests. In the south it is desert dry. In Peru it's the same way, only everything is on a much longer scale.

In Peru and Ecuador the coastal lowlands are farmed because nearby rivers provide water for irrigation.

It's High! The Andes Highland is high land that cuts through the center of Ecuador and continues all the way through a large portion of Peru. High plateaus bridge the parallel mountain ridges that run north to south. Mountains peak over 6,000 meters (20,000 feet) high.

It's High, Alive, Active, and Well! Cotopaxi, in Ecuador's Andes Highlands, is the world's highest active volcano at 5,897 meters (19,347 feet).

Whether it is called the Ecuadorian eastern lowland or the Peruvian high selva and low selva, the area east of the Andes is a *jungle!*

What's a jungle without a river? In Ecuador there are two major rivers — the Napo and the Pastaza — each flowing its separate way and eventually running together as part of the Amazon River system.

The Amazon River is a river's river! It starts as a little stream called the Apurímac River high in the Peruvian Andes — 5,240 meters (17,200 feet) high! This river flows northwest to another, the Ucayali. Going with the flow it is north, then east, to join the Marañón River at Iquitos in Peru. It is here that the Amazon River becomes an amazing amazon of a river — the second-longest river in the world!

Naturally

Animals used as plows and trucks? Two such work animals are the llama and alpaca. Their wool is used to make sweaters, blankets, and other warm things. These animals, along with woolly sheep, graze on the grassy highland plateaus.

In the Peruvian Andes there's more than just gold in these mountains! Some of the richest deposits in the world of copper, silver, lead, zinc, and petroleum are found in these Andes. In fact, Peru is one of the world leaders in silver production.

Peru is a key country when it comes to fish — it's really rich! Peru has the world's largest commercial fishing industry!

Ecuador is named after the equator, which passes right on through it. *Ecuador* is the Spanish spelling of equator.

Ecuador is one of the world's top exporters of bananas and, like Panama, also makes Panama hats.

Six hundred miles off the coast of Ecuador are the Galápagos Islands, a one-time pirate refuge. Times have changed. They are now a protected refuge for many forms of wildlife, especially the giant sea-turtle for which the islands are named. *Galápagos* is the Spanish word for turtle.

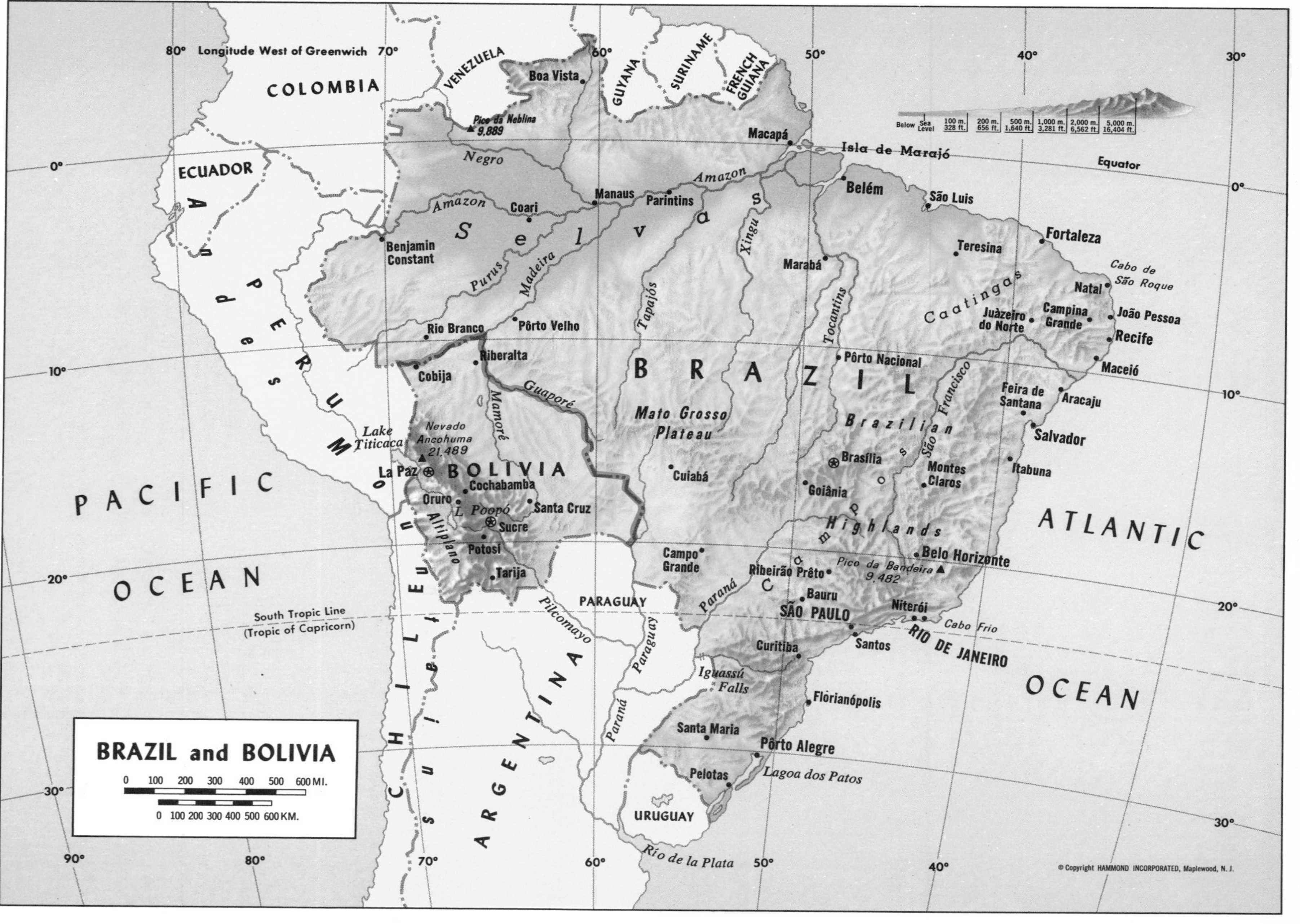
BRAZIL and BOLIVIA
0 100 200 300 400 500 600 MI.
0 100 200 300 400 500 600 KM.
Longitude West of Greenwich
Below Sea Level
100 m. 328 ft.
200 m. 656 ft.
500 m. 1,640 ft.
1,000 m. 3,281 ft.
2,000 m. 6,562 ft.
5,000 m. 16,404 ft.
Equator
South Tropic Line
(Tropic of Capricorn)
BRAZIL
BOLIVIA
COLOMBIA
VENEZUELA
GUYANA
SURINAME
FRENCH GUIANA
ECUADOR
PERU
PARAGUAY
ARGENTINA
URUGUAY
CHILE
PACIFIC OCEAN
ATLANTIC OCEAN
Andes Mountains
Selvas
Caatingas
Brazilian Highlands
Campos
Mato Grosso Plateau
Altiplano
Isla de Marajó
Cabo de São Roque
Cabo Frio
Pico da Neblina 9,889
Nevado Ancohuma 21,489
Pico da Bandeira 9,482
Lake Titicaca
L. Poopó
Lagoa dos Patos
Iguassú Falls
Río de la Plata
Amazon
Negro
Purus
Madeira
Tapajós
Xingu
Tocantins
São Francisco
Mamoré
Guaporé
Paraná
Paraguay
Pilcomayo
Boa Vista
Macapá
Manaus
Parintins
Coari
Benjamin Constant
Belém
São Luis
Fortaleza
Teresina
Marabá
Natal
João Pessoa
Recife
Campina Grande
Juàzeiro do Norte
Maceió
Aracaju
Feira de Santana
Salvador
Itabuna
Rio Branco
Pôrto Velho
Riberalta
Cobija
Pôrto Nacional
Brasília
Goiânia
Cuiabá
Montes Claros
Belo Horizonte
La Paz
Cochabamba
Oruro
Santa Cruz
Sucre
Potosí
Tarija
Campo Grande
Ribeirão Prêto
Bauru
São Paulo
Niterói
Rio de Janeiro
Santos
Curitiba
Florianópolis
Santa Maria
Pôrto Alegre
Pelotas

Brazil and Bolivia

Geographically Speaking

Brazil is the largest South American country, covering half of the continent. It is the fifth-largest country in the world following Russia, Canada, China, and the United States.

"Big Blue Marble" Photograph

The Amazon River cuts from west to east across the entire country of Brazil, just below the equator. More water flows through this river than all the waters of the Mississippi, the Nile, and the Yangtze rivers combined, thanks to the Amazon's 200 contributing tributaries.

The Amazon River is from 2.4 kilometers to 10 kilometers (1.5 miles to 6 miles) wide. It's got a big mouth! Ah! It opens wide to 140 kilometers (90 miles). It is deep too — anywhere from 12 meters (40 feet) to 91 meters (300 feet)!

How long is the second-longest river in the world? The Amazon is 6,437 kilometers (4,000 miles) long, from the Andes Mountains all the way to the Atlantic Ocean.

Along the Amazon River is the Amazon River basin, which contains the world's largest tropical rain forest, or *selva*. The area of this basin is equal to two-thirds the size of the United States! This basin is part of South America's central plains.

Naturally

Did you know that Brazil has more farmland than all the farmland in Europe? It is no surprise, then, to learn that Brazil is "number one" in the world when it comes to growing bananas, beans, cassava, and coffee. Brazil ranks in the world's top ten in producing cacao, oranges, pineapples, and sugar cane, and shares the world title for production of cattle and hogs! And, if that isn't enough, Brazil leads South America in corn, rice, tobacco, and cotton! If you think that's nuts, Brazil leads in growing Brazil nuts and cashews too.

Brazil measures up worldwide in iron ore and manganese!

In the western part of Bolivia the Andes Mountains are at their widest — 724 kilometers (450 miles).

Tin can be, and is, found in abundance in Bolivia — a leading world producer.

Would you believe that Brazil is second only to the USSR when it comes to forests, and 40 percent of Bolivia, Brazil's neighbor, is covered with trees! From both of these South American countries comes a lot of the world's rubber!

One potato, two potato. Bolivia grows 200 different kinds of potatoes!

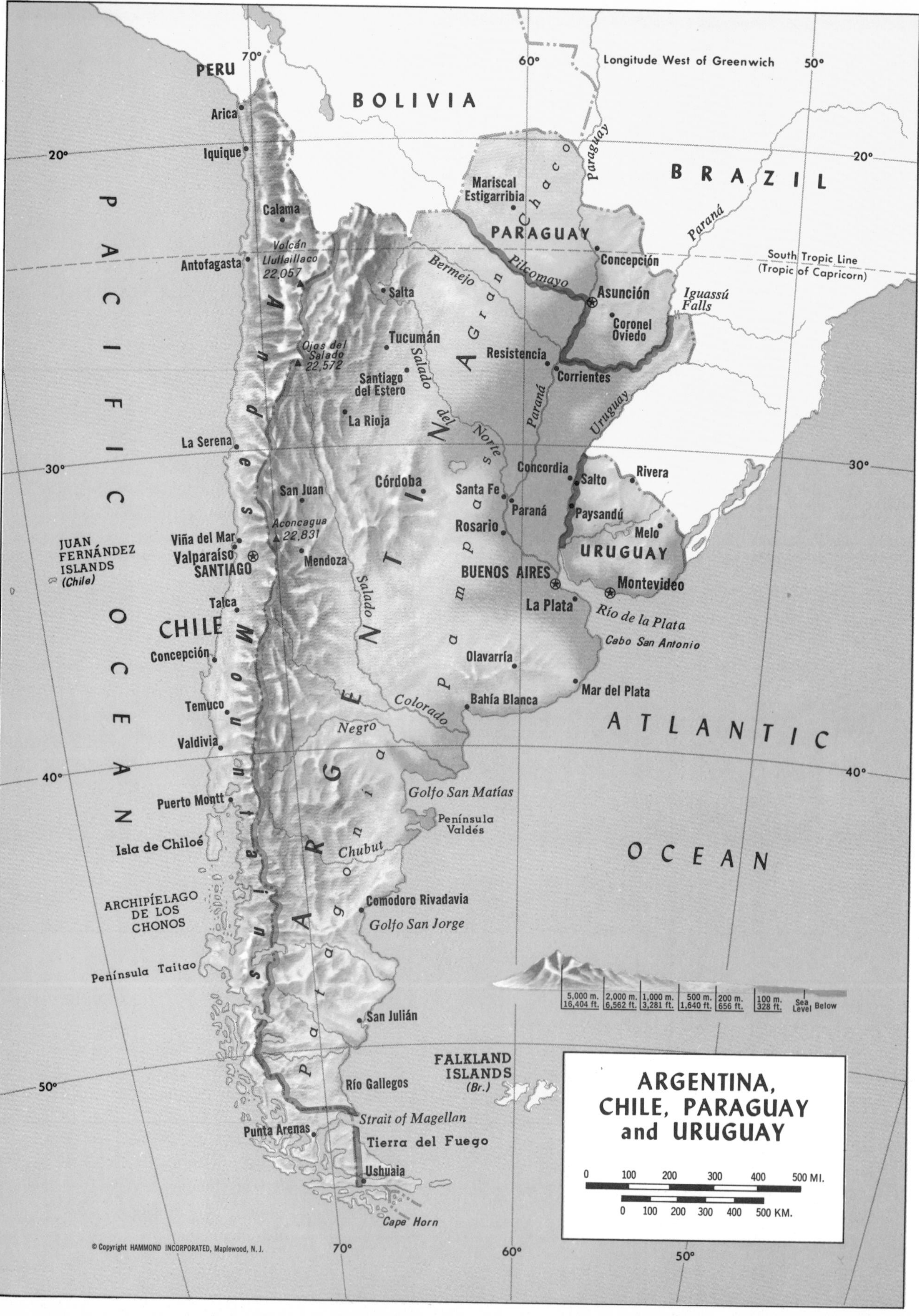
ARGENTINA, CHILE, PARAGUAY and URUGUAY
PERU
BOLIVIA
BRAZIL
PARAGUAY
URUGUAY
CHILE
ARGENTINA
PACIFIC OCEAN
ATLANTIC OCEAN
Longitude West of Greenwich
South Tropic Line (Tropic of Capricorn)
70°
60°
50°
20°
30°
40°
Arica
Iquique
Calama
Antofagasta
Volcán Llullaillaco 22,057
Salta
Tucumán
Ojos del Salado 22,572
Santiago del Estero
La Rioja
La Serena
San Juan
Córdoba
Aconcagua 22,831
Viña del Mar
Valparaíso
SANTIAGO
Mendoza
JUAN FERNÁNDEZ ISLANDS (Chile)
Talca
Concepción
Temuco
Valdivia
Puerto Montt
Isla de Chiloé
ARCHIPÍELAGO DE LOS CHONOS
Península Taitao
Mariscal Estigarribia
Gran Chaco
Concepción
Asunción
Coronel Oviedo
Iguassú Falls
Paraguay
Paraná
Pilcomayo
Bermejo
Salado
Resistencia
Corrientes
Uruguay
Salado del Norte
Concordia
Salto
Rivera
Santa Fe
Paraná
Paysandú
Rosario
Melo
BUENOS AIRES
Montevideo
La Plata
Río de la Plata
Cabo San Antonio
Pampas
Olavarría
Mar del Plata
Bahía Blanca
Colorado
Negro
Patagonia
Golfo San Matías
Península Valdés
Chubut
Comodoro Rivadavia
Golfo San Jorge
San Julián
Río Gallegos
FALKLAND ISLANDS (Br.)
Strait of Magellan
Punta Arenas
Tierra del Fuego
Ushuaia
Cape Horn
Andes Mountains
5,000 m. 16,404 ft.
2,000 m. 6,562 ft.
1,000 m. 3,281 ft.
500 m. 1,640 ft.
200 m. 656 ft.
100 m. 328 ft.
Sea Level
Below
0 100 200 300 400 500 MI.
0 100 200 300 400 500 KM.

Argentina, Chile, Paraguay, and Uruguay

Geographically Speaking

Uruguay is one of the smallest countries in South America. The southern end of the Eastern Highlands covers most of this tiny but rich country. Uruguay has nothing to beef about! That's right! There are plenty of cattle and sheep here.

Chile is long and skinny. It runs the length of half of the Pacific coast of South America for 4,265 kilometers (2,650 miles). The northern third of Chile is Andes country and is chock full of minerals. Chile is one of the world's largest producers of copper. What's more, there is plenty of iron ore. Are you ready for a shocker? Ouch! Most of the world's crude iodine comes from Chile.

Argentina shares with Chile the Andes Mountains as a common border. Argentina outdoes them all when it comes to mountains being tall. Mount Aconcagua is 6,960 meters (22,834 feet) high. That's more than four miles! Mount Aconcagua is the highest mountain in Argentina, South America, and even the entire Western Hemisphere.

Gauchos, or cowboys, who ride the Argentine *pampas* tend the cattle that graze on this rich soil of the South American central plain. Argentina is the number-one exporter of beef in the world. And, half of all the leather used in the world was once grazing on the Argentine pampa.

Paraguay is landlocked but has access to the sea via the Paraná River, which joins the Río de la Plata on Paraguay's southeastern border. This river connection is part of the most important inland waterway of South America. The Río de la Plata flows through Bolivia, Brazil, Paraguay, Argentina, and Uruguay—all the way to the Atlantic Ocean!

"Big Blue Marble" Photograph

Tierra del Fuego, the Land of Fire, is so named not because it is hot. It is a group of islands located at the very southern tip of South America. When the explorer, Magellan, first sighted the islands he saw the fires of the natives who kept a constant blaze going to keep warm. Magellan named these islands Tierra del Fuego.

Naturally

Paraguay is a world-leading source of *quebracho* trees. The bark of these trees produces a material known as *tannin.* This tannin tans Argentina's hides!

Petitgrain oil is used in the manufacture of both perfumes and marmalades. Paraguay is the world's largest producer of petitgrain oil.

Argentina measures up minerally when it comes to lead, zinc, iron ore, and nickel. Argentina has precious amounts of gold and silver. They "fuel" around with oil, natural gas, and uranium!

EARTH'S NEIGHBORHOOD

There was a time, about 1,800 years ago, when the Earth was thought to be the center of the universe and all things revolved around it—the sun, the moon, the planets, and the stars.

Since that time, other ideas have been advanced and discoveries made so that today the form, structure, and composition of the universe seem to fall into more understandable patterns and relationships.

Astronomy, the science of stars, planets, galaxies, and all other heavenly bodies, helps us to learn more about the Earth and its neighborhood.

The Moon

The moon is the Earth's original satellite. It is one-fourth the size of the Earth.

The moon rotates on an axis, just like the Earth, only very slowly. It takes about 28 Earth-days to complete one revolution. That means one moon day is 28 Earth-days. Now that's a long day!

The moon, like the Earth, has gravity. But the moon's gravity is one-sixth that of Earth's. That means a girl or boy weighing 27 kilograms (60 pounds) would weigh only 4.5 kilograms (10 pounds) on the moon. And any girl or boy who can jump over a .9-meter- (3-feet) high hurdle on Earth could jump over a 5.4-meter (18-feet) barrier on the moon.

The moon's gravitational attraction has a powerful effect on the Earth's tides. The moon has more effect on the Earth's tides than the sun only because the moon is closer to the Earth.

Mountains on the moon are as high as the ones on Earth. And, to top it off, there are over a half-million craters that are more than 1.6 kilometers (1 mile) wide. Some of these craters were probably formed when meteors traveling at great speeds through outer space struck the moon's surface. Remember, the moon has no atmosphere like the Earth's to protect it.

It never rains on the moon.
It never snows on the moon.
There is never a cloudy day.
Nothing grows on the moon.
Nothing lives on the moon.
There is no air on the moon.
There is no sound, because sound
is carried by air.

An **eclipse** is a darkening of the sun when some heavenly body is in a position that partly or completely cuts off its light. The usual eclipse of the sun occurs when the moon passes between the Earth and the sun. An eclipse of the moon is when the Earth passes between the sun and the moon.

The moon as photographed from the Apollo 13 spacecraft on its return voyage to Earth. Even though there isn't any water on the moon, some of its surface features have been given the following names: the Sea of Crisis, the Sea of Fertility, the Sea of Tranquility. Other names include the Crater Langrenus and the Crater Tsiolkovsky. ▶

Is That a Fact?

	Moon
Total area:	37,943,000 sq. km. (14,650,000 sq. mi.)
Diameter:	3,476 km. (2,160 mi.)
Age:	Estimated to be about the same as the Earth's — 4.6 billion years
Distance from Earth:	382,171 km. (238,857 mi.)

The Apollo Missions

Man first landed on the moon in July 1969. It was then that Neil A. Armstrong, Edwin E. Aldrin, Jr., and Michael Collins conducted an 8-day, 3-hour-and-18-minute flight that resulted in the first manned landing on the moon. "One small step for Man, one giant leap for Mankind."

Since then, astronauts have spent 166 hours exploring the surface of the moon: have traveled 96 kilometers (60 miles) across the surface of the moon; and have collected 387 kilograms (850 pounds) of lunar samples.

We learned many things from these explorations. For example, the moon, like Earth, is about 4.6 billion years old. The moon had active volcanoes, but for the last 2 to 3 billion years, it has been very "quiet." There haven't been any eruptions.

NASA Photograph

NASA Photograph

The Apollo 16 lunar module "Orion" landed on target, permitting astronauts John W. Young (pictured above) and Charles H. Duke, Jr., (the photographer) to set up their many experiments and carry out their other assignments while on the surface of our moon. ▲

The Sun

The sun is our star. It provides us with out heat, our light, and makes possible life. It is a huge ball of extremely hot elements, mostly hydrogen and helium gases.

The sun's temperature and gravitational pressure are far higher than those of the Earth. A man weighing 81 kilograms (180 pounds) on Earth would weigh 2,272 kilograms (5,048 pounds) on the sun. The same man would weigh only 13.5 kilograms (30 pounds) on the moon.

Like a ball of fire, the sun photographed from space shows the intense activity of our star. A great gaseous eruption of the sun can be seen at the top of the picture. These "prominences," as they are called, shoot great waves of energy into the solar atmosphere that often affect weather and agriculture on Earth, to say nothing of what they can do to radio and television reception. ▼

Is That a Fact?

	Sun
Diameter:	The sun is an average-size star. 1,392,000 km. (865.000 mi) in diameter
Volume:	About 1.3 million times that of Earth
Mass:	The sun has 99.85 percent of the mass (weight) of the entire solar system; about 322,000 times that of Earth
Estimated surface temperature:	6,000°C (10,832°F)
Estimated interior temperature:	15,000,000°C (27,000,032°F)
Gravity force:	About 28 times that on the surface of Earth
Age:	About 4.6 billion years
Distance from Earth:	148,000,000 km. (93,000,000 mi.)

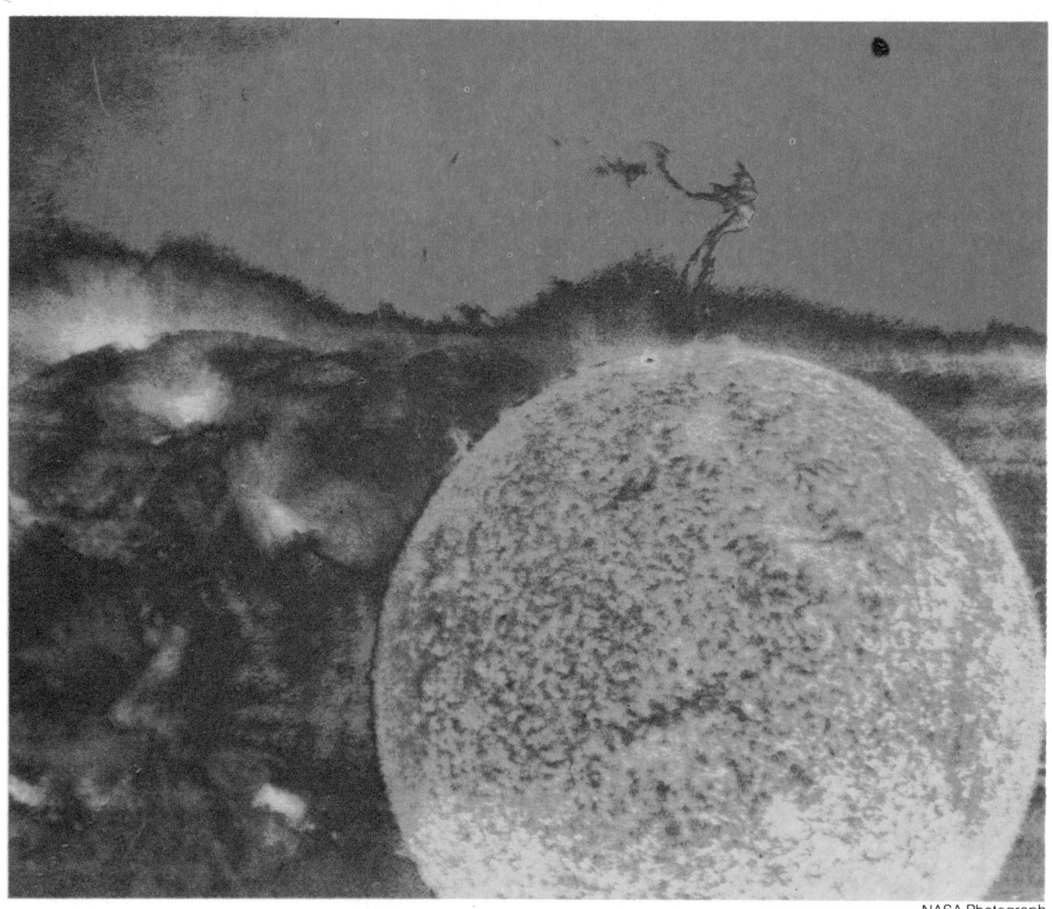

NASA Photograph

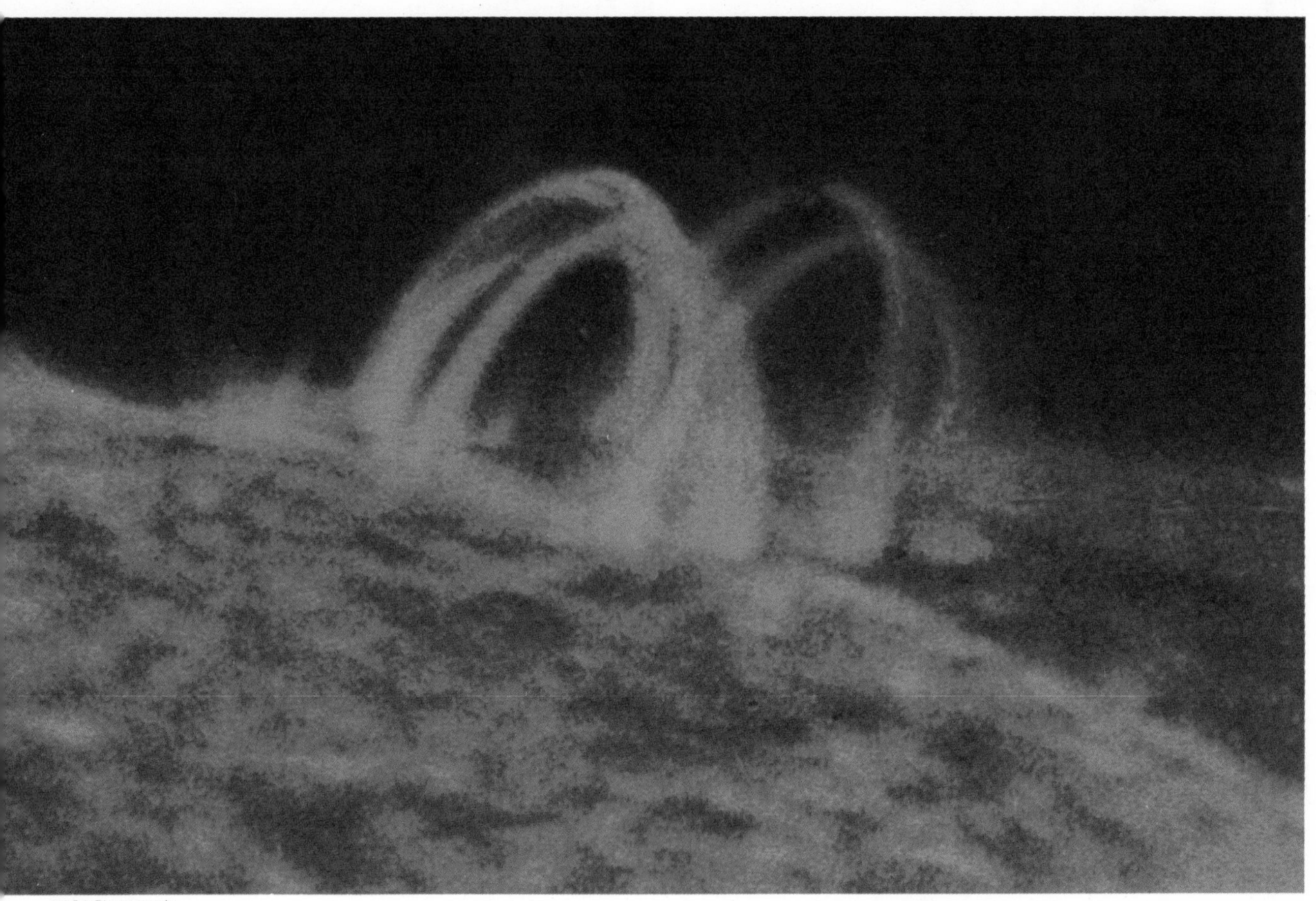

NASA Photograph

Magnetic loops of the sun sometimes reach a height of 48,000 kilometers (30,000 miles) and cover a distance of 200,000 kilometers (125,000 miles) across the sun's surface. Periods of increased solar activity — magnetic loops, sunspots, solar flares — occur in about 11-year cycles. This regular surging of energy affects our weather. Even the growth of trees on Earth is affected — it is increased — during these cycles.▲

The Solar System

Introducing:
The solar system
Starring:
The sun. (Affectionately referred to as "Old Sol"; *sol* means sun in Latin.) It is not only a star in its own right, but also is the entire source of energy for the solar system.
Featuring:
The planets and their satellites (moons) in order of their distance from the sun
And a cast of thousands:
Asteroids, pieces of broken planet
Meteoroids, pieces of iron and stone
Comets, dust and frozen gases
Interplanetary dust particles and gases

The solar system is made possible by the sun's "pull." It creates the gravitation that keeps all the elements of the solar system in order or, should we say, in orbit. Without the sun, where would we be?

The gravitational pull acts like a magnet, but it is a different and even more mysterious force.

Imagine a gigantic game of crack the whip being played by the solar system. The sun is at the center and its planets with their moons all spin out from the sun, clockwise. And then crack the whip! All the planets fly out into their orbits on the same plane. All except Pluto, on the end; its orbit is a little crooked. It's a little more *elliptical*, meaning it is oval shaped. Do you suppose that in reality this has anything to do with the decrease in the sun's gravitational pull, because Pluto is so far away?

Asteroids, over 3,000 very small "planets," maintain a constant orbit between Mars and Jupiter. Some of the best-known are: Ceres, the largest, with a 768-kilometer (480-mile) diameter; Pallas, with a 480-kilometer (300-mile) diameter; Vesta, with a 384-kilometer (240-mile) diameter; and Juno, with a 192-kilometer (120-mile) diameter.

Is That a Fact?

The Solar System

	Distance from sun	Satellites	"Year"*	Diameter
Mercury	57,600,000 km./ 35,991,000 mi.	0	88 days	4,656 km./ 2,910 mi.
Venus	107,200,000 km./ 67,000,000	0	225 days	12,128 km./ 7,580 mi.
Earth	148,000,000 km./ 93,000,000 mi.	1	1 year	12,656 km./ 7,910 mi.
Mars	227,200,000 km./ 142,000,000 mi.	2	1.9 years	6,624 km./ 4,140 mi.
Jupiter	774,700,000 km./ 483,879,000 mi.	14	11.9 years	138,560 km./ 86,600 mi.
Saturn	1,419,403,000 km./ 887,127,000 mi.	15 **	29.7 years	115,680 km./ 72,300 mi.
Uranus	2,854,400,000 km./ 1,783,740,000 mi.	5	83.7 years	47,200 km./ 29,500 mi.
Neptune	3,328,000,000 km./ 2,795,580,000 mi.	2	166 years	44,480 km./ 27,800 mi.
Pluto	5,884,800,000 km./ 3,667,920,000 mi.	1	247.7 years	5,920 km./ 3,700 mi.

* Number of Earth-days/years it takes to complete one orbit around the sun.

** Number of Saturn's satellites could change depending on new information from Voyager 2 in the summer of 1981.

NASA Photograph

The Martian terrain. This remarkable photograph taken from the landed Viking I camera shows the reddish soil, rocks, and atmosphere of Mars, our neighboring planet. ▲

NASA Photograph

This exciting photo of Jupiter and Europa, one of its moons, was taken from a distance of about 350,000 kilometers (220,000 miles) above the Red Spot. A theory is that Europa is one of the few places in the solar system where life might exist or might have existed once — because it has water! It seems to be covered with a crust of ice. ▲

NASA Photograph

Saturn. This photograph was taken at a distance of 2.4 million kilometers (1.5 million miles) from the planet, and shows not only Saturn's rings but also the shadows the rings cast on Saturn itself. The satellite seen in the picture is Rhea, one of Saturn's moons. It is 1,450 kilometers (900 miles) in diameter, or one-half the size of our moon. ▲

The Universe

The universe is all existing or created things, including all of the Earth and everything on it and around it, including the sun, the moon, the solar system, the stars, and infinite space. The universe is everything there is — as far as we know!

The basic building block of the universe is the galaxy. Our solar system is part of a galaxy called the Milky Way. The shape of our galaxy — like a discus — is maintained by a force of gravity in much the same way as our solar system holds its shape.

On a clear night you can see the Milky Way in the sky. It is like a mist of starlight. The Milky Way is the galaxy of which our solar system and our Earth are but a very small part. It is estimated that a typical galaxy has about 250 billion stars. (Remember the sun is but *one* of the stars in our galaxy.) It is also estimated that the universe contains as many as 100 billion galaxies. If you figure 100 billion galaxies, each with about 250 billion stars, it adds up to a universe of 25 sextillion stars — quite a few at which to gaze. Actually, the most stars you see on a clear evening in the overhead sky is about 2,000. Quite a difference in what you see and what's really out there in space.

"Star light, star bright!"

Just how big is this star-studded universe? There's no certain answer, but we do know it's *big!* Its size is almost beyond comprehension.

Astronomers invented a new measurement for dealing with the vastness of space. It's called a *light-year.*

When you use a flashlight, the light actually takes time to travel from the bulb to the subject it's shining on.

The speed of light is 298,080 kilometers (186,300 miles) per second! So the "star light" traveling from the sun to the Earth, a distance of 148,800,000 kilometers (93 million miles), takes eight minutes!

In one Earth-year light travels about 9.6 trillion kilometers (6 trillion miles). To use miles as a basis for measuring distances in the universe is as impractical as taking the Earth's measurements in inches. The measurement used is a light-year and it is equal to 6 trillion miles, the distance light travels in an Earth-year.

The closest star, after the sun, is Proxima Centauri. It's four light-years away! The light from Proxima that you see when you observe the star actually started out from the star four years ago.

Astronomers think *quasars,* starlike objects giving off radio pulses at perhaps the ends of the universe, are as far away as 10 billion light-years from Earth.

$$
\begin{array}{rl}
6{,}000{,}000{,}000{,}000 & \text{miles (one light-year)} \\
\times\ 10{,}000{,}000{,}000 & \text{light-years} \\
\hline
 & \text{miles}
\end{array}
$$

As yet the definite size of the universe is still unknown!

A nebula, like the one pictured here, can be either a mass of luminous gas if it's within our galaxy, or a cluster of stars if it's much farther out in space. ▶

NASA Photograph

There are so many stars in the clustered area of this photo that the area has been named the Star Cloud of Sagittarius. ▲

NASA Photograph

Big Blue Marble®

Book of Lists

Earth's Renewable Resources

NOTE: In all resource lists, countries or states are listed alphabetically, but the world's major producer is identified by *"No. 1!"*

GRAINS

Leading *wheat*-growing countries
- Australia
- Canada
- China
- France
- India
- Italy
- Turkey
- United States
- USSR *(No. 1!)*
- West Germany

Leading *wheat*-growing states
- Colorado
- Kansas *(No. 1!)*
- Montana
- Nebraska
- North Dakota
- Oklahoma
- Washington

Leading *corn*-growing countries
- Brazil
- China
- France
- India
- Mexico
- Rumania
- South Africa
- United States *(No. 1!)*
- USSR
- Yugoslavia

Leading *corn*-growing states
- Illinois
- Indiana
- Iowa *(No. 1!)*
- Michigan
- Minnesota
- Missouri
- Nebraska
- Ohio
- South Dakota
- Wisconsin

Leading *oat*-growing countries
- Canada
- Poland
- United States *(No. 1!)*
- USSR
- West Germany

Leading *oat*-growing states
- Minnesota *(No. 1!)*
- North Dakota
- South Dakota

Leading *rice*-growing countries
- Bangladesh
- Burma
- Brazil
- China *(No. 1!)*
- India
- Indonesia
- Japan

Leading *rice*-growing states
- Arkansas
- California
- Louisiana
- Texas *(No. 1!)*

LIVESTOCK

Leading *cattle*-raising countries
- Argentina
- Australia
- Bangladesh
- Brazil
- China
- Ethiopia
- India *(No. 1!)*
- Mexico
- United States
- USSR

Leading *beef-cattle*-raising states
- California
- Colorado
- Iowa
- Kansas
- Missouri
- Nebraska
- Oklahoma
- Texas *(No. 1!)*
- South Dakota

Leading *dairy-cattle*-raising states
- California
- Iowa
- Michigan
- Minnesota
- New York
- Ohio
- Pennsylvania
- Wisconsin *(No. 1!)*

Leading *hog*-raising states
- Georgia
- Illinois
- Indiana
- Iowa *(No. 1!)*
- Kansas
- Minnesota
- Missouri
- Nebraska
- Ohio

Leading *sheep*-raising countries
- Argentina
- Australia *(No. 1!)*
- Brazil
- China
- India
- Iran
- New Zealand
- South Africa
- Turkey
- USSR

Leading *sheep*-raising states
- California
- Colorado
- Idaho
- Iowa
- Montana
- New Mexico
- South Dakota
- Texas *(No. 1!)*
- Utah
- Wyoming

FRUIT TREES

Leading *banana*-growing countries
- Brazil *(No. 1!)*
- Costa Rica
- Ecuador
- Honduras
- India
- Mexico
- Panama
- Philippines
- Thailand
- Venezuela

Leading *apple*-growing states
- California
- Michigan
- New York
- Pennsylvania
- Virginia
- Washington *(No. 1!)*
- West Virginia

Leading *orange*-growing countries
- Argentina
- Brazil
- Italy
- Japan
- Mexico
- Spain
- United States *(No. 1!)*

Leading *orange*-growing states
- Arizona
- California
- Florida *(No. 1!)*
- Texas

Leading *coffee*-growing countries
- Angola
- Brazil *(No. 1!)*
- Colombia
- El Salvador
- Ethiopia
- Guatemala
- Indonesia
- Ivory Coast
- Mexico
- Uganda

Leading *cacao*-growing countries
- Brazil
- Cameroon
- Colombia
- Dominican Republic
- Ecuador
- Ghana *(No. 1!)*
- Ivory Coast
- Mexico
- Nigeria
- Papua New Guinea

NATURAL FIBERS

Leading *cotton*-growing countries
- Brazil
- China
- Egypt
- India
- Mexico
- Pakistan
- Sudan
- Turkey
- United States
- USSR *(No. 1!)*

Leading *cotton*-growing states
- Alabama
- Arkansas
- Arizona
- California
- Georgia
- Louisiana
- Mississippi
- Missouri
- Tennessee
- Texas *(No. 1!)*

Leading *wool*-producing states
- California
- Colorado
- Idaho
- Montana
- New Mexico
- Ohio
- South Dakota
- Texas *(No. 1!)*

Leading *natural rubber*-producing countries
- India
- Indonesia
- Malaysia *(No. 1!)*
- Sri Lanka
- Thailand

Leading *synthetic rubber*-producing countries
- France
- Japan
- United States *(No. 1!)*
- USSR
- West Germany

Leading *jute*-exporting countries
- Bangladesh
- India
- Thailand

Earth's Nonrenewable Resources

MINERALS

Countries with greatest *bauxite* deposits
- Australia
- France
- Guinea
- Guyana
- Hungary
- Jamaica *(No. 1!)*
- Malaysia
- Suriname
- USSR
- Yugoslavia

States with greatest *bauxite* deposits
- Alabama
- Arkansas *(No. 1!)*
- Georgia

Countries mining the most *bauxite*
- Australia
- France
- Greece
- Guinea
- Guyana
- Hungary
- Jamaica *(No. 1!)*
- Suriname
- USSR

Countries with leading *cobalt* deposits
- Morocco
- Zaire *(No. 1!)*
- Zambia

States with leading *cobalt* deposits
- Idaho
- Missouri
- Pennsylvania *(No. 1!)*

Countries mining the most *copper*
- Austraila
- Canada
- Chile
- Peru
- Philippines
- United States *(No. 1!)*
- USSR
- Zaire
- Zambia

States mining the most *copper*
- Arizona *(No. 1!)*
- Michigan
- Montana
- Nevada
- New Mexico
- Utah

Countries mining the most *lead*
- Australia
- Bulgaria

Canada
China
Mexico
Peru
Sweden
United States *(No. 1!)*
USSR
Yugoslavia

States mining the most *lead*
Colorado
Idaho
Missouri *(No. 1!)*
Utah

Countries mining the most *iron ore*
Australia
Brazil
Canada
China
France
India
Liberia
United States
USSR *(No. 1!)*
Sweden

States mining the most *iron ore*
California
Michigan
Minnesota *(No. 1!)*
Missouri
Utah
Wyoming

States producing the most *steel*
Illinois
Indiana
Michigan
Ohio
Pennsylvania *(No. 1!)*

Countries mining the most *zinc*
Australia
Canada *(No. 1!)*
Peru
United States
USSR

Countries mining the most *tungsten*
Australia
Bolivia
Brazil
Canada
China *(No. 1!)*
Korea, North and South
United States
USSR

Countries mining the most *tin*
Australia
Bolivia
China
Indonesia
Malaysia *(No. 1!)*
Nigeria
Thailand
USSR

Countries mining the most *manganese*
Australia
Brazil
China
Gabon
India
South Africa
USSR *(No. 1!)*

Countries producing the most *magnesium*
Canada
France
Great Britain
Italy
Japan
Norway
Poland
United States *(No. 1!)*
USSR

Countries mining the most *chromium*
Cuba *(No. 1!)*
New Caledonia
Philippines
Turkey
South Africa
USSR
Zimbabwe

PRECIOUS METALS
A Nonrenewable Resource

Countries mining the most *gold*
Australia
Canada
Colombia
Ghana
Japan
Philippines
Rhodesia
South Africa *(No. 1!)*
USSR
Zimbabwe

States mining the most *gold*
Arizona
Nevada
South Dakota *(No. 1!)*
Utah
Washington

Countries mining the most *silver*
Australia
Bolivia
Canada
East Germany
Honduras
Japan
Mexico *(No. 1!)*
Peru
United States
USSR

States mining the most *silver*
Arizona
Colorado
Idaho *(No. 1!)*
Montana
Utah

Countries producing the most *platinum*
Canada
Colombia
South Africa
United States
USSR *(No. 1!)*

METALS made by people

Countries manufacturing the most *aluminum*
Australia
Canada
France
India
Italy
Japan
United States *(No. 1!)*
USSR
West Germany

States manufacturing the most *aluminum*
Alabama
Louisiana
Ohio
Oregon
New York
Tennessee
Texas
Washington *(No. 1!)*

MANUFACTURING NATIONS

Leading ten countries
Canada
East Germany
France
Great Britain
Italy
Japan
Poland
United States *(No. 1!)*
USSR
West Germany

Leading states
California
Illinois
Indiana
New Jersey
New York *(No. 1!)*
Ohio
Pennsylvania
Texas

Top U.S. product lines in order of size
Transportation equipment
Machinery
Food products
Electrical machinery
Chemicals

Primary metals
Metal products
Printing and publishing
Clothing
Paper and allied products

FISHING INDUSTRY

Leading countries
- China
- India
- Japan
- Norway
- Peru *(No. 1!)*
- South Africa
- Spain
- Thailand
- United States
- USSR

FOSSIL FUELS
A Nonrenewable Energy Source

Countries mining the most *coal*
- Australia
- China
- Czechoslovakia
- East Germany
- Great Britain
- India
- Poland
- USSR *(No. 1!)*
- United States
- West Germany

States mining the most *coal*
- Alabama
- Colorado
- Illinois
- Indiana
- Kentucky
- Ohio
- Pennsylvania
- Tennessee
- Virginia
- West Virginia *(No. 1!)*

Countries producing the most *petroleum*
- Algeria
- Canada
- Iran
- Iraq
- Kuwait
- Libya
- Saudi Arabia
- United States *(No. 1!)*
- USSR
- Venezuela

States producing the most *petroleum*
- Alaska
- California
- Kansas
- Louisiana
- New Mexico
- Oklahoma
- Texas *(No. 1!)*
- Wyoming

Countries producing the most *natural gas*
- Canada
- Iran
- Italy
- Mexico
- Netherlands
- Rumania
- United States *(No. 1!)*
- USSR
- West Germany

States producing the most *natural gas*
- California
- Kansas
- Louisiana
- New Mexico
- Oklahoma
- Texas *(No. 1!)*
- Wyoming

NUCLEAR FUEL
A Nonrenewable Energy Source

Countries producing the most *uranium*
- Australia
- Canada
- France
- Gabon
- Portugal
- South Africa
- United States *(No. 1!)*

States producing the most *uranium*
- Colorado
- New Mexico *(No. 1!)*
- Utah
- Wyoming

WATER POWER
A Renewable Energy Source

Areas *with* adequate rain
- Southeast Asia
- Much of China
- Most of Europe
- India
- Eastern United States
- Northwestern USSR

Areas *without* adequate rain
- Most of North Africa
- Most of Asia
- Central Australia
- Middle East

Earth has enough water: 326 million cubic miles, or 1,000,000,000,000 gallons (one trillion gallons). Ninety-seven percent of the water is salty, 2 percent is fresh, but in glaciers and icecaps. One percent is in rain, snow, rivers, lakes — mostly fresh.

Hydroelectricity is electricity (energy) made by using the force of moving water. One of the most spectacular evidences of water's power is a waterfall. To harness this power, dams are built near waterfalls, rivers, and lakes.

Waterfalls — The World's Ten Largest

Angel	979 m./3,212 ft.	Venezuela
Kukenaan	610 m./2,000 ft.	Venezuela
Ribbon	491 m./1,612 ft.	California
King George VI	488 m./1,600 ft.	Guyana
Yosemite	436 m./1,430 ft.	California
Gavarnie	422 m./1,385 ft.	France
Tugela	411 m./1,350 ft.	South Africa
Krimml	381 m./1,250 ft.	Austria
Takakkaw	380 m./1,248 ft.	British Columbia, Canada
Silver Strand	357 m./1,170 ft.	California

Dams — The World's Ten Greatest

Highest	*Height*
Nurek, USSR	305 m./1,017 ft.
Grand Dixence, Switzerland	280 m./932 ft.
Inquri, USSR	268 m./892 ft.
Vaiont, Italy	266 m./888 ft.
Mica, Canada	240 m./800 ft.

Largest Volume

Tarbela — Pakistan
120,840 cu.ms./159,000,000 cu. yds.
Fort Peck—Fort Peck, United States
95,456 cu.ms./125,600,000 cu. yds.
Oahe — Oahe, United States
69,920 cu. ms/92,000,000 cu. yds.
Gardiner — Gardiner, Canada
65,161 cu. ms./85,739,000 cu. yds.
Mangla — Mangla, Pakistan
64,220 cu. ms./84,500,000 cu. yd.

The *widest* dam in the world, Fort Peck, stretches four miles across the Missouri River in northeastern Montana.

OTHER EARTHLY DIMENSIONS

Continents	Area	% of world's land
Asia	43,976,000 sq. km./ 16,979,000 sq. mi.	29.7
Africa	30,320,000 sq. km./ 11,707,000 sq. mi.	20.0
North America	24,399,000 sq. km./ 9,420,000 sq. mi.	16.3
South America	17,830,000 sq. km./ 6,884,000 sq. mi.	12.0
Antarctica	13,209,000 sq. km./ 5,100,000 sq. mi.	9.6
Europe	10,523,000 sq. km./ 4,063,000 sq. mi.	7.0
Australia	7,687,000 sq. km./ 2,968,000 sq. mi.	5.1

Oceans	Area	% of world's water
Pacific	166,884,000 sq. km./ 64,186,000 sq. mi.	46.0
Atlantic	82,841,000 sq. km./ 31,862,000 sq. mi.	22.9
Indian	73,710,000 sq. km./ 28,350,000 sq. mi.	20.3
Arctic	14,110,000 sq. km./ 5,427,000 sq. mi.	3.9

Largest Seas	Area
South China Sea	3,380,000 sq. km./1,300,000 sq. mi.
Caribbean Sea	2,764,000 sq. km./1,063,000 sq. mi.
Mediterranean Sea	2,514,000 sq. km./967,000 sq. mi.
Bering Sea	2,278,000 sq. km./876,000 sq. mi.
Sea of Okhotsk	1,534,000 sq. km./590,000 sq. mi.

Longest rivers	Length	Location
Nile	6,738 km./4,187 mi.	Africa
Amazon	6,437 km./4,000 mi.	South America
Mississippi–Missouri	5,971 km./3,710 mi.	North America
Yangtze	5,527 km./3,424 mi.	Asia
Ob'-Irtysh	5,411 km./3,362 mi.	Asia

Largest Natural Lakes	Area
Caspian Sea	373,438 sq. km./144,000 sq. mi.
Lake Superior	82,420 sq. km./31,700 sq. mi.
Lake Victoria	69,488 sq. km./28,828 sq. mi.
Aral Sea	66,716 sq. km./25,660 sq. mi.
Lake Huron	59,930 sq. km./23,050 sq. mi.

Largest Deserts	Area	Location
Sahara	9,100,000 sq. km./ 3,500,000 sq. mi.	Africa
Gobi	1,300,000 sq. km./ 500,000 sq. mi.	Asia
Great Victoria	650,000 sq. km./ 250,000 sq. mi.	Australia
Rub' al Khali	611,000 sq. km./ 235,000 sq. mi.	Asia
Kalahari	585,000 sq. km./ 225,000 sq. mi.	Africa

Highest peaks of each continent	Size	Location
Mount Everest	8,848 m./29,028 ft.	Asia
Mount Aconcagua	6,960 m./22,834 ft.	South America
Mount McKinley	6,194 m./20,320 ft.	North America
Mount Kilimanjaro	5,895 m./19,340 ft.	Africa
Mount Elbrus	5,633 m./18,481 ft.	Europe
Vinson Massif	5,140 m./16,864 ft.	Antarctica
Mount Kosciusko	2,228 m./ 7,316 ft.	Australia

Largest Islands	Area
Greenland	2,175,600 sq. km./840,000 sq. mi.
New Guinea	789,950 sq. km./305,000 sq. mi.
Borneo	751,100 sq. km./290,000 sq. mi.
Madagascar	569,800 sq. km./220,000 sq. mi.
Baffin	507,454 sq. km./195,928 sq. mi.
Sumatra	424,760 sq. km./164,000 sq. mi.
New Zealand	268,676 sq. km./103,736 sq. mi.
Great Britain	229,899 sq. km./88,764 sq. mi.
Honshu	227,920 sq. km./88,000 sq. mi.
Victoria	217,291 sq. km./83,896 sq. mi.

Largest countries by geographical area

USSR	22,402,000 sq. km./8,649,500 sq. mi.
Canada	9,976,200 sq. km./3,851,800 sq. mi.
China	9,561,000 sq. km./3,691,523 sq. mi.
United States	9,371,781 sq. km./3,618,465 sq. mi.
Brazil	8,511,965 sq. km./3,286,488 sq. mi.
Australia	7,686,848 sq. km./2,967,909 sq. mi.
India	3,287,590 sq. km./1,269,346 sq. mi.
Argentina	2,776,889 sq. km./1,072,163 sq. mi.
Sudan	2,505,813 sq. km./967,500 sq. mi.
Algeria	2,381,741 sq. km./919,595 sq. mi.

Smallest countries of the world

	Area		
	sq. km.	sq. mi.	Population
Vatican City	0.44	0.17	1,000
Monaco	1.49	0.58	27,000
Macao	16	6.2	300,000
Nauru	21	8	9,000
San Marino	61	24	21,000
Liechtenstein	157	61	27,000
Seychelles	280	108	63,000
Maldives	298	115	145,000
Malta	316	122	331,000
Grenada	344	133	98,000
Mayotte	374	144	40,000

NUMBERS OF PEOPLE

Most populous countries*

China	869,424,000
India	649,940,000
USSR	266,403,000
United States	220,806,000
Indonesia	152,582,000
Brazil	120,593,000
Japan	116,375,000
Bangladesh	84,459,000
Pakistan	79,078,000
Mexico	69,018,000

Most populous cities

Shanghai	10,000,000
Tokyo	8,646,000
Mexico City	8,591,000
Cairo	8,500,000
Moscow	8,011,000
Peking	7,570,000
Seoul	7,500,000
New York	7,312,000
London	7,028,000
Bombay	5,970,000

Most populous urban areas

New York	16,485,000
Mexico City	11,943,000
Tokyo	11,683,000
Shanghai	10,820,000
Los Angeles	10,605,000
Paris	9,863,000
Buenos Aires	8,435,000
Moscow	8,011,000
Chicago	7,661,000

* Populations are estimates based on the latest figures (1979) from official government and United Nations sources.

Seven Wonders of the Ancient World

The Pyramids of Egypt

The Hanging Gardens of Babylon

The Temple of Artemis at Ephesus

The Statue of Zeus at Olympia

The Mausoleum of Halicarnassus

The Colossus of Rhodes

The Lighthouse of Alexandria

Seven Natural Wonders of the World

Mount Everest, Asia

Victoria Falls, Africa

Grand Canyon, North America

Great Barrier Reef, Australia

Prehistoric Cave Paintings, Altamira, Spain

Paricutin, a young volcano, Mexico

Harbor at Rió de Janeiro, Brazil

Seven Wonders of the Modern World

Suez Canal — Egypt

Dneproges Dam — Dneiper River, USSR

Atomic Energy Research Establishment — Harwell, England

Alcan Highway — Alaska/Canada/United States

Golden Gate Bridge — San Francisco, United States

Eiffel Tower — Paris, France

Sears Tower — Chicago, United States

Map Facts

		Page
AFGHANISTAN		62
Area:	649,497 sq. km. (250,000 sq. mi.)	
Population:	21,199,000	
Capital city:	Kabul	
ALABAMA		108
Area:	133,667 sq. km. (51,609 sq. mi.)	
Population:	3,742,000	
Capital city:	Montgomery	
ALASKA		102
Area:	1,518,807 sq. km. (586,412 sq. mi.)	
Population:	403,000	
Capital city:	Juneau	
ALBANIA		48
Area:	28,748 sq. km. (11,100 sq. mi.)	
Population:	2,794,000	
Capital city:	Tirane	
ALBERTA		98
Area:	661,188 sq. km. (255,284 sq. mi.)	
Population:	1,838,037	
Capital city:	Edmonton	
ALGERIA		76
Area:	2,381,741 sq. km. (919,595 sq. mi.)	
Population:	19,029,000	
Capital city:	Algiers	
ANDORRA		40
Area:	453 sq. km. (175 sq. mi.)	
Population:	36,000	
Capital city:	Andorra la Vella	
ANGOLA		82
Area:	1,246,700 sq. km. (481,354 sq. mi.)	
Population:	7,819,000	
Capital city:	Luanda	
ANTIGUA AND BARBUDA		122
Area:	440 sq. km. (177 sq. mi.)	
Population:	72,000	
Capital city:	St. John's	
ARGENTINA		134
Area:	2,776,889 sq. km. (1,072,163 sq. mi.)	
Population:	23,983,000	
Capital city:	Buenos Aires	
ARIZONA		116
Area:	295,023 sq. km. (113,909 sq. mi.)	
Population:	2,354,000	
Capital city:	Phoenix	
ARKANSAS		112
Area:	137,539 sq. km. (53,104 sq. mi.)	
Population:	2,186,000	
Capital city:	Little Rock	
AUSTRALIA		84
Area:	7,686,848 sq. km. (2,967,909 sq. mi.)	
Population:	14,336,000	
Capital city:	Canberra	

		Page
AUSTRIA		46
Area:	83,849 sq. km. (32,374 sq. mi.)	
Population:	7,614,000	
Capital city:	Vienna	
BAHAMAS		122
Area:	13,935 sq. km. (5,380 sq. mi.)	
Population:	235,000	
Capital city:	Nassau	
BAHRAIN		60
Area:	622 sq. km. (240 sq. mi.)	
Population:	294,000	
Capital city:	Manama	
BANGLADESH		62
Area:	143,998 sq. km. (55,598 sq. mi.)	
Population:	84,459,000	
Capital city:	Dacca	
BARBADOS		122
Area:	431 sq. km. (166 sq. mi.)	
Population:	251,000	
Capital city:	Bridgetown	
BELGIUM		34
Area:	30,514 sq. km. (11,781 sq. mi.)	
Population:	9,914,000	
Capital city:	Brussels	
BELIZE		120
Area:	22,965 sq. km. (8,867 sq. mi.)	
Population:	158,000	
Capital city:	Belmopan	
BENIN		76
Area:	112,622 sq. km. (43,484 sq. mi.)	
Population:	3,462,000	
Capital city:	Porto-Novo	
BERMUDA		94
Area:	53 sq. km. (21 sq. mi.)	
Population:	60,000	
Capital city:	Hamilton	
BHUTAN		62
Area:	47,000 sq. km. (18,147 sq. mi.)	
Population:	1,275,000	
Capital city:	Thimphu	
BOLIVIA		132
Area:	1,098,581 sq. km. (424,165 sq. mi.)	
Population:	6,268,000	
Capital city:	Sucre (judicial) La Paz (administrative)	
BOTSWANA		82
Area:	600,372 sq. km. (231,805 sq. mi.)	
Population:	796,000	
Capital city:	Gaborone	
BRAZIL		132
Area:	8,511,965 sq. km. (3,286,488 sq. mi.)	
Population:	90,840,000	
Capital city:	Brasília	
BRITISH COLUMBIA		98
Area:	948,601 sq. km. (366,255 sq. mi.)	
Population:	2,466,608	
Capital city:	Victoria	

Page

BRUNEI — 68
Area: 5,765 sq. km. (2,226 sq. mi.)
Population: 162,000
Capital city: Bandar Seri Begawan

BULGARIA — 48
Area: 110,912 sq. km. (42,823 sq. mi.)
Population: 8,941,000
Capital city: Sofia

BURMA — 70
Area: 676,552 sq. km. (261,218 sq. mi.)
Population: 34,483,000
Capital city: Rangoon

BURUNDI — 80
Area: 27,834 sq. km. (10,747 sq. mi.)
Population: 4,150,000
Capital city: Bujumbura

CALIFORNIA — 116
Area: 411,013 sq. km. (158,693 sq. mi.)
Population: 22,294,000
Capital city: Sacramento

CAMEROON — 80
Area: 475,442 sq. km. (183,569 sq. mi.)
Population: 6,898,000
Capital city: Yaounde

CANADA — 98
Area: 9,976,200 sq. km. (3,851,800 sq. mi.)
Population: 23,901,000
Capital city: Ottawa

CAPE VERDE — 72
Area: 4,033 sq. km. (1,557 sq. mi.)
Population: 317,000
Capital city: Praia

CENTRAL AFRICAN REPUBLIC — 80
Area: 622,984 sq. km. (240,535 sq. mi.)
Population: 1,800,000
Capital city: Bangui

CHAD — 78
Area: 1,284,000 sq. km. (495,755 sq. mi.)
Population: 4,379,000
Capital city: N'djamena

CHILE — 134
Area: 756,945 sq. km. (292,258 sq. mi.)
Population: 11,011,000
Capital city: Santiago

CHINA (mainland) — 64
Area: 9,561,000 sq. km. (3,691,523 sq. mi.)
Population: 869,424,000
Capital city: Peking

CHINA (Taiwan) — 64
Area: 35,961 sq. km.(13,885 sq. mi.)
Population: 17,350,000
Capital city: Taipei

COLOMBIA — 128
Area: 1,138,914 sq km. (439,737 sq. mi.)
Population: 26,289,000
Capital city: Bogotá

Page

COLORADO — 116
Area: 269,998 sq. km. (104,247 sq. mi.)
Population: 2,670,000
Capital city: Denver

COMOROS — 72
Area: 2,171 sq. km. (838 sq. mi.)
Population: 338,000
Capital city: Moroni

CONGO — 80
Area: 342,000 sq. km. (132,047 sq. mi.)
Population: 1,485,000
Capital city: Brazzaville

CONNECTICUT — 104
Area: 12,973 sq. km. (5,009 sq. mi.)
Population: 3,099,000
Capital city: Hartford

COSTA RICA — 120
Area: 50,700 sq. km. (19,575 sq. mi.)
Population: 2,181,000
Capital city: San José

CUBA — 122
Area: 114,524 sq. km. (44,218 sq. mi.)
Population: 10,020,000
Capital city: Havana

CYPRUS — 60
Area: 9,251 sq. km. (3,572 sq. mi.)
Population: 660,000
Capital city: Nicosia

CZECHOSLOVAKIA — 46
Area: 127,869 sq. km. (49,371 sq. mi.)
Population: 15,161,000
Capital city: Prague

DELAWARE — 106
Area: 5,328 sq. km. (2,057 sq. mi.)
Population: 583,000
Capital city: Dover

DENMARK — 32
Area: 43,070 sq. km. (16,629 sq. mi.)
Population: 5,161,000
Capital city: Copenhagen

DJIBOUTI — 78
Area: 22,000 sq. km. (8,494 sq. mi.)
Population: 116,000
Capital city: Djibouti

DOMINICA — 122
Area: 751 sq. km. (290 sq. mi.)
Population: 70,302
Capital city: Roseau

DOMINICAN REPUBLIC — 122
Area: 48,734 sq. km. (18,816 sq. mi.)
Population: 5,287,000
Capital city: Santo Domingo

ECUADOR — 130
Area: 283,561 sq. km. (109,484 sq. mi.)
Population: 7,846,000
Capital city: Quito

Page

EGYPT 78
Area: 1,001,449 sq. km. (386,662 sq. mi.)
Population: 40,619,000
Capital city: Cairo

EL SALVADOR 120
Area: 21,041 sq. km. (8,124 sq. mi.)
Population: 4,510,000
Capital city: San Salvador

ENGLAND 30
Area: 130,837 sq. km. (50,516 sq. mi.)
Population: 46,417,600
Capital city: London

EQUATORIAL GUINEA 80
Area: 28,051 sq. km. (10,830 sq. mi.)
Population: 326,000
Capital city: Malabo

ESTONIAN SSR 52
Area: 45,274 sq. km. (17,413 sq. mi.)
Population: 1,356,100
Capitai city: Tallinn

ETHIOPIA 78
Area: 1,221,900 sq. km. (471,778 sq. mi.)
Population: 30,968,000
Capital city: Addis Ababa

FIJI 88
Area: 18,272 sq. km. (7,055 sq. mi.)
Population: 627,000
Capital city: Suva

FINLAND 32
Area: 337,009 sq. km. (130,120 sq. mi.)
Population: 4,783,000
Capital city: Helsinki

FLORIDA 108
Area: 151,670 sq. km. (58,560 sq. mi.)
Population: 8,594,000
Capital city: Tallahassee

FRANCE 38
Area: 547,026 sq. km. (211,208 sq. mi.)
Population: 54,040,000
Capital city: Paris

FRENCH GUIANA 128
Area: 91,000 sq. km. (35,135 sq. mi.)
Population: 67,000
Capital city: Cayenne

FRENCH POLYNESIA 88
Area: 4,000 sq. km. (1,544 sq. mi.)
Population: 142,000
Capital city: Papeete

GABON 80
Area: 267,667 sq. km. (103,347 sq. mi.)
Population: 1,039,000
Capital city: Libreville

GAMBIA 76
Area: 11,295 sq. km. (4,361 sq. mi.)
Population: 578,000
Capital city: Banjul

Page

GEORGIA 108
Area: 152,488 sq. km. (58,876 sq. mi.)
Population: 5,084,000
Capital city: Atlanta

GERMANY, EAST 36
Area: 108,178 sq. km. (41,768 sq. mi.)
Population: 16,716,000
Capital city: East Berlin

GERMANY, WEST 36
Area: 248,468 sq. km. (95,934 sq. mi.)
Population: 62,827,000
Capital city: Bonn

GHANA 76
Area: 238,537 sq. km. (92,100 sq. mi.)
Population: 10,975,000
Capital city: Accra

GIBRALTAR 40
Area: 6 sq. km. (2.3 sq. mi.)
Population: 33,000
Capital city: Gibraltar

GREECE 48
Area: 131,944 sq. km. (50,944 sq. mi.)
Population: 9,302,000
Capital city: Athens

GREENLAND 92
Area: 2,175,600 sq. km. (840,000 sq. mi.)
Population: 61,000
Capital city: Godthaab

GRENADA 122
Area: 344 sq. km. (133 sq. mi.)
Population: 98,000
Capital city: St. George's

GUAM 88
Area: 549 sq. km. (212 sq. mi.)
Population: 107,000
Capital city: Agana

GUATEMALA 120
Area: 108,889 sq. km. (42,042 sq. mi.)
Population: 6,820,000
Capital city: Guatemala City

GUINEA 76
Area: 245,857 sq. km. (94,926 sq. mi.)
Population: 4,855,000
Capital city: Conakry

GUINEA-BISSAU 76
Area: 36,125 sq. km. (13,938 sq. mi.)
Population: 557,000
Capital city: Bissau

GUYANA 128
Area: 214,970 sq. km. (83,000 sq. mi.)
Population: 863,000
Capital city: Georgetown

HAITI 122
Area: 27,750 sq. km. (10,714 sq. mi.)
Population: 4,884,000
Capital city: Port-au-Prince

Page

HAWAII 102
Area: 16,705 sq. km. (6,450 sq. mi.)
Population: 897,000
Capital city: Honolulu

HONDURAS 120
Area: 112,088 sq. km. (43,277 sq. mi.)
Population: 3,539,000
Capital city: Tegucigalpa

HONG KONG 64
Area: 2,916 sq. km. (1,126 sq. mi.)
Population: 4,400,000
Capital city: Victoria

HUNGARY 46
Area: 93,030 sq. km. (35,919 sq. mi.)
Population: 10,710,000
Capital city: Budapest

ICELAND 32
Area: 103,000 sq. km. (39,769 sq. mi.)
Population: 221,000
Capital city: Reykjavik

IDAHO 114
Area: 216,412 sq. km. (83,557 sq. mi.)
Population: 878,000
Capital city: Boise

ILLINOIS 110
Area: 146,075 sq. km. (56,400 sq. mi.)
Population: 11,243,000
Capital city: Springfield

INDIA 62
Area: 3,287,590 sq. km. (1,269,346 sq. mi.)
Population: 649,940,000
Capital city: New Delhi

INDIANA 110
Area: 93,993 sq. km. (36,291 sq. mi.)
Population: 5,374,000
Capital city: Indianapolis

INDONESIA 68
Area: 1,919,270 sq. km. (741,034 sq. mi.)
Population: 152,582,000
Capital city: Djakarta

IOWA 110
Area: 145,790 sq. km. (56,290 sq. mi.)
Population: 2,896,000
Capital city: Des Moines

IRAN 60
Area: 1,648,000 sq. km. (636,296 sq. mi.)
Population: 37,019,000
Capital city: Tehran

IRAQ 60
Area: 434,924 sq. km. (167,925 sq. mi.)
Population: 12,667,000
Capital city: Baghdad

IRELAND 30
Area: 70,283 sq. km. (27,136 sq. mi.)
Population: 3,280,000
Capital city: Dublin

Page

ISRAEL 60
Area: 20,770 sq. km. (8,019 sq. mi.)
Population: 3,809,000
Capital city: Jerusalem

ITALY 42
Area: 301,253 sq. km. (116,314 sq. mi.)
Population: 57,618,000
Capital city: Rome

IVORY COAST 76
Area: 322,463 sq. km. (124,504 sq. mi.)
Population: 7,897,000
Capital city: Abidjan

JAMAICA 122
Area: 10,991 sq. km. (4,244 sq. mi.)
Population: 2,171,000
Capital city: Kingston

JAPAN 66
Area: 377,389 sq. km. (145,711 sq. mi.)
Population: 116,375,000
Capital city: Tokyo

JORDAN 60
Area: 97,740 sq. km. (37,738 sq. mi.)
Population: 3,077,000
Capital city: Amman

KAMPUCHEA (CAMBODIA) 70
Area: 181,035 sq. km. (69,898 sq. mi.)
Population: 9,057,000
Capital city: Phnom Penh

KANSAS 110
Area: 213,063 sq. km. (82,264 sq. mi.)
Population: 2,348,000
Capital city: Topeka

KENTUCKY 108
Area: 104,623 sq. km. (40,395 sq. mi.)
Population: 3,498,000
Capital city: Frankfort

KENYA 80
Area: 582,646 sq. km. (224,961 sq. mi.)
Population: 15,366,000
Capital city: Nairobi

KOREA, NORTH 66
Area: 120,538 sq. km. (46,540 sq. mi.)
Population: 17,635,000
Capital city: Pyongyang

KOREA, SOUTH 66
Area: 98,484 sq. km. (38,025 sq. mi.)
Population: 37,547,000
Capital city: Seoul

KUWAIT 60
Area: 20,118 sq. km. (7,768 sq. mi.)
Population: 1,257,000
Capital city: Al-Kuwait

LAOS 70
Area: 236,800 sq. km. (91,429 sq. mi.)
Population: 3,603,000
Capital city: Vientiane

		Page
LATVIAN SSR		52
Area:	63,947 sq. km. (24,595 sq. mi.)	
Population:	2,364,100	
Capital city:	Riga	
LEBANON		60
Area:	10,398 sq. km. (4,105 sq. mi.)	
Population:	3,649,000	
Capital city:	Beirut	
LESOTHO		82
Area:	30,355 sq. km. (11,720 sq. mi.)	
Population:	1,133,000	
Capital city:	Maseru	
LIBERIA		76
Area:	111,369 sq. km. (43,000 sq. mi.)	
Population:	1,871,000	
Capital city:	Monrovia	
LIBYA		78
Area:	1,759,540 sq. km. (679,362 sq. mi.)	
Population:	2,881,000	
Capital city:	Tripoli	
LIECHTENSTEIN		44
Area:	157 sq. km. (61 sq. mi.)	
Population:	27,000	
Capital city:	Vaduz	
LITHUANIAN SSR		52
Area:	65,452 sq. km. (25,174 sq. mi.)	
Population:	3,128,000	
Capital city:	Vilna	
LOUISIANA		112
Area:	125,674 sq. km. (48,523 sq. mi.)	
Population:	3,966,000	
Capital city:	Baton Rouge	
LUXEMBOURG		34
Area:	2,586 sq. km. (998 sq. mi.)	
Population:	371,000	
Capital city:	Luxembourg	
MACAO		64
Area:	16 sq. km. (6.2 sq. mi.)	
Population:	286,000	
Capital city:	Macao	
MADAGASCAR		82
Area:	587,041 sq. km. (226,658 sq. mi.)	
Population:	8,138,000	
Capital city:	Antananarivo	
MAINE		104
Area:	86,026 sq. km. (33,215 sq. mi.)	
Population:	1,091,000	
Capital city:	Augusta	
MALAWI		82
Area:	118,484 sq. km. (45,747 sq. mi.)	
Population:	5,589,000	
Capital city:	Lilongwe	
MALAYSIA		70
Area:	329,749 sq. km. (127,316 sq. mi.)	
Population:	13,664,000	
Capital city:	Kuala Lumpur	

		Page
MALDIVES		62
Area:	298 sq. km. (115 sq. mi.)	
Population:	145,000	
Capital city:	Malé	
MALI		76
Area:	1,240,000 sq. km. (478,767 sq. mi.)	
Population:	6,288,000	
Capital city:	Bamako	
MALTA		42
Area:	316 sq. km. (122 sq. mi.)	
Population:	331,000	
Capital city:	Valletta	
MANITOBA		98
Area:	650,090 sq. km. (251,000 sq. mi.)	
Population:	1,021,506	
Capital city:	Winnipeg	
MARYLAND		106
Area:	27,394 sq. km. (10,577 sq. mi.)	
Population:	4,143,000	
Capital city:	Annapolis	
MASSACHUSETTS		104
Area:	21,385 sq. km. (8,257 sq. mi.)	
Population:	5,774,000	
Capital city:	Boston	
MAURITANIA		76
Area:	1,030,700 sq. km. (397,956 sq. mi.)	
Population:	1,461,000	
Capital city:	Nouakchott	
MAURITIUS		56
Area:	2,045 sq. km. (790 sq. mi.)	
Population:	954,000	
Capital city:	Port Louis	
MEXICO		118
Area:	1,972,547 sq. km. (761,605 sq. mi.)	
Population:	69,018,000	
Capital city:	Mexico City	
MICHIGAN		110
Area:	150,779 sq. km. (58,216 sq. mi.)	
Population:	9,189,000	
Capital city:	Lansing	
MINNESOTA		110
Area:	217,735 sq. km. (84,068 sq. mi.)	
Population:	4,008,000	
Capital city:	St. Paul	
MISSISSIPPI		108
Area:	123,584 sq. km. (47,716 sq. mi.)	
Population:	2,404,000	
Capital city:	Jackson	
MISSOURI		110
Area:	180,486 sq. km. (69,686 sq. mi.)	
Population:	4,860,000	
Capital city:	Jefferson City	
MONACO		38
Area:	1.49 sq. km. (0.58 sq. mi.)	
Population:	27,000	
Capital city:	Monaco	

		Page
MONGOLIA		64
Area:	1,565,000 sq. km. (604,250 sq. mi.)	
Population:	1,500,000	
Capital city:	Ulan Bator	
MONTANA		114
Area:	381,086 sq. km. (147,138 sq. mi.)	
Population:	785,000	
Capital city:	Helena	
MOROCCO		76
Area: *	712,000 sq. km. (275,117 sq. mi.)	
Population: *	19,635	
Capital city:	Rabat	
	*Includes Western Sahara	
MOZAMBIQUE		82
Area:	783,030 sq. km. (302,330 sq. mi.)	
Population:	10,119,000	
Capital city:	Maputo	
NAMIBIA (SOUTH WEST AFRICA)		82
Area:	823,172 sq. km. (317,827 sq. mi.)	
Population:	883,000	
Capital city:	Windhoek	
NAURU		88
Area:	21 sq. km. (8 sq. mi.)	
Population:	9,000	
Capital city:	Yaren	
NEBRASKA		110
Area:	200,017 sq. km. (77,227 sq. mi.)	
Population:	1,565,000	
Capital city:	Lincoln	
NEPAL		62
Area:	140,797 sq. km. (54,362 sq. mi.)	
Population:	12,900,000	
Capital city:	Katmandu	
NETHERLANDS		34
Area:	41,160 sq. km. (15,892 sq. mi.)	
Population:	14,151,000	
Capital city:	The Hague, Amsterdam	
NEVADA		116
Area:	286,297 sq. km. (110,540 sq. mi.)	
Population:	660,000	
Capital city:	Carson City	
NEW BRUNSWICK		98
Area:	73,437 sq. km. (28,354 sq. mi.)	
Population:	677,250	
Capital city:	Fredericton	
NEWFOUNDLAND		98
Area:	404,520 sq. km. (156,185 sq. mi.)	
Population:	557,725	
Capital city:	St. John's	
NEW HAMPSHIRE		104
Area:	24,097 sq. km. (9,304 sq. mi.)	
Population:	871,000	
Capital city:	Concord	
NEW JERSEY		106
Area:	20,295 sq. km. (7,836 sq. mi.)	
Population:	7,327,000	
Capital city:	Trenton	

		Page
NEW MEXICO		116
Area:	315,115 sq. km. (121,666 sq. mi.)	
Population:	1,212,000	
Capital city:	Santa Fe	
NEW YORK		106
Area:	128,401 sq. km. (49,576 sq. mi.)	
Population:	17,748,000	
Capital city:	Albany	
NEW ZEALAND		84
Area:	268,704 sq. km. (103,747 sq. mi.)	
Population:	3,328,704	
Capital city:	Wellington	
NICARAGUA		120
Area:	130,000 sq. km. (50,193, sq. mi.)	
Population:	2,454,000	
Capital city:	Managua	
NIGER		76
Area:	1,267,000 sq. km. (489,191 sq. mi.)	
Population:	5,117,000	
Capital city:	Niamey	
NIGERIA		76
Area:	923,768 sq. km. (356,669 sq. mi.)	
Population:	69,667,000	
Capital city:	Lagos	
NORTH CAROLINA		108
Area:	136,197 sq. km. (52,586 sq. mi.)	
Population:	5,577,000	
Capital city:	Raleigh	
NORTH DAKOTA		110
Area:	183,021 sq. km. (70,665 sq. mi.)	
Population:	652,000	
Capital city:	Bismarck	
NORTHERN IRELAND		30
Area:	14,122 sq. km. (5,452 sq. mi.)	
Population:	1,537,200	
Capital city:	Belfast	
NORTHWEST TERRITORIES		98
Area:	3,379,700 sq. km. (1,304,903 sq. mi.)	
Population:	42,609	
Capital city:	Yellowknife	
NORWAY		32
Area:	324,219 sq. km. (125,182 sq. mi.)	
Population:	4,027,000	
Capital city:	Oslo	
NOVA SCOTIA		98
Area:	55,490 sq. km. (21,425 sq. mi.)	
Population:	828,571	
Capital city:	Halifax	
OHIO		110
Area:	106,764 sq. km. (41,222 sq. mi.)	
Population:	10,749,000	
Capital city:	Columbus	
OKLAHOMA		112
Area:	181,090 sq. km. (69,919 sq. mi.)	
Population:	2,880,000	
Capital city:	Oklahoma City	

Page

OMAN — 60
Area: 212,457 sq. km. (82,030 sq. mi.)
Population: 865,000
Capital city: Muscat

ONTARIO — 98
Area: 1,068,587 sq. km. (412,582 sq. mi.)
Population: 8,264,465
Capital city: Toronto

OREGON — 114
Area: 251,180 sq. km. (96,981 sq. mi.)
Population: 2,444,000
Capital city: Salem

PACIFIC ISLANDS, TRUST TERRITORY OF THE — 88
Area: 1,857 sq. km. (717 sq. mi.)
Population: 127,000
Capital city: Kolonia (administrative)

PAKISTAN — 62
Area: 803,943 sq. km. (310,404 sq. mi.)
Population: 79,078,000
Capital city: Islamabad

PANAMA — 120
Area: 75,650 sq. km. (29,209 sq. mi.)
Population: 1,885,000
Capital city: Panama City

PAPUA NEW GUINEA — 68
Area: 461,691 sq. km. (178,260 sq. mi.)
Population: 2,983,000
Capital city: Port Moresby

PARAGUAY — 134
Area: 406,752 sq. km. (157,048 sq. mi.)
Population: 2,784,000
Capital city: Asunción

PENNSYLVANIA — 106
Area: 117,412 sq. km. (45,333 sq. mi.)
Population: 11,750,000
Capital city: Harrisburg

PERU — 130
Area: 1,285,216 sq. km. (496,225 sq. mi.)
Population: 17,896,000
Capital city: Lima

PHILIPPINES — 68
Area: 300,000 sq. km. (115,831 sq. mi.)
Population: 47,663,000
Capital city: Manila

POLAND — 50
Area: 312,677 sq. km. (120,725 sq. mi.)
Population: 35,261,000
Capital city: Warsaw

PORTUGAL — 40
Area: 91,082 sq. km. (35,553 sq. mi.)
Population: 8,832,000
Capital city: Lisbon

PRINCE EDWARD ISLAND — 98
Area: 5,657 sq. km. (2,184 sq. mi.)
Population: 118,229
Capital city: Charlottetown

Page

PUERTO RICO — 122
Area: 8,897 sq. km. (3,435 sq. mi.)
Population: 3,421,000
Capital city: San Juan

QATAR — 60
Area: 11,000 sq. km. (4,247 sq. mi.)
Population: 104,000
Capital city: Doha

QUÉBEC — 98
Area: 1,540,690 sq. km. (594,860 sq. mi.)
Population: 6,234,445
Capital city: Québec

RHODE ISLAND — 104
Area: 3,144 sq. km. (1,214 sq. mi.)
Population: 935,000
Capital city: Providence

RUMANIA — 48
Area: 237,500 sq. km. (91,699 sq. mi.)
Population: 21,951,000
Capital city: Bucharest

RWANDA — 80
Area: 26,338 sq. km. (10,169 sq. mi.)
Population: 4,670,000
Capital city: Kigali

SAINT LUCIA — 122
Area: 616 sq. km. (238 sq. mi.)
Population: 101,100
Capital city: Castries

SAINT VINCENT AND THE GRENADINES — 123
Area: 389 sq. km. (150 sq. mi.)
Population: 167,646
Capital city: Kingstown

SÃO TOMÉ and PRÍNCIPE — 76
Area: 964 sq. km. (372 sq. mi.)
Population: 86,000
Capital city: São Tomé

SAN MARINO — 42
Area: 61 sq. km. (24 sq. mi.)
Population: 21,000
Capital city: San Marino

SASKATCHEWAN — 98
Area: 651,903 sq. km. (251,700 sq. mi.)
Population: 921,323
Capital city: Regina

SAUDI ARABIA — 60
Area: 2,153,090 sq. km. (831,313 sq. mi.)
Population: 7,200,000
Capital city: Riyadh
Mecca (religious capital)

SCOTLAND — 30
Area: 78,772 sq. km. (30,414 sq. mi.)
Population: 5,261,000
Capital city: Edinburgh

SENEGAL — 76
Area: 196,192 sq. km. (75,750 sq. mi.)
Population: 4,078,000
Capital city: Dakar

		Page
SEYCHELLES		**56**
Area:	280 sq. km. (108 sq. mi.)	
Population:	63,000	
Capital city:	Victoria	
SIERRA LEONE		**76**
Area:	71,740 sq. km. (27,699 sq. mi.)	
Population:	3,440,000	
Capital city:	Freetown	
SINGAPORE		**70**
Area:	581 sq. km. (224 sq. mi.)	
Population:	2,397,000	
Capital city:	Singapore	
SOLOMON ISLANDS		**88**
Area:	28,446 sq. km. (10,983 sq. mi.)	
Population:	209,000	
Capital city:	Honiara	
SOMALIA		**80**
Area:	637,657 sq. km. (246,201 sq. mi.)	
Population:	3,513,000	
Capital city:	Mogadishu	
SOUTH AFRICA		**82**
Area:	1,221,037 sq. km. (471,445 sq. mi.)	
Population:	28,115,000	
Capital city:	Pretoria (administrative) Cape Town (legislative)	
SOUTH CAROLINA		**108**
Area:	80,432 sq. km. (31,055 sq. mi.)	
Population:	2,918,000	
Capital city:	Columbia	
SOUTH DAKOTA		**110**
Area:	199,551 sq. km. (77,047 sq. mi.)	
Population:	690,000	
Capital city:	Pierre	
SPAIN		**40**
Area:	504,750 sq. km. (194,885 sq. mi.)	
Population:	37,210,000	
Capital city:	Madrid	
SRI LANKA		**62**
Area:	65,610 sq. km. (25,332 sq. mi.)	
Population:	15,258,000	
Capital city:	Colombo	
SUDAN		**78**
Area:	2,505,813 sq. km. (967,500 sq. mi.)	
Population:	19,600,000	
Capital city:	Khartoum	
SURINAME		**128**
Area:	163,265 sq. km. (63,037 sq. mi.)	
Population:	481,000	
Capital city:	Paramaribo	
SWAZILAND		**82**
Area:	17,363 sq. km. (6,704 sq. mi.)	
Population:	560,000	
Capital city:	Mbabane	
SWEDEN		**32**
Area:	449,964 sq. km. (173,732 sq. mi.)	
Population:	8,327,000	
Capital city:	Stockholm	

		Page
SWITZERLAND		**44**
Area:	41,288 sq. km. (15,941 sq. mi.)	
Population:	6,584,000	
Capital city:	Bern	
SYRIA		**60**
Area:	185,180 sq. km. (71,498 sq. mi.)	
Population:	8,375,000	
Capital city:	Damascus	
TANZANIA		**80**
Area:	954,087 sq. km. (364,000 sq. mi.)	
Population:	16,850,000	
Capital city:	Dar es Salaam	
TENNESSEE		**108**
Area:	109,414 sq. km. (42,244 sq. mi.)	
Population:	4,357,000	
Capital city:	Nashville	
TEXAS		**112**
Area:	692,402 sq. km. (267,339 sq. mi.)	
Population:	13,014,000	
Capital city:	Austin	
THAILAND		**70**
Area:	514,000 sq. km. (198,457 sq. mi.)	
Population:	47,768,000	
Capital city:	Bangkok	
TOGO		**76**
Area:	56,000 sq. km. (21,622 sq. mi.)	
Population:	2,453,000	
Capital city:	Lome	
TONGA		**88**
Area:	699 sq. km. (207 sq. mi.)	
Population:	115,000	
Capital city:	Nuku' alofa	
TRINIDAD and TOBAGO		**122**
Area:	5,128 sq. km. (1,980 sq. mi.)	
Population:	1,120,000	
Capital city:	Port-of-Spain	
TUNISIA		**76**
Area:	163,610 sq. km. (63,170 sq. mi.)	
Population:	6,346,000	
Capital city:	Tunis	
TURKEY		**60**
Area:	780,576 sq. km. (301,382 sq. mi.)	
Population:	44,100,000	
Capital city:	Ankara	
TUVALU		**88**
Area:	10 sq. km. (4 sq. mi.)	
Population:	5,887	
Capital city:	Funafuti	
UGANDA		**80**
Area:	236,036 sq. km. (91,134 sq. mi.)	
Population:	13,151,000	
Capital city:	Kampala	
UKRANIAN SSR		**52**
Area:	603,320 sq. km. (232,046 sq. mi.)	
Population:	47,126,517	
Capital city:	Kiev	

Page

UNION OF SOVIET SOCIALIST REPUBLICS 52
Area: 22,402,200 sq. km. (8,649,500 sq. mi.)
Population: 266,403,000
Capital city: Moscow

UNITED ARAB EMIRATES 60
Area: 83,600 sq. km. (32,278 sq. mi.)
Population: 252,000
Capital city: Abu Dhabi

UNITED KINGDOM 30
Area: 244,108 sq. km. (94,251 sq. mi.)
Population: 56,387,000
Capital city: London

UNITED STATES 102
Area: 9,371,781 sq. km. (3,618,465 sq. mi.)
Population: 220,806,000
Capital city: Washington, D.C.

UPPER VOLTA 76
Area: 274,200 sq. km. (105,869 sq. mi.)
Population: 6,729,000
Capital city: Ouagadougou

URUGUAY 134
Area: 177,508 sq. km. (68,536 sq. mi.)
Population: 2,820,000
Capital city: Montevideo

UTAH 116
Area: 219,931 sq. km. (84,916 sq. mi.)
Population: 1,307,000
Capital city: Salt Lake City

VANUATU 88
Area: 14,760 sq. km. (5,700 sq. mi.)
Population: 112,596
Capital city: Vila

VATICAN CITY STATE 42
Area: 0.44 sq. km. (0.17 sq. mi.)
Population: 1,000
Capital city: Vatican City

VENEZUELA 128
Area: 912,050 sq. km. (352,145 sq. mi.)
Population: 13,446,000
Capital city: Caracas

VERMONT 104
Area: 24,887 sq. km. (9,609 sq. mi.)
Population: 487,000
Capital city: Montpelier

VIETNAM 70
Area: 322,559 sq. km. (128,402 sq. mi.)
Population: 50,690,000
Capital city: Hanoi

VIRGINIA 108
Area: 105,716 sq. km. (40,817 sq. mi.)
Population: 5,148,000
Capital city: Richmond

VIRGIN ISLANDS 122
Area: 344 sq. km. (133 sq. mi.)
Population: 120,000
Capital city: Charlotte Amalie

Page

WALES 30
Area: 20,763 sq. km. (8,017 sq. mi.)
Population: 2,778,000
Largest city: Cardiff

WASHINGTON 114
Area: 176,616 sq. km. (68,192 sq. mi.)
Population: 3,744,000
Capital city: Olympia

WESTERN SAMOA 88
Area: 2,842 sq. km. (1,097 sq. mi.)
Population: 173,000
Capital city: Apia

WEST VIRGINIA 108
Area: 62,628 sq. km. (24,181 sq. mi.)
Population: 1,860,000
Capital city: Charleston

WHITE RUSSIAN SSR (BYELORUSSIAN SSR) 52
Area: 208,400 sq. km. (80,154 sq. mi.)
Population: 9,002,338
Capital city: Minsk

WISCONSIN 114
Area: 145,438 sq. km. (56,154 sq. mi.)
Population: 4,679,000
Capital city: Madison

WYOMING 110
Area: 253,596 sq. km. (97,914 sq. mi.)
Population: 424,000
Capital city: Cheyenne

YEMEN ARAB REPUBLIC 60
Area: 195,000 sq. km. (77,290 sq. mi.)
Population: 7,476,000
Capital city: San'a

YEMEN, PEOPLES DEMOCRATIC REPUBLIC OF 60
Area: 332,968 sq. km. (128,560 sq. mi.)
Population: 1,910,000
Capital city: Aden (national)
Madinat ash Shab (administrative)

YUGOSLAVIA 48
Area: 255,804 sq. km. (98,766 sq. mi.)
Population: 22,131,000
Capital city: Belgrade

YUKON TERRITORY 98
Area: 536,327 sq. km. (207,076 sq. mi.)
Population: 21,836
Capital city: Whitehorse

ZAIRE 80
Area: 2,345,409 sq. km. (905,568 sq. mi.)
Population: 27,810,000
Capital city: Kinshasa

ZAMBIA 82
Area: 752,618 sq. km. (290,586 sq. mi.)
Population: 5,553,000
Capital city: Lusaka

ZIMBABWE 82
Area: 390,580 sq. km. (150,803 sq. mi.)
Population: 6,600,000
Capital city: Harare

Glossary

alluvial rich soil, deposited by a river

altitude a height above sea level

Antarctic Circle an imaginary line of latitude 66°30′ (66 degrees, 30 minutes) south of the equator. On June 21 the sun does not rise along the Circle and on December 22 it does not set.

archipelago a group of nearby islands

Arctic Circle an imaginary line of latitude 66°30′ (66 degrees, 30 minutes) north of the equator. On December 22 the sun does not rise along the Circle and on June 21 it does not set.

artesian well formed when water, trapped underground, rises and reaches the surface of the land

atoll a coral reef surrounding a central lagoon

basin 1) a land area surrounded by higher borderlands, or 2) the entire area drained by a river and its branches.

bay a branch of the sea indenting the land, generally with a wide opening

canal a narrow, man-made channel of water joining lakes or rivers, or connecting them with the sea, and used for navigation or irrigation

canyon a deep, narrow valley

cape (or point) a piece of land extending into the water

channel 1) a narrow passage of water, wider than a strait, connecting two large bodies of water, or 2) the deepest part of a river or harbor

continent one of the large, continuous areas of the Earth into which the land surface is divided

degree a unit of measurement of a circle, represented by the symbol °. There are 180° of latitude, 90° north of the equator to the North Pole and 90° south of the equator to the South Pole. 360° of longitude circle the earth, stretching 180° in either direction from the prime meridian of Greenwich. Degrees are subdivided into 60 *minutes* (represented by the symbol ′).

delta a low, usually fan-shaped area of alluvial land at a river's mouth

depression a low land area, often below sea level, without drainage outlet

desert a barren land area so dry as to support little or no vegetation and with few people

Eastern Hemisphere the half of the global sphere that embraces Europe, Asia, Africa, and Australia, and their waters; also called the "Old World"

equator an imaginary line of latitude (0°) midway between the two poles

estuary a branch of the ocean at the mouth of a large river, that is affected by ocean tides as well as the flow of the river

fall a sudden drop of a river from a high level to a much lower one

fiord (or fjord) a long, narrow arm of the ocean into the land, bordered by high cliffs

forest a large area of land densely covered with trees and underbrush

gap a notch or an opening in the crest of a mountain formed by wind or water

geyser a spring that shoots hot water and / or steam into the air

glacier a large mass of ice that moves slowly down a valley from highlands toward sea level

grasslands prairies, plains, savannas, and steppes

gulf a branch of the ocean indenting the land, generally with a narrow opening to the sea between islands or parts of continents

highland an elevated area of land with irregular base levels, but generally with fairly even heights

hill a slightly elevated point of land rising above its surroundings

ice shelf a thick, floating area of ice adjoining a land area

inland waterway generally connects two distant bodies of water via rivers, lakes, canals, channels, or locks

international dateline an imaginary line of longitude generally 180° east or west of the prime meridian, along which the date changes by one day. Going west, for instance, the moment at which one crosses the dateline becomes the corresponding moment of the following day.

island an area of land completely surrounded by water

isthmus a narrow strip of land connecting two larger land areas, located between two bodies of water

jungle an area that is thickly covered with tropical vegetation

key (or cay) 1) a low island, usually composed of sand, or 2) a reef

lagoon a shallow area of water separated from the ocean by a sand bank, by a strip of low land, or a coral reef

lake an area of fresh or salt water entirely surrounded by land

latitude distance measured in degrees north or south of the equator

levee a wide wall built along banks of rivers to prevent floods

longitude the distance measured in degrees east or west of the prime meridian

massif a compact mass of high elevations with sharply defined borders

meridian an imaginary line of longitude running between the two poles

mountain an unusually high elevation rising steeply above its surroundings

North Pole the northern extremity of the Earth, 90° north of the equator

North Tropic Line (or Tropic of Cancer) an imaginary line of latitude 23°30′ north of the equator. It is the most northerly position at which the sun's rays fall vertically on the earth (only June 21).

oasis a desert area made fertile by the presence of water

ocean one of the large, continuous areas of the Earth into which the water surface is divided

parallel latitude lines running east and west parallel to the equator

peak 1) the highest point of a mountain, or 2) a mountain that has a pointed top

peninsula an area of land extending into the sea, surrounded by water on three sides

permafrost permanently frozen soil

plain a flat or level area of land

plateau (or tableland) a highland plain, or elevated area of generally level land, sometimes containing deep canyons

polder a Dutch name for a low area, at or below sea level, reclaimed from the sea, from which it is protected by *dikes*

prairie see **plain**

prime meridian the starting point (0°), passing through Greenwich, England, for the lines of longitude running east and west

range (or mountain range) a connecting chain of high elevations

reef a chain of rocks, sand, or coral usually just below sea level, but often with dry areas above the surface

reservoir a man-made lake, the amount of water being controlled by a *dam*

river a stream of water generally flowing to another stream, a lake, or to the ocean

savanna see **plain**

scale the relationship of the length between two points as shown on a map and the true distance between the two points on the Earth

sea a large area of salt water smaller than an ocean, sometimes occurring within a land area with no outlet to the ocean

selva see **tropical rain forest**

sound a body of water connecting two larger bodies of water, generally wider than a channel or strait

South Pole the southern extremity of the Earth, 90° south of the equator

South Tropic Line (or Tropic of Capricorn) an imaginary line of latitude 23° 30′ south of the equator. It is the most southerly position at which the sun's rays fall vertically on the Earth (only December 21).

steppes mid-latitude grasslands

strait a narrow body of water connecting two larger bodies of water

swamp a low area of wet, spongy ground, usually containing reedlike vegetation

taiga subarctic evergreen forest land

tropical rain forest made up of tall, broad-leaved evergreen trees

tundra cold, barren (treeless) land

valley a long hollow, usually with an outlet, lying between two areas of higher elevation and generally containing a stream

volcano a mountain that has (active) or had (inactive) openings in the Earth's crust from which lava escapes, making it more or less cone shaped

wadi a dry valley that fills up during a rainy season

watershed elevated land located between two drainage areas, dividing them

Western Hemisphere the half of the global sphere that embraces North and South America and their waters; also called the "New World"

Abbreviations

A

Afgh., Afghan.–Afghanistan
Afr.–Africa
Ala. (AL)–Alabama
AK–Alaska
Alb.–Albania
Alg.–Algeria
Alta.–Alberta
Amer. Samoa–American Samoa
arch.–archipelago
Arg.–Argentina
Ariz. (AZ)–Arizona
Ark. (AR)–Arkansas
Arm. SSR–Armenian Soviet Socialist Republic
Aust.–Australia
Azer. SRR–Azerbaidzhan Soviet Socialist Republic

B

Bah.–Bahrain
Bang.–Bangladesh
Barb.–Barbados
Belg.–Belgium
Ben.–Benin
Bh.–Bhutan
Bol.–Bolivia
Bots.–Botswana
Braz.–Brazil
Br.–British
Br. Ind. Oc. Terr.–British Indian Ocean Territory
Bulg.–Bulgaria

C

c.–cape
Calif. (CA)–California
Cam.–Cameroon
Camb.–Cambodia
cap.–capital
Cent. Afr. Emp.–Central African Empire
chan.–channel
Col.–Colombia
Colo. (CO)–Colorado
Conn. (CT)–Connecticut
C.R.–Costa Rica
Czech.–Czechoslovakia

D

Del. (DE)–Delaware
Den.–Denmark
des.–desert
Dom. Rep.–Dominican Republic

E

E. Ger.–East Germany
Ec.–Ecuador
El. Sal.–El Salvador
Eng.–England
est.–estuary
Est. SSR–Estonian Soviet Socialist Republic
Eth.–Ethiopia
Eur. – Europe

F

Fla. (FL)–Florida
Fr.–France, French
Fr. Gu.–French Guiana
Ft.–Fort

G

Ga. (GA)–Georgia
Gamb.–Gambia
Ger.–Germany
Gr.–Greece
Gren.–Grenada
Guat.–Guatemala
Gui.-Bis.–Guinea-Bissau
Guy.–Guyana

H

Hond.–Honduras
Hung.–Hungary

I

i., isl.–island
I.C.–Ivory Coast
Ice.–Iceland
ID–Idaho
Ill. (IL)–Illinois
Ind. (IN)–Indiana
Indon.–Indonesia
IA–Iowa
Ire.–Ireland
is., isls.–islands
Isr.–Israel
It.–Italy

J

Jam.–Jamaica
Jap.–Japan, Japanese
Jor.–Jordan

K

Kans. (KS)–Kansas
Ky. (KY)–Kentucky

L

l.–lake
La. (LA)–Louisiana
Lat. SSR–Latvian Soviet Socialist Republic
Liech.–Liechtenstein
Lith. SSR–Lithuanian Soviet Socialist Republic
Lux.–Luxembourg

M

Mal.–Malawi
ME–Maine
Man.–Manitoba
Mass. (MA)–Massachusetts
Maur.–Mauritania
Md. (MD)–Maryland
Mex.–Mecixo
Mich. (MI)–Michigan
Minn. (MN)–Minnesota
Miss. (MS)–Mississippi
Mo. (MO)–Missouri
Mold. SSR–Moldavian Soviet Socialist Republic
Mont. (MT)–Montana
Mor.–Morocco
Moz.–Mozambique
mt., mte.–mount
mts.–mountains

N

N. Amer.–North America
nat'l–national
N.B.–New Brunswick

N.C. (NC)–North Carolina
N. Cal.–New Caledonia
N. Dak. (ND)–North Dakota
Nebr. (NB)–Nebraska
Neth.–Netherlands
Neth. Ant.–Netherlands Antilles
Nev. (NV)–Nevada
Newf.–Newfoundland
N.H. (NH)–New Hampshire
Nic.–Nicaragua
Nig.–Nigeria
N. Ire.–Northern Ireland
N.J. (NJ)–New Jersey
N. Kor.–North Korea
N.Mex. (NM)–New Mexico
N.S.–Nova Scotia
N.S.W.–New South Wales
N. Terr.–Northern Territories
N.W.T.–Northwest Territories
N.Y. (NY)–New York
N.Z.–New Zealand

O

OH–Ohio
Okla. (OK)–Oklahoma
Ont.–Ontario
Oreg. (OR)–Oregon

P

Pa. (PA)–Pennsylvania
Pak.–Pakistan
Pan.–Panama
Par.–Paraguay
P.D.R. Yemen–Peoples Democratic Republic of Yemen
P.E.I.–Prince Edward Island
pen.–peninsula
Phil.–Philippines
plat.–plateau
Pol.–Poland
Port.– Portugal, Portuguese
P.R. (PR)–Puerto Rico
pt., pte.–point

Q

Que.–Québec
Queens.–Queensland

R

r., riv.–river
ra.–range
reg.–region
rep.–republic
res.–reservoir
R.I. (RI)–Rhode Island
Rum.–Rumania

S

sa.–serra, sierra
S. Afr.–South Africa
S. Amer.–South America
S. Aust.–South Australia
Sask.–Saskatchewan
Saudi Ar.–Saudi Arabia
S.C. (SC)–South Carolina
Scot.–Scotland
sd.–sound
S. Dak. (SD)–South Dakota
Sen.–Senegal
S. Kor.–South Korea
Sp.–Spain, Spanish
sprs.–springs
st., ste.–saint, sainte
sta.–station
str.–strait
Sur.–Suriname
Swaz.–Swaziland
Switz.–Switzerland
Syr.–Syria

T

Tan.–Tanzania
Tenn. (TN)–Tennessee
terr.–territory
TX–Texas
Thai.–Thailand
Trin. & Tob.–Trinidad and Tobago
Tun.–Tunisia
Turk.–Turkey

U

U.A.E.–United Arab Emirates
U.K.–United Kingdom
un.–united
Urug.–Uruguay
USA–United States of America
USSR–Union of Soviet Socialist Republics
UT–Utah

V

Va. (VA)–Virginia
Ven.–Venezuela
Vic.–Victoria
vol.–volcano
Vt. (VT)–Vermont

W

Wash. (WA)–Washington
W. Ger.–West Germany
W.I.–West Indies
Wis. (WI)–Wisconsin
W. Samoa–Western Samoa
W. Va. (WV)–West Virginia
Wyo. (WY)–Wyoming

Y

Yugo.–Yugoslavia

Z

Zim. — Zimbabwe

Index of the World

A

B

C

D

E

F

G

H

I

J

K

L

M

N

O

P

Q

R

S

T

U

V

W

Y

Z

B C 2 D 3 E 4 F 5 G 6 H 7 I 8 J 9 K 0 L 1